STIMSON BULLITT

River
Dark
&
Bright

RIVER DARK
AND BRIGHT

STIMSON BULLITT

Willows Press 1995

Published by
Willows Press
1204 Minor Avenue
Seattle, Washington 98101

Library of Congress Catalog Card Number: 95-60988

ISBN: Case Bound 0-9631630-5-1
       Perfect Bound 0-9631630-6-X

Other books by Stimson Bullitt, available from Willows Press
To Be A Politician, ISBN: 0-9631630-2-7 (Case Bound)
          0-9631630-3-5 (Perfect Bound)
Ancestral Histories of Scott Bullitt and Dorothy Stimson,
          ISBN: 0-9631630-4-3

Cover Photo: Prussik Peak, Cascades 8/92
Cover and text designed by Virginia Hand
Printed in the USA on 50% recycled, acid-free paper

To My Children
May their rivers flow long and bright

for KB for always
Shining Bright.
With Affection and of course
Immer Lieb
S/

Acknowledgments

My gratitude goes to friends who did much to improve the quality of this book. David Brewster, Jim Frush, Peter Potterfield, Michael Roemer, Shelby Scates, Cynthia Wilson and Bagley Wright generously plowed through crude early drafts, saved me from embarrassing errors, called attention to what was opaque or liable to be misunderstood and suggested fruitful lines of thought. Katherine Raff and Linda Armstrong edited the work with meticulous and intelligent care.

CONTENTS

FOREWORD

One that walketh after the
imagination of his own heart

—JEREMIAH

This book seeks to please us both. The prospect of reaching you by observing what has seemed important to me and by sharing thoughts and feelings with you gives me pleasure. So does the prospect of your enjoying what may interest or amuse you. Yet omitted are actions that would give me shame to admit, memories that would give me pain to describe, and scenes that dignity, delicacy or fairness to others forbids me to reveal.

H.W. Tilman wrote: "A man's experiences are said to be the name he gives to his mistakes." The reader may apply the label of mistake to those recited experiences that appear to deserve it. Tilman went on: "And his reminiscences are often written when his mistakes have been forgotten." Having kept and preserved a daily diary throughout my adult life may have limited the degree to which forgetfulness—among reasons for selection—has omitted past mistakes from these recollected events.

Chapter | 1

REFERENCE POINTS

A. Labels

This tale is told by a seventy-five-year-old who dwells on a wooded hillside looking westward across Puget Sound. Seattle has been my lifelong home.

A parlor game calls on each player to answer the question "What am I?" with a series of nouns (e.g., a dentist, a debtor, a doting grandmother, a dry-fly fisherman, a misunderstood artist, God's gift to _____, etc.). The game reveals something of how the player identifies himself, how he ranks his values, and what are the windows through which he sees the world. Were the question addressed to me, my answer would be: man, lawyer, father, son, brother, American, friend of my friends, citizen of my city and state, Bertrand Russell rationalist, self-pitying stoic (a Peter DeVries term), and then lesser categories such as bachelor (divorced), upper class WASP, war veteran, mountaineer, student, writer, sinner....

Franklin Roosevelt identified himself as an Episcopalian and a Democrat. The term "Episcopalian" applies to my background but not continuing affiliation; if asked my party affiliation, I would answer "Democrat," but would not advance this.

One peers up the causal procession in order to discover the shaping past, to try to trace those ancestral chains by which we all are bound. One would like to know personal details about one's forebears' characters and lives, to help discover how, from a blend of inheritance and experience, one man was made.

As a historian studies a nation's past in order to explain its present, I have sought to discover my ancestors' behavior and character for help to understand why (and even what) I came to be what I have been becoming. My Father's forebears lived in Virginia and Kentucky, and my Mother's lived in New England, making me a blend of South and North, Cavalier and Roundhead.

B. Models and Goals

Man is born a predestined idealist, for he is born to act. To act is to affirm the worth of an end, and to persist in affirming the worth of an end is to make an ideal....the root of joy as of duty is to put out all one's powers toward some great end....even while we think that we are egotists we are living to ends outside ourselves.

—HOLMES

I only half believe that and think that Holmes did too. However, idealism can be pursued in every walk of life in which one is not wholly driven down a groove of circumstance. For such pursuit, one need not endow universities, write a constitution, cure disease or dive one's plane into an enemy's deck.

As sons commonly do, I took my Father as my principal human model. My other models tended less often to be humans whom I knew and admired (e.g., Father Sill, Paul Robeson, Lonnie Austin) than composites, abstracted from figures in history and literature. Many of those whom I admired seemed too exalted for me to take as a model. Unlike Marcus Aurelius, I cannot enumerate those from whom I learned, by precept or example, aspects of wise and virtuous conduct.

Some men have stirred my admiration. One is

David Riesman of the Harvard Social Science faculty, for his rare combination of strong convictions with open-mindedness and fair-mindedness, his willingness to overcome his attachment to privacy by making sustained public efforts as a citizen, his quality as a parent and the contribution he has made to American society as a teacher. Although no longer does any living person appear to me larger than life, if any living person is my hero, he is David Riesman.

A few people's lives or deaths have inspired me. Like many in my generation I had models who were idealized, yet whom I took as real and subject to emulation. But now no more; we know too much. This paralyzing knowledge of how our models are in part our own creation is illustrated by an exchange in a movie. A man accused Woody Allen: "You think you're God!" Allen replied, "I've got to model myself on someone."

When one of my children asked me if the master boxer Archie Moore (a friendly acquaintance) was the man I most admired (no), his question reminded me how little in later years the thought of living models had occurred to me. There could not be repeated now the incident of the youth in tears, crying, "Say it ain't so, Joe," to the Chicago center fielder implicated in the 1919 Black Sox scandal; or of the young Peter the Great (not thought of as recognizing superiority to himself), catching sight of Richelieu's monument in Paris, running to it, embracing it and declaring: "Ah! Great man, if thou wert still alive, I would give thee half my kingdom to teach me to govern the other."

In all ages, admirably distinguished behavior has been easier for some to sneer at than to emulate. Recently, hero worship has almost disappeared. Human models exert such a strong force for setting standards of conduct that in turn, through habit, form character, that it is puzzling how some young people, without apparent heroes, nonetheless turn out well. Perhaps some do emulate models, but it is the fashion to conceal this.

In reincarnation, my thought has been to take a wardrobe of three skins: one each to wear for work, play and ceremony. For work, to be Pericles, Marcus Aurelius, Lorenzo, Milton, Mozart or Jefferson. For play, to be Pinza or Cellini—in the working role (singing or sculpting) of one of these two men, not to be he at his own play. And for parades, rituals and receptions, Scipio Africanus the Younger or Sir Philip Sidney (as depicted by his posthumous reputation). Although some aspects of each man have appealed to my taste, none has been a model whom I have sought to emulate.

Both Holmes and Morris Cohen remarked how life is more like painting a picture than doing a sum. This metaphor reflects life's complexity, the different efforts for the sets of roles that each of us is asked to fill, multiple pursuits, whether one recognizes them or not. The lives of men who have done well in more than one field or function – like decathlon champions – have intrigued me: Caesar, Leonardo, Spinoza (as philosopher and lens-maker), Bach (as performer, composer and progenitor), Jefferson, Byron White, Leonard Bernstein (as teacher, conductor, composer and pianist). Why has France been the only national society in recent generations to produce several men who combined high gifts in both letters and action (e.g., Francois Guizot, Antoine de Sainte-Exupèry, Jean Jacques Cousteau, André Malraux and Charles de Gaulle)?

Some young men's effort and direction are seen to flow from an aim to vindicate a father who had been defeated in some inspiring cause (e.g., Churchill, Mountbatten and Robert La Follette, Jr.), perhaps augmented by the father's encouragement, seeking consolation by vicarious success. But to me my Father had not seemed an embattled warrior; as a child and youth I regarded him as an awesome success. When awareness came that he was not as triumphant a figure as supposed, my course of conduct had been set long enough to make habits that restricted shifts in attitude.

In stories and biographies a youth reacts to an adverse experience by vowing never again to repeat it; then, through resolute determination, this vow is kept. I never made such promises to myself, probably from lack of confidence in controlling any part of my destiny. Of course, as with all of us, early experiences have set or altered attitudes or practices.

Observers have remarked that my family has been distinguished from others for its members seeking to direct their lives according to abstract principles. Either to confirm this observation or to answer its implied question has been beyond me.

The first occupation to which I can remember aspiring was that of a high rigger who tops trees for a high-lead logging operation, the equivalent of wanting to become a fireman. For a while, idle dreams would place me in the prow of a whaleboat, harpoon poised, one foot forward, like George Washington in the picture, the swells foaming under the trade wind and sparkling under the tropic sun.

By about the end of high school my hopes had begun to aim toward public service, preferably through politics, concentrated primarily on my community and secondarily on the country. While the shells were hitting LST 452, the blood that trickled down my chest provoked in me the thought: "How useful some day for politics!" On return from the War, this aim developed until it became fixed by conviction and habit of mind. In time it was given force, by growing confidence and by ambition to rise, to make good as well as do good.

In the college course that meant the most to me, Ralph Henry Gabriel's "American Thought and Civilization," his last lecture (May, 1941) concluded with the words, as best remembered, "We have one of the greatest civilizations the world has ever known. This civilization is now threatened by strong forces. To preserve it are needed the services of educated men." This made me want to become an educated man and, as such, to serve my country.

At college I learned little but received one important thing. Yale strengthened an enduring ambition to excel in education and general achievement. The examples of schoolmates and teachers and the spirit of the place fostered attitudes and expectations of excellence and success. Many students were smart, ambitious, hard-working and the sons of high-achieving, and often illustrious, fathers. Living among them spurred me to seek the high standards of performance to which most subscribed, which some of them sought and a few attained.

Following several years of a vague and indifferent expectation of being "in business," the thought of law school solidified from a notion to an intention. Even then my confidence did not permit presuming to plan a career or to set any goals of achievement that were high or far off.

At the end of 1946, I wrote that my year had been more productive than any other since that in which I learned to speak, hold a spoon and tie my shoes: "I hope to plow a deeper furrow through the year to come."

In the first half-dozen postwar years the memory of the war dead spurred me to step up the pace of work. The sight of people enjoying themselves at a lively party or at the crowded park around Green Lake, bathing, loafing and playing in the sunshine, would return my thoughts to those fellows under the sand out there in the islands. We lucky survivors were left with a duty by their lost chance to live out their lives on this often-happy earth. The contrast between their fate and mine drove me to pull my weight in order to justify my presence, to make compensatory payment for my chance to enjoy life, and to try to fulfill the ideals for which they died. How different were these feelings from those that some other wars inspired!

C. Work

[W]hether a man accepts from Fortune her spade, and will look downward and dig, or from Aspiration her ax and cord, and will scale the ice, the one and only success which it is his to command is to bring to his work a mighty heart. . . . We cannot live our dreams. We are lucky enough if we can give a sample of our best, and if in our hearts we can feel that it has been nobly done.

—HOLMES

A conventional outlook on work's importance has made me define myself probably more through work than through play, family relationships, fulfillment of social expectations or opinions of peers.

One summer the brush caught fire on the bluff below my grandparents' home. The gardeners and some other men fought it with shovels and mattocks. Aged ten or eleven, I helped and was glad to be allowed to take part, although smoke stung my eyes, and my feet got hot. A few times I sold Christmas seals, knocking on the doors of neighbors who were relatives or family friends. Sometimes—unsupervised and unpaid—I helped a gardener dig a hole or burn out a stump.

In the summers, from ages twelve to sixteen, I worked from time to time on my grandparents' place, supervised by the head gardener, raking leaves, weeding and some lawn mowing. I do not remember the rate of pay except that it exceeded the 10 cents an hour that my Father paid me for pulling out dandelions from our lawn with a pronged tool.

One day at thirteen, I went into town to a field south of Mercer Street and joined a crowd of city boys, convoked by a newspaper ad, picking up stones and dropping them in wheelbarrows and trucks. A hot dog and a bottle of pop were offered us for lunch, but the supply ran out before Edward Ohata and I reached the head of the long line. The balance of our pay was a ticket for a baseball game to be played on the field. It was becoming the ball park of the local Coast League team (Joe Dimaggio played there), and in later years was used for high school sports.

At Kent School, we boys did all the work of keeping the physical plant operated, maintained and clean except for cooking, laundry and repairs; that is, we did the janitorial work for the buildings, the housekeeping for the living quarters, setting and waiting on tables, dishwashing and care of the yards and athletic fields.

This work program and other aspects of student life were directed by a student government of certain seniors appointed by the headmaster and faculty. Six days a week we gathered for the morning assembly, where the prefects arrayed upon the platform handed down justice related to job performance, e.g., assigning more waits on tables as a penalty for dustballs on the floor of one's assigned sweeping territory. The first year the awe-inspiring senior prefect who presided in the center, with his arms resting on the chair arms, was Cyrus Vance.

On turning seventeen, I spent the summer at work for the Black Manufacturing Company in its over-all factory on Rainier Avenue at $13 a week (32 1/2 cents an hour). My duties included bringing up supplies of denim from the cutting floor to the sewing floor, repairing broken sewing machine belts and sweeping up the scraps and lint that accumulated on the floor. At least half of the workers were of Italian extraction. Our time was recorded on a card punched by a clock when we came and left. This made me proud, the first work that seemed to be a "real job."

The next summer, after a time spent searching, I worked at several jobs for short periods, starting in the office of cousin Cully Stimson's lumber mill (where the men resented me as the boss's kin). The work was dull and insignificant. When an injury (not work-connected) cost me the job, there followed a few weeks' work for my Mother, mainly tearing down a brick wall with a sledge hammer and crow bar and then sawing up a tree and digging out the stump.

After that, a few days' work picking pears near Peshastin in the Wenatchee Valley—35 cents an hour, a ten-hour day; the work was monotonous but not hard. The farmer upset me when he scolded me for breaking off the pears not at the knuckle joint of the stem, leaving a blunt stub, but short of the joint, splitting the stem, so that the sharp point would spear and mar the neighbor pears in the crate. My only previous farm experience had been on the Kent School farm where I sometimes helped milk the cows and enjoyed playing in the hay.

At nineteen, my summer was spent at a place my Mother owned on Icicle Creek in the Cascade foothills: clearing land of thorns and brush, building fences, fixing pipes, cutting wood, irrigating an alfalfa field.

At summer's end I worked in the wheat harvest on a ranch near Sprague. This was the hardest physical work I ever have done (the hardest play: carrying loads up McKinley). At 4:00 A.M., we would harness horses and hitch them to a wagon. In a shack between the farm house and the barn, I shared a sheetless bunk under a sweaty blanket with a coworker who was as dirty as I. A farm laborer by trade, he was a rodeo bronco rider by avocation. Our toil exhilarated us: our ancient and fundamental function, the dry heat from the blazing sun in the blue bowl overhead, the golden grain and the hills rolling with a rhythm that touched one's heart.

From time to time I worked as an usher at concerts given at college. One had to wear a tuxedo, was paid $1 and attended the show. Many were good: Yehudi Menuhin, Marian Anderson, The Helsinki University Glee Club. Once Paul Robeson sang with the Yale Glee Club. The experience inspired me, not so much from the singing as from the man himself. His figure, presence, address and the character he radiated made otherwise dignified and forceful men look like chickens. In Boston a few years later, at a performance of the play *Othello*, Jose Ferrer as Iago was the more supple and subtle actor, but Robeson in the title role impressed me by his appearing to be what he represented: a beleaguered alien of stature.

The latter part of the summer when I turned twenty was spent on a State highway maintenance crew. We lived in a work camp west of Chinook Pass. My crosscut saw partner and most of the others in the crew were college football players. The mess tent sometimes saw thrown food.

From boys' fiction I had come to think that men who worked with their hands outdoors, such as sailors, loggers, cowboys and longshoremen, spoke with colorful and variegated imagery, using phrases like "ring-tailed wowsers." Association with men of these callings, however, disappointed me to discover their speech, whether of anger or of adornment, to be little more than the monotonous handful of obscenities, set in the impoverished vocabulary of those who know few words and lack experience of their good use.

The following summer was spent in tedium as a messenger for the Seattle Trust & Savings Bank at $65 per month. On my every journey up the street to make deliveries in the first weeks, the newsstands showed the German line advanced another inch across the map of France.

At twenty-two, wanting to serve the public in some capacity, I was offered work (with my Mother's help) for the State Health Department in the Smith Tower basement as a combination janitor, handyman and stockroom clerk. Because to decline this unappealing job seemed high-hat, and none other was in prospect, I took it.

After a few months a new job came my way, as an "administrative assistant" (semi-clerical worker) for the U.S. Housing Authority on the Yesler Terrace slum clearance residential housing project. Before long, I quit to go to war.

The Navy service was civic service, although in some respects, of course, it was another job. Most of those four years were dull, some frustrating, some frightening. They delayed career progress, but did me no harm. At the end of 1945 the Navy let me go and permitted a return to Seattle after eleven years away in school and the War. Joining a profession came next.

A man may live greatly in the law as well as elsewhere; his thought may find its unity in an infinite perspective; there as well as elsewhere he may wreak himself upon life, may drink the bitter cup of heroism, may wear his heart out after the unattainable.

—HOLMES

After law school, I began work for a firm headed by my Mother's lawyer. My monthly salary was $50. On my admission to the Bar, it was raised to $75. My total compensation for the first two years was $4,025. I felt grateful to be given this job, although in retrospect my rate of pay suggested that my professional worth had been under-estimated. After six years employed there, three more in partnership with a friend, Marvin Mohl, and a short time solo, I joined the firm in which I remain a partner for the rest of my career as a lawyer. Its name later became Riddell, Williams, Bullitt & Walkinshaw. At the end of law school, Charlie and Dick Riddell had offered me a job in this, their firm. Later, hindsight let me see that to have accepted them then would have been the better course. I mistakenly had thought that to join the "establishment" firm that I did join would reduce disapproval of me for political positions critical of the establishment.

For the eleven years away at school and war, my thoughts had been beamed at Seattle, where were the things that mattered most: family, friends, outdoor beauties, familiar sights, and perhaps opportunities. Then for three years of law school, my thoughts remained projected ahead to the time when this preparation would be applied. Upon starting law practice, my attention was no longer split in time or space. A radical adjustment, this integration in the here and now satisfied by raising efficiency at work.

When we filled out a marriage license application, under "occupation" my first wife had written "writer," while I wrote "student." On admission to the bar, it was gratifying to be able, at last, to sit at the table with the other grownups as one who had a trade. Also, it felt good to shake off the anxiety of always trying to catch up, staying awake to do not what should be done but what had to be done.

Much of the early work was trivial to me, although not, of course, to the people whose interests were involved: making an inventory of the furniture and furnishings in a decedent's estate; helping a woman who refused to pay her hospital bill because hospital employees had lost her teeth; a woman's claim against a drug store for selling her a home permanent wave liquid that made her hair fall out. An old man who had formed a corporation and wanted me to do things to help it prosper thought my refusal to work for stock rather than cash was unreasonable since he offered to let me have 11 billion shares.

At a trial I attended in Melbourne during the War, a man was charged with having shot his wife through the head because she had refused to allow him a divorce that would let him marry a twenty-year old. His lawyer argued that if he really had wanted to do her in, he would have used a shotgun rather than a .22. When the "other woman" testified, the prosecutor asked her what the defendant did when he called on her on such-and-such an evening. She replied, "Nothing. He just sat in a chair." "Well, what did he say?" "Nothing at all. He didn't say anything." "How long did he stay?" "Oh, about five hours." This was preposterous, but I discovered that in trials the preposterous was not uncommon.

A couple of months after my admission to the bar, a negotiation in which my role was mainly that of an observer took place one night. After a long evening in my Mother's living room, she agreed to buy, and the owner (who had been losing money) agreed to sell, for $375,000, his television station (which became KING-TV). Each party fearing a possible overnight change of mind by the other, we lawyers went to a downtown office where a memorandum agreement was typed and signed at 3:00 a.m.

In time my work became more effective, from knowing more and gaining confidence to speak out and to think rather than do research as a substitute for thinking. The Japanese Relocation from the West Coast had destroyed a Nisei's soft drink distributorship business. With my help on his behalf, he recovered a sum said to have been the largest recovery to date under the Evacuation Claims Act. Nonetheless, he objected to the previously agreed fee.

In my lifetime, both the law and the administration of justice have changed, and largely to the good. Now no one can be prosecuted for a crime without a lawyer's help, if he wishes it, while in my childhood, at the time of the IWW/American Legion violence in Centralia, the local bar association pledged its members not to defend an IWW member, "no matter what the charge." In 1941, people living on the present site of the Yesler Terrace Housing Project told me how, living as they did near the Public Safety Building, their nights had been disturbed by interrogated prisoners' screams.

Much has been asserted in recent years about the protections granted the accused by the requirement that they be told their rights before they are interrogated and by the rules excluding evidence obtained by improper means, such as extorted confessions and searching private zones without a warrant. But none does more to protect an innocent person from a jail sentence than the right to counsel, because it keeps the authorities from charging a person with a crime on scant evidence, confident that the defendant could not put that evidence to a rigorous test.

Over four decades, I took occasional cases defending people charged with crime. This work was done without pay—on behalf of those who could not pay—as a duty to the profession and to uphold the system of justice. I did not enjoy this. The cases tended not to challenge the mind. And one's clients were people hard to help and hard to enjoy helping. Most of them distrusted me. None told me the truth.

My practice grew, and by the time I took charge of King Broadcasting I had many clients, although none who was rich. However, after I left King and started Harbor Properties, although my time available for law expanded some, the practice never came back. Except for some assignments from my partners, no one employed me for important services. Nor was my advice sought in the alternative fields of business or politics. Others asked me for money: for investment, philanthropy, political campaigns, personal succor and other causes. To be asked to contribute to the cost of retaining, for some litigation to preserve good environment, a lawyer I thought my inferior could not help but gall.

After having become well-known and ranked a(v) by Martindale-Hubbell, this lack of acknowledgment in the professional market place—not the only test of competence but an important one—both puzzled and discouraged me. For my work seeming to be thought worth little, with its consequence of bringing in negligible revenue to the firm, made me feel likewise and, as we would sit together around a long table at firm meetings, made it hard to look my partners in the face.

Aptitude and pleasure drew me more to solve problems than to anticipate them, to find a way around an obstacle than to discern it ahead, to discover a loophole than to foresee a pitfall. I have preferred the role of counselor or advocate to that of draftsman or lobbyist. I have known highly moral men who were effective lobbyists without selling their personalities, but I lacked their skills.

Among those areas of law I know a bit about I most enjoy litigation. And among its forms, I prefer appeals and have learned to do them better than other work. They permit digging deeper into questions than trial practice permits, and their requirements do not impede one whose mind often is not quick. Recognition in the profession as a good appellate advocate has been satisfying. (An implied compliment was a State Supreme Court opinion, signed by a good judge, that took most of its language, word for word, from the arguments I had presented the Court. This gave me a sense of contributing to shaping the law.)

I enjoy making an argument—whether written or oral—in a case that challenges, not with hopeless odds but with adverse odds, where one can give a small lemon a hard squeeze.

I never learned to cross-examine witnesses with high skill. Part of this depends on keeping in mind, helped with notes, what the witness has said and done. Dana described a fellow seaman:

> With an iron memory, he seemed to have your whole past conversation at command, and if you said a thing now which ill agreed with something said months before, he was sure to have you on the hip.

A greater problem is the process of adjusting questions in series to the answers as given, so as to elicit those aspects of the truth that you seek to show.

Others' approval of my performance as a lawyer has given me pleasure when coming from judges or from lawyers who had been on the other side. After I had appeared before the Bar Association's judicial selection committee, the chairman, later a U.S. Judge, remarked to its members, ". . .makes a guy proud to be a lawyer." Of course, my daughter Dorothy's choice of our profession was an implied high compliment.

Presidents and governors have been heard to murmur that every political appointment makes several enemies and one ingrate. However, judges receive enough respect and trust that each judicial decision does not make one enemy and one ingrate. Of all occupations, that of politician calls for a higher degree of sophisticated moral courage than any other. But a judge rarely needs courage. The pressures and threats that he or she must withstand mainly come from within.

Before court experience, I imagined judges to resemble Charles Evans Hughes or Sir Stafford Cripps. This notion was dispelled.

At first, it seemed to me that little mattered in a

judge but absence of bias and enough brains to understand the problem. Then I came to realize that a mind
that is fair is not enough unless it is open as well, a
willingness to consider evidence and listen to arguments. The two are not always combined.

A not uncommon type has a sharp mind and
knowledge of the law combined with imperviousness to
argument, so that on reading the file and listening to the
opening statements he determines the question and
turns down his mind's receiving system. This owes to
laziness, rigidity, impatience with the tedious process of
receiving evidence and argument, and an arrogant sense
that his experience enables him to learn from these
preliminary items of information all he needs to know.

Another frustrating personality among judges is
one who plays Mr. Nice Guy, trying to please both
parties by compromising their differences.

Although the law is one of organized society's
great constructions, it has limitations, of course, as a
method for solving human problems.

> The law's our yardstick, and it measures well
> Or well enough when there are yards to measure.
> —STEVEN VINCENT BENET,
> *JOHN BROWN'S BODY*

Likewise, some lawyers suffer from the limitation of
seeking to apply legal thinking to all problems that
confront them as humans.

In recent years law practice in this country has
become more combative outside the courtroom, less
polite, less a profession and more a hustling business. It
might improve itself by shifting some of its training
emphasis from craftsmanship, where we have achieved

such excellence, to fundamental principles—recognizing that they be learned, remembered and applied. In Wallace Loh's words, "to educate not only merchants of law, but servants of justice."

The popular notion that most lawyers are dishonest is false. Among vocations, my observations have found lawyers' average standard of truthfulness among the highest. And they are sophisticated about practical truth, as well as about many ethical questions, especially those that involve conflicting interests. Where a person is called on to play more than one distinct role, lawyers can recognize the separate duties that go with each. An incident in early Kentucky illustrated the distinction of duties. A young man waylaid some travelers in the forest, robbed and killed them. He was convicted and sentenced to hang. Governor Desha resigned his office after he had pardoned the young man, who was his son. (The resignation is supported by tradition, not confirmed by records.)

Law practice offers an honest living, a social contribution, challenge to the mind, the company of some of the world's best companions, and a never-ending diversity (unless your practice is confined to intersection collision cases) of human situations that amuse, enlighten and absorb.

My choice of vocation has never given me a day's regret. Having entered law intending to use it as a step to political life, I discovered pleasure in law as an end as well as a means—a good thing, of course, to find you enjoy what necessity compels. Though far less constricted by circumstances, my life in the law has made me feel like Pierre Maury (described by Ladourie in *Montaillou*), the cheerful shepherd of Arriège, born seven hundred years ago, who, "with a deep sense of occupational continuity," followed his austere calling with contentment and energy, rather than enduring it, first frustrated, then resigned.

One wonders how so many people can find freedom in service to an exacting profession and how some can even feel free in dedication to vows of poverty, chastity and obedience.

> Nuns fret not at their convent's narrow room,
> And hermits are contented with their cells
> —WORDSWORTH

Such puzzlement does not bother me; pleasure comes from so many things I do not understand. However, the changes in this profession over the last score years have made me think that if it were mine again to choose my work, the law would not be such an easy choice.

My little teaching I have enjoyed and—of the intellectual sort—done well. At college, I coached boxing at the Dixwell Avenue Community House. Owing to these teenagers' lack of discipline and my lack of assertiveness only a few learned something, but others enjoyed healthy play. During my first few weeks in the Navy, the training program required me one evening to give a swimming lesson to a unit of about fifty Black recruits, aged seventeen to twenty-one. My inability to induce them to stop hollering and splashing led to an hour of splashes and shouts.

At the San Diego NTS, some of my duties were to teach recruit companies marching drill, the manual of arms, making up bunks, folding clothes, and some other basic military procedures. On the USS *Bogue* and in the Solomon Islands, I taught boxing to some white sailors and "colored mess cooks" (diary entry). My Bible class to inattentive seventh grade boys at St. Mark's Cathedral transmitted little. More productive for both teacher and students have been service as moderator of a world politics study group; as a lecturer to lawyers; as a visiting professor in law schools, teaching several subjects; and lecturing and teaching classes in government on a one-shot basis at a number of Northwest colleges. An especially satisfying week was spent teaching in the Political Science Department at Berkeley. The law school experience taught me a good deal about teaching but, I fear, at my students' expense.

In politics, many of the processes—campaign speeches, civic causes, party platform creation—enable one to exercise the teaching function: to inform, interpret, illuminate and explain. This aspect of politics I enjoyed and, after practice, did pretty well.

If reincarnated and offered another run through life, in a different vocation, my choice might be to teach and write some aspect of history. But looking back, my regrets apply more to performance than to calling. Appealing as teaching, writing and learning history are for me, it would be hard to forego work that in part has a direct impact on concrete events rather than playing with ideas, despite the fact that improving and filling others' minds is "getting things done."

My work in business has been family-related. For the first sixteen years after returning from the War, it was part time work for my Mother's company. Then,

at her request, I succeeded her as President of King
Broadcasting Company, which she had started with the
resources of the real estate holding company that her
father had built. During the next decade, covering my
age from forty-two to fifty-two, I served in this job.

My approach to work at King aimed for high
achievement: social justice and a product that would set
moral, intellectual and aesthetic examples to all. These
aims included profit, of course. As breathing is to life,
making a profit in business, even if not the main purpose, is an essential means to every other worthwhile
corporate end.

However, I sought more than to corrupt other
people's children to gain the means with which to corrupt my own. My approach to our programming I stated
in our Policy Manual to be:

> like at least one theory of constitutional gov-
> ernment—a compromise between aristocratic and
> democratic doctrines. In part it is to serve as a teacher,
> leader and guide to choose our content on the basis of
> our own taste and judgment of merit. And in part it is
> to be obediently responsive to popular tastes. It blends
> the Grand Inquisitor and Oliver Cromwell ("It is not
> what they want but what is good for them—that is the
> question") with Cleon and Marshall Field. We aim to
> supply our audience with creations of our own, not to
> hold up a mirror to the mob, not to treat the public as
> the sun which we worship as though we were some
> shivering pagan or which we passively reflect as though
> we were a sort of electronic moon. The aristocratic
> element of our approach rests on our duty to provide
> something of our own; the responsive element rests on
> the public's right to have some of what it prefers; both

elements are necessary to hold our audience, the former over the long run, and the latter over the short.

The Company's net worth on my departure exceeded what it was when I came but fell short of what it would have been if the Company had been better managed. I took it into some business ventures that failed.

On the other hand, I established divisions for videocable and for mobile TV service, and they both prospered, the former, after I was gone, coming to provide half the Company's cash flow, and the latter becoming the largest such enterprise in the world. I reorganized some of the internal structure to make it more efficient and established a system of budgets and financial controls. The accounting system was made more informative by the laborious and expensive shift to computers from adding machines and boxes of canceled checks, so that the term "ledger" came to mean a system of recording the final accounts of an enterprise, rather than a folio-sized book with lined pages. The Company logo has been used ever since I commissioned its design and adopted it. The employees' profit-sharing plan, which I had drafted years before, was improved. A substantial number of the staff were made stockholders. After long delay (from Mother's sustained resistance), I established an employees' retirement program. The quality of the Board of Directors and the executive staff was raised, a couple of relatives were removed from sinecures, and uniform personnel policies were established.

The news departments were strengthened, and some competent news commentators were brought in: Herb Altschul, Forrest Amsden (later a King executive) and Charles Royer (later Seattle's Mayor); and a radio talk show host, Irv Clark (an amusing, witty lawyer, the first Harvard student to swallow a goldfish), who raised the standards of spoken English over the air in Seattle. The pipsqueak nonentities who served as disk jockeys annoyed me: their vain and vulgar inanities; their sniggers and giggles evoked by matters that should be taken seriously; and sedulously courting popularity with their audience and taking positions that they thought would thrill the rabble, while they sneered at politicians at whom they railed for following majority wishes. But my efforts to improve this aspect of radio failed.

For the Portland and Spokane operations, good quality buildings were built. Over the years, on behalf of King and other companies, and for myself as well, I have engaged a number of architects and worked with them on the design and construction of buildings. More than some other forms of artistic expression, architectural beauty allows me to appreciate it, and working out functional problems of design gives me pleasure. When I told Mies van der Rohe that the office building he was designing for us needed to be built in a way that the vibration from passing trucks would not be allowed to rattle the TV studios that it also was to contain, he replied, in his heavily-accented voice, with an intensity of feeling that made me regret having raised the matter, "Our buildings do not rattle!"

Some business ventures turned out to be adventures in the sense of struggle, risk and colorful events, although they did not exhilarate and most of them tended to discourage and frustrate.

One unsuccessful venture was a plywood mill on Okinawa. I had acquired it for a company in my charge by winning a proxy fight, mainly by buying shares. To have lost would have been better. That mill made me feel the way the kidnappers felt toward the obnoxious boy in O. Henry's "Ransom of Red Chief."

The only labor negotiations in which I ever have taken direct part were in Naha. Wages at the mill were in line with those paid for similar work on that Island but compared with the United States, they were low. On my first walk through the mill, the humid heat made me remark to the manager that a Coke machine would be popular. He replied that since some of the women were earning ten cents per hour, they might take home nothing.

New in their roles and unaware of traditions or practices of collective bargaining, the union leaders with whom I dealt were naive and rigid, in contrast with their shrewd and elastic counterparts in cities where labor bargaining has long been carried on. The language barrier caused further confusion. One of the leaders (not long out of prison for arson) would bellow a tirade, while pounding on the table hard enough to make the water pitcher hop, and the translator would tell us: "He asks if you would please be so kind to. . . ."

After making a settlement that seemed fair I came home, but the manager there—perhaps my worst ever hiring mistake—thinking my concessions had been unnecessary, refused to honor the contract and thereby brought on a strike. Absence of union solidarity and absence of public respect for picket lines made picketing ineffective. However, strikers used a resourceful method. One night, a few men hauled a thick plywood panel, the factory's product, to the top of the plant smokestack, which towered above the city. They camped on the panel, which capped the stack. In America, customs might have permitted the furnace to be lit, but on Okinawa the risk to the sitters on top made a fire unthinkable, so for a long time the mill was shut down.

Two other business misadventures that I undertook at King Broadcasting were *Seattle Magazine* and the film-making division. Both recruited and trained professional talent who in later years established themselves among the country's better film makers and journalists. The *Magazine* often annoyed me by its tone and content, although its editorial standards set an example for the community. We folded it when hope was lost that its losses ever would stop.

The Screen Division made some constructive educational films. But it lost so much money that its educational, political and esthetic ends might have been better pursued by giving the money to appropriate worthy causes. (Historians have observed that the Crisis of 1860 would have cost less than it did if the Union had bought all slaves at going prices, then freed them—as Lincoln sought consent to do from the Border States in 1862.) One feature film was made, *The Plot Against Harry*. The Company put up the whole of the cost and lost it all when no distributor would take it. Twenty years later, it was discovered, praised and shown throughout the world.

The credit due to a creator for the merit of his work is deserved regardless of the time elapsed between creation and recognition, e.g., the cave dweller who left the drawings at Lascaux. But to questions whether *Harry's* belated acclaim made me feel vindicated, my response was "no." When you are employed to produce that for which others will pay, and they do not, a later discovery that you had been a patron of art does not make your experience any less a business failure.

Bagley Wright invited me to invest in a venture he was organizing. I declined, thinking how board members' eyebrows would rise at a proposal to invest in a bizarre structure called a "space needle" when the last venture had been a plywood mill on Okinawa. Alas, the regret with which I declined this longtime loyal friend's invitation was multiplied when the Needle became a big financial success.

Some films were made that encouraged protecting the natural physical environment before the movement to do so had gained strength. A KING-TV News documentary won a Sierra Club award, and King Screen made a couple of such films, one of which "The Redwoods," won an Oscar.

My program to hire Blacks and women before popular or legal pressure to do so had begun was thrust hard enough that when I left, the Company employed more Blacks in responsible positions (i.e. not as hewers of wood or drawers of water) than all the other mass communication companies in the Northwest combined.

In hiring for jobs in programming, news and administration (as distinguished from engineering and accounting), I gave too much weight to brains, not enough to experience. In most cases I gave more weight to a liberal arts education than to vocational training for these areas of work, but that was not a mistake. Hostile resistance was expressed against the well-educated young whom I recruited. In their ignorant populism, many in the Company and out charged me with snobbish elitism. However, I made manager of station KING a high school dropout who had spent time doing penance in the penitentiary for armed robberies. And in later years, after I had left the Company, the Board elected as vice presidents two of the men whom I had recruited from their Ivy League colleges.

In my office hung a picture (a framed page torn

from Life Magazine) of Verrochio's bust of Lorenzo de Medici. In the whole decade, no one appeared to recognize it except for my friend Michael Roemer, whose glance took it in and whose polite smile showed he grasped not only its identity but its significance on that wall.

My efforts were ineffectual to induce the staff to pursue both money and aesthetic and educational goals. Because few people are willing and able to pursue multiple goals (e.g. seeking to attract a large audience without triviality or degrading vulgarity), I tried without success what amounted to two teams of people, conflicting with mutual suspicion and incomprehension, as each pursued a separate single goal.

On leaving King, under strained and awkward circumstances, I formed Harbor Properties, owned by me and by those (kin and friends) to whom I gave stock. This enterprise made money after it had been gradually transformed from a set of assets with little in common into a diversified real estate company. Having less social significance than King Broadcasting in what it does, Harbor was easier for me to concentrate on the goal of profit, modified sometimes by community utility or esthetic considerations. Not only were this Company's goals easier to pursue, because of their narrower scope, but my own effectiveness was increased by accumulated experience and by my authority no longer being undercut.

After twelve years of operation, when I had passed age sixty-five, Harbor sustained reverses from a development project, shrinking its net worth by a quarter. The fault was shared by a couple of executives, who had made errors of judgment, and by me, who had failed to pay enough attention to what was done. This—plus some severe intra-company turmoil—compelled me to plunge into the detailed affairs of the enterprise and drive hard for another decade. Having only recently discovered the pleasures of play, after two score years of assiduous work, I begrudged this necessity. The work was a kind that did not much fit either my aptitude or taste. It annoyed me to be made to work when ready for play and also to work not for the rewards of success but to escape the shame of failure. Soon, however, the challenge, the struggle and the encouraging results swept away the resentment; in part, drudgery was replaced by fun.

One example of my ineffectual administration at both King and Harbor was my failure to establish a sound system for preserving records and making the information they contained easy to find. My efforts could not overcome the attitude of some people that after a decade pieces of paper become uniformly worthless and others' wish to obliterate the record of their immediate predecessors so as to magnify the appearance of their own.

As between business and law, the latter suits me better. With many exceptions, the company of lawyers gives me more pleasure than that of executives, pleasure from enjoyment of argument, more shared interests and experiences, a stronger taste for playing with ideas and an often wider range of shoptalk.

On the other hand, although some individual lawyers have high capacity to get things done, I would rather try to take action on a committee composed of executives than one composed of lawyers because too many of the latter enjoy extending argument for its own sake.

By contrast with the law, argument in business is neither as widely practiced nor as well done. The people have not been trained in the process. In a hierarchy, an argument by a superior may be felt as overbearing, and by a subordinate may be regarded as insubordinate, in contrast to the law, where the Supreme Court Justice and his clerk may debate the afternoon away in social ease. The strongest constraint on argument in business is that in contrast to lawyers' argument about others' follies and misdeeds, in business one argues about your mistake or mine.

In law practice, your thinking is tested by argument, but in business, where dealing with people and organizing work are comparatively more important, you have a greater need for advice. Yet your subordinates may withhold that critical advice that you invite from them in your hope of improving your effectiveness. By showing they regard you as a paranoiac egotist whom such advice would offend they thereby give you offense.

The business jobs distorted one's perspective, giving the false impressions that one is a fine fellow, liked and respected by almost everyone and that almost all other people are affable and pleasant. Law practice presents no such risk.

In law, often a caller would ask for what he/she styled "information" (for which there would be no charge), but what in fact was advice. Yet in business subordinates purported to seek my advice as an executive when they sought information about what I thought.

The higher levels of business afford more scope for idealism than law; what one does has a greater social impact. Providing a framework for a hundred people to do constructive work may contribute more to society than a successful argument over skidmarks, mortgage recording priorities or custody of the Volkswagen. A legislator or a business executive may affect a whole category, while a lawyer, though performing an important social function and exercising strong analytical powers, may affect only the blurred boundaries where the lawyer is called upon to draw a sharp line.

In modern business one is offered a wide range of opportunity between creating wealth for one's society and wasting it. But the range of justice versus injustice available to a business leader is narrow. Tocqueville pointed out that when the Ancien Régime in France engaged in the large-scale program of selling public offices, "its greed frustrated its ambition." Staffing the government with people who were disobedient or disloyal, often incapable, made the bureaucracy unresponsive to policy directions. Thus the governors did not get their way, and some despotic excesses were mitigated, as this condition "often acted as a political check on the absolutism of the central power." Likewise, although neither corruption, despotism nor gross incompetence afflicts American business, external pressures limit the wickedness and the good that one can do beyond providing goods and services that people want enough to buy.

"It is not the beginning but the continuing the same until it be thoroughly finished that yieldeth the true glory." So Drake told his men before they sailed into the harbor at Cadiz to strike the Spanish fleet. Observation of people's progress in the world of affairs over the years, has impressed me with how important are the factors of energy and directness of purpose. With these two, in most walks of life one can go far without a lot of brains.

In the 1830s, Dana recorded that because his ship was in port, rain was falling and it was Christmas, the crew was given its first day off in sixteen months. He remarked that "There's no danger of Catholicism spreading in New England; Yankees can't afford the time to be Catholics."

Among those who lived before us in this country, knowledge of past material improvement and the presence of resources not yet exploited evoked much effort, with success breeding more effort, which in turn bred more success. Their hard work won material rewards far greater than those enjoyed by their forbears in Europe. In early years, with an unbroken chain of experience, an expectation of material improvement was assumed because the encouraging prospect seemed to everyone so self-evident that it was not articulated. Then after a time, in some of the inhabitants, this assumption hardened into a belief in such improvement not merely as probability but as destiny.

It always has puzzled me why people put out effort to bring to pass what they think has been predestined. You might expect one convinced that the river of life would carry him to a certain place would lean back and relax in the sunshine, knowing he would reach the same destination no matter which way he paddled or how hard he rowed. Yet in matters of more abstract belief people seem to try to assist destiny, as though destiny needed help. For example, Calvinists as to moral and theological deserts and Communists as to providing goods and services. Despite faith that their fate is inexorable, many Calvinists tried hard to be good and Communists to be efficient. Their efforts are not belied by the mixed results. And those who believe that the planets and stars direct our destiny nonetheless follow astrologers' advice, as though the heavenly bodies had only limited authority to determine our fate.

Some people disagree with the notion that opportunity evokes energy. They assert the premise that human energies are solely a function of our bodies and what we put in them, a matter of calories and metabolism, so that motivation may direct energies but not increase or diminish them. They point out that lack of purpose does not keep a river from running downhill, and argue that an aimless person puts out no less energy than he would if he were purposeful, the only difference being that his energy is dispersed or shifted rather than concentrated and maintained.

However, the human personality can be compared not to an open hose, which constantly flows, whether by torrent or by drip, but rather to a battery that either can hold energy or dispense it, depending on whether it is tapped. In France, in the score of years that straddled 1800, the sense of opening doors (e.g., society can be anything we make it, a marshal's baton in every private's knapsack) released explosive energies: the Terror, a radical alteration of the social structure, a code of laws, a conquering army, a school system, trees planted along the roads to enable soldiers to march beneath their shade.

Perhaps we can expect a similar burst of energy from those who have obtained opportunities that had been closed to members of the groups to which they belonged. This seems likely unless social policies diminish the rewards for self-improvement and the penalties for indolence, encouraging some to coast on personal magnetism as their own offering carrot and on truculence as their offering stick.

✧ ✧ ✧

Sometimes as a child, on asking, "What does so-and-so do?" I would be told, "Oh, he's got some money, he doesn't do anything." The notion of awakening each morning, faced with the prospect of doing nothing all day, at first perplexed me and later appalled. To regard work as a grim necessity, to be avoided if any alternative is offered, is common to many, mostly those who lack the opportunity or capacity for fulfilling or rewarding work. This outlook I can understand, but never have shared. As a youth and young man I would feel scorn for colleagues who, in Benjamin Franklin's phrase, would "declare a Saint Monday." Novels have bored and frustrated me where most of their characters seemed either to do little work *(David Copperfield)* or none *(Fathers and Sons)*, and whose lives were neither justified by constructive effort nor enlivened by dashing behaviour.

Money for all our needs and many of our wishes was provided my sisters and me as we grew up. We were neither required nor requested to work, yet we started early and have continued to work throughout our lives. To be allowed to work, even at jobs that fell far below my preference of things to do, has made me grateful. I have worked throughout the night more nights than I have so played (few of both). On the whole, work always has given me pleasure, and for one not driven by the lash of material scarcity, I have worked hard (since ceasing to be a college student), content to take some other pleasures as a by-product, like those of Joshua's soldiers who splashed up the water in transit.

Dick Riddell 7/62

Randy Gordon & Steve DeForest 6/94

Bob Ivie & Walt Walkinshaw 6/94

Vern Williams

Doug Raff, Cynthia & Bart Wilson 6/89

Kathy Raff, Jon & Judy Whetzel 6/89

Bill & Emily Glueck, Dave & Nancy Buck

Chapter | 2
ATTACHMENTS

> If it were now to die,
> 'Twere now to be most happy; for I fear
> My soul has her content so absolute
> That not another comfort like to this
> Succeeds in unknown fate.
>
> —OTHELLO

Twice during our earthly sojourn—when we arrive and when we leave—life is ineluctably unjust. One injustice is the range of differences between us in the personal gifts we bring with us at birth. The other, truly life's worst, is mortality. As at birth, life at death is unequal: Some are allowed an ample span, while others are cut down when just out of the starting gate. And it is universal: Each of us, even if not notably wicked, even the most blameless of us all, is condemned to capital punishment. The question is not whether, only when. One day the bell rings, telling you the party's over. You don't go home, you go outside in the dark.

Along this lonely road that all travel, we reach toward those with whom we wish to connect. Words, gestures, glances, caresses, serenades: measures often serving little more than flares and flags exchanged by passing ships. In our isolation, or at best tenuous contact, to accept a final parting is difficult, and to endure it is harsh.

The purpose of a funeral or words at a grave seems to be farewell to one who is not there to get the message, as though the mourners had come down to the dock and waved their handkerchiefs after the ship had sailed. Most phrases for affectionate parting do not fit because they ring changes on the phrase "until we meet again." When the coffin passes, we declare no graceful and gracious *au plaisir de vous revoir,* no hearty *auf wiedersehen.* We turn to the Roman simplicity of *ave atque vale.* When aware we are dying, we may say the same even to ourselves.

> I'm going away, I know not where,
> Or to what fortune, or whether I may ever
>   see you again,
> So Good-bye my Fancy.
>
>   —WHITMAN

However, a funeral not only fills us with death's bleak horror, its despairing finality. It also reminds us of how precious is life, what sweetness it can offer, making us treasure life all the more.

On a late summer afternoon, sister Priscilla and I were playing on the porch under an awning when Father came running around the corner from the driveway in front and told us (and the nurse who was tending us) that we had a new baby sister. In response to this happy and total surprise, Patsy, about to become four, and I, then five, ran up to the attic to pick out toys for her. We agreed on the name of Mary, which we urged on Father, but the baby was named Harriet Overton after her maternal grandmother. We were taken to the Seattle General Hospital, where we found Mother. Harriet was brought in and put on the bed where she yawned. She was the first member of our family to have been born in a hospital.

At the center of the garden south of the house was a small circular pool with a rounded light blue bottom. We used to splash around in this when we were very young. Once Patsy pushed in Wetherill ("Bubby") Collins who was a big boy and classified by us as one of the grownups, and whose elder brother she later married.

When cousin Johnny Bullitt (who later was to teach 18th Century English Literature at Harvard for a generation) threw our cat in the pool, I retaliated by pushing John in. He said, "At our house we don't treat little boys that way," and I replied, "At our house we don't treat cats that way." Or maybe he made the reply to my statement. At a party at the Harvard Faculty Club the night before I was married, he told this anecdote in the course of his toast to the groom.

We would go out on grandfather Stimson's 93-foot motor yacht. Wearing a yachting cap that fell over my ears, I would speak the command "On Deck!," imitating grandfather. While the *Wanda* lay alongside the low concrete pier that he had built at the Highlands Beach, the tide went out, letting the boat lurch over to port. Falling against the low rail beside the deckhouse frightened me. Going through the Locks, grandfather let me stand by him as we both (he with his one arm) pushed against the wet and slimy wall to hold the boat off; a bystander looking down from above remarked, "Helping your grandfather, eh?"

One evening, Mother told me, "If you do not stop what you are doing, you will have no breakfast." I continued the forbidden conduct. She forgot the incident and at breakfast time next morning was surprised when I did not come down.

Another evening when my parents had company for dinner, a pig was set on the table. On being brought in to say goodnight, I looked carefully at the pig but said nothing, then, in a serious voice and looking at each in turn said, "Goodnight, Daddy. Goodnight, Mummy. Goodnight, Pig." (Cf. little Rousseau bidding good night to the joint on the spit)

When Patsy and I were five and six, respectively, we had some baby ducks in the back yard. To give them a treat, we put them in a tub for a swim until they became chilled, and grownups revived them in the oven.

We children played on the lawns around the house: rolled, wrestled, sunbathed, ran through sprinklers in bathing suits, played in the sandbox, and played mumblety-peg and catch. Once under the madronas Father saw me holding a hatchet, when Patsy was nearby; he told me to watch out, that a boy by accident had chopped off his sister's hand. I surmised that he probably had made up this story but did not resent it as he had not used it to take advantage of me, and the moral had use. A few times there on the lawn he played with me with a football, teaching me about the game.

Father would read passages from the Bible to us children and tell us Bible stories. He had me memorize the Ten Commandments and the Lord's Prayer. An adult reported that after repeated attempts to teach Patsy how to say "Deliver us from temptation," I gave up and told her, "Well, you'll just have to wait till you grow up to be four like me."

Sometimes during childhood our parents took me to church services at the Highlands Chapel. I did not realize until later that Father was indifferent to religious beliefs and ceremonies, but we both enjoyed hearing Mother sing in the choir in her clear contralto.

In the winter, he would go down to the basement and shovel coal into the furnace. When we children would help him build a fire in the fireplace, we would crumple a piece of newspaper into a ball and hand it to him, and he would say, "That's the ticket!"

In summer, he would wear a stiff straw hat. He would go out on the kitchen porch and make ice cream by cranking the metal cylinder embedded in a bucket of salted ice.

One evening, the extended family had a picnic on the beach. The men took turns paddling—while standing up—one of the little wooden boats, about five feet long, in which we children had been playing. After Uncle Thomas had negotiated his voyage successfully, Father tipped over, falling on his face in his white flannels. He told me this later, observing with pleasure that this was the first time that Mother had laughed heartily since her father had died the year before.

On his frequent trips out of town he would send us children letters and postcards. On his return, we children would ask him: "Did you bring me a little something, Daddy?" And usually he would bring out a present for each of us.

At the Olympic (later Four Seasons) Hotel he took me to meet Jack Dempsey and Helene Madison, the swimming champion.

He took me with him to civic events in town. One was a banquet at the Chamber of Commerce. I sat at the long high table between Father, who made a speech, and the aged Professor Edmond Meany, who impressed and saddened me when he remarked that one day I might attend the University where he taught, but that he by then would be long dead.

Another was a breakfast meeting on the University Street sidewalk. A couple of uniformed police walked over to our table and lifted the table cloth beside Father, exposing a flat pint bottle containing a brown liquid. Father was led away in handcuffs amid noise of laughter and applause. This alarmed me until it was explained that this was a joke related to Father's strong advocacy that the 18th Amendment be repealed. After a few moments he was released and returned to breakfast.

He was a courtly gentleman, always socially at ease, his manners less notable for polish than for warmth and grace. He spoke with a pronounced Southern accent and used "mighty" and "right" as adverbs. He inspired several young men to enter politics, Warren Magnuson for one.

When he would take me by the hand and we would walk down Fourth Avenue, he would exchange greetings with what seemed to be every other passerby, even though he lived in Seattle for only twelve years. Everywhere he went he would be greeted with enthusiasm, reciprocating his own radiant warmth. He had a great gift for friendship and was the most loved man I have ever known. A decade after his death I got to chatting with a man; when he learned that Scott Bullitt was my father, this hard-boiled old Swede started to cry.

My parents gave me a crystal set radio. I strung the aerial to the cedar tree in the southern part of the lower lawn. Harriet would annoy me when she would forget that she was wearing the earphones and would run off, jerking the set to the floor.

When Father and Mother were going out for the evening, Patsy and I, kneeling on the window seat at the stair landing between the first and second floors of our home, would look out the window and cry as we watched them drive away in the car.

After a visit from Senator C. C. Dill who told us about his recent trip abroad and a delicious drink he had enjoyed in France, we children discussed what delights awaited us when we grew up, such as the taste treat he had called "cafiola with milk."

Once when we had been put to bed on the balcony on a summer night, Patsy became enchanted by the moon and said she wished to have it as her toy. I responded that she could not because I would not let her have it. At this, she cried so loudly that Mother came upstairs.

Patsy and I used to tease Harriet, who would react with a hot temper. Sometimes we shut her in a closet. Once she came out swinging a baseball bat. Another time she came out throwing milk from a glass; we dodged aside, and the milk splashed on some grownup who had come in the front door.

When we were taken to the Metropolitan Theater to see our first play (William Gillette in "Sherlock Holmes"), Patsy asked the meaning of the word "AS-BESTOS" on the hem of the curtain; I told her it meant "welcome" in Greek.

Until middle age I knew little about my forebears more distant than grandparents. Although curiosity has led me since to discover much about many of them, they have not come often into my mind beyond the process of discovery, and insofar as their dead hands have pushed the levers of my conduct, they have left me unaware of the weight.

On the other hand, during my developing years, direct experience of my parents and maternal grandparents and knowledge of their lives gave me a sense of family. Although much of our time was spent with nurses and other servants, we children nonetheless belonged to the extended family. Five houses in a row were occupied by related families: Our grandparents' Norcliffe, our home, the Downeys' (related by marriage), Mother's cousin Cully Stimson's, and, at the far end, her brother Thomas's big house. Other children living nearby were so few that siblings and cousins, with whom we felt at ease to play, were our main playmates. Our lives were affected by this group that was happy, loyal and warm.

In those days, children tended to derive some emotional security from facing a narrower range of choices than do present day children and from knowing clear and certain rules and roles. Children were not given special care—counselling, therapy, instruction in sensitivity, grieving support—for upsetting experience or other hard knocks. For example, when a car smashed into the gas pumps at 145th and Greenwood, Patsy, age twelve, on her way home from school watched the occupants burn to death: Saw them rolling on the pavement in flames, heard their screams and smelt their burning flesh. Thereafter, nothing ever was said to her about that.

As years passed, we responded in different ways to our Mother's powerful exercise of authority on us. I fought back until sullenly obeying, Patsy obeyed, and Harriet cheerfully evaded or deflected. Yet each of us grew up to be uncommonly stubborn (although our parents were not). I was less pugnacious than either of them; Patsy did not become docile or tractable any more than did the other two of us; and Harriet did not manipulate others but in her relationships became direct. Throughout the period of our growing up together my sisters treated me with affection and respect.

On my return from the War, Priscilla was running a Red Cross Service Center between Kobe and Osaka, while Harriet was newly married to a medical student at Columbia. In later years, after they had borne and raised children, my sisters returned to Seattle and directed the mass communications business that they controlled. They both made their marks, Priscilla in several business enterprises and as a writer and in civic affairs; Harriet as an editor, publisher, conservationist and developer of an unusual conference center.

Long after I was grown, after about a year of intermittent negotiation I made a deal to sell the office building at 4th and Union that had been Mother's principal object of business attention before she entered broadcasting. Hindsight has shown that the sale probably would have been advantageous. When I told her, she listened with interest and made no objection, but a tear rolled down her cheek. I canceled the deal. Thirty-five years later I was happy that we had it still.

Over the years, my practice shifted from seeking her permission to consulting her for advice on conduct in the world of affairs. In her old age, I would tell her the same sorts of things but with the aim of entertaining her.

Romantic love did not play a part in my two marriages. Both women were introduced to me in Seattle by mutual friends, Joanna Eckstein and Dorothy Block. In some respects the wives were similar: each a bright graduate of a good Northeastern women's college; politically liberal; about the same height and weight; born a few months apart; no brother; from upper-middle class Protestant families of mixed American stock (of Northwest European origins); both parents college graduates; both mothers well-educated women who had careers before marriage at almost forty; both fathers previously married and widowed without children, then aged about fifty when daughter born. In most other aspects of personality and values they stood in polar contrast. In generosity and humility, Kay approached sainthood; she made no demands on me and seldom complained.

Appetite for Carolyn put me on the short and slippery slope to a marriage that was, like the life of early humankind, "solitary, poor, nasty, brutish and short." Like the loss of a kneecap in an accident, this marriage was accepted with resignation as a condition to be endured for life. Although it had laughter and stimulating conversation, it was devoid of love, friendship or trust. By her I had two daughters and a son. After five and a half years of marriage, we were separated and then divorced. To perform the joint custody of the children was a nightmare.

During court proceedings with Carolyn, I met Kay, and we were married after the divorce. I was thirty-five. Kay's beauty attracted me, and her pure integrity reassured me; I knew she would wear well, would not betray me and would serve as a kind and conscientious stepmother to my three little children. In our lives together we had mutual affection and respect but we were not intimate. Discussion of personal matters was infrequent and tended to end promptly and inconclusively in disappointing misunderstandings. By her I begot two daughters and a son. This marriage was dissolved after twenty-four years.

Many things may be said of marriage, but in my own experience humiliation, frustration and loneliness were the worst, and children were the best.

Three weeks before her death, I visited my grandmother in her bedroom at Norcliffe to say goodbye before taking the train east for prep school. She told me not to forget I was head of the family. For the next twenty years it appeared to me that she had been the only one who thought there was such a thing to remember. Among my kin, I received more heed after becoming single and old than ever before. This was puzzling, but one takes his satisfactions where they come.

Since growing up, I have enjoyed children. From before turning twenty, I wanted children and wanted to be a good father to them, so that they might receive from me what my Father had provided me, and so they would not miss what I had missed when he was gone. He was often away from home during the years our lives overlapped and he did not spend much time with us children. However, when we were together he was attentive, affectionate and kind. I adored him (as he had adored his father), grieved at his loss and still miss him some. He is the only person who has appeared in my dreams long after his death.

The casual attitude of some men toward sowing wild oats always has disgusted and horrified me. To think of my baby out there somewhere without me to care for it and delight in it is intolerable.

Duty and pleasure combined to devote to my children a substantial proportion of my time and attention from age twenty-nine to fifty-six. Pleasure came from their company, their pleasures, their development and their kindnesses to me. To measure the whole experience, the plusses substantially outweighed the minuses. When one of my children repeated my first mother-in-law's remark to them that I was "always out looking for votes," it reminded me (among other things) of how much my children's company meant to me.

Of all the terms and titles by which I have been addressed, the one that has given me the most pleasure is "Daddy." My Mother deeply gratified me by saying I was the best father she had ever known. Now in a public place, on hearing a child cry out, "Daddy!" I spin around, then subside on realizing that the call was not for me.

Children surprise you. Often their adult shape does not match the mold of ingredients from which they came. Frederick of Prussia earned the title of Great despite a brutally harsh upbringing. Sydney Smith lamented that "The life of a parent is the life of a gambler." True, but gamblers often win.

When my oldest child Ashley's ballet class gave a recital at the Cornish Institute, most of the family attended. Dorothy cheered loudly when her big sister skipped out on the stage. In my lap sat son Benjamin Logan (named after my great-great-great grandfather, the frontier leader, who was noted for bravery at a time and place when this quality was common). I had bought seats for each, but little Ben ate his ticket.

When my older son, Scott, was five and a half, and a Sunday paper puzzle that he had asked me to solve had stumped me, I confessed to him that I was not very bright. He looked up with a sweet smile and replied in a sympathetic tone, "But you're very strong."

When my youngest child Margaret was eight, I came upon a scrap of paper bearing her handwriting. After dating it I put it away, returning it to her when her age had tripled. The words on the paper:

Nobody loves me.
But kitty loves me.

Among devices that I built or had installed in the yard for the children, the most successful (except the pool) was a four-foot plywood cube, open on one side and hung against a tree trunk five feet from the ground. From a branch overhanging the slope above the tree, a rope permitted a child to swing into the box, making this swing the only access.

While my children were growing up I enjoyed teaching them bits and scraps: answering questions, helping with homework; reading aloud perhaps twenty-five educational books (*The Count of Monte Cristo* was the most popular), with occasional interruptions for comment, discussion and explanations; also methods for sailing a boat, skiing, mountaineering, camping, football, tennis, boxing and chess. In the use of tools I had little to contribute. I caused them to hear good music but taught them nothing about it. I sought to teach each of them plane geometry, the subject I had most enjoyed in school. Scott learned more than the others; sitting in my lap at age five, he followed the steps of the theorems; his mind wandered seldom, as when from the apex of an isosceles triangle he drew upward-curling smoke. One season I helped to coach a Little League football team; Benjamin was one of three white players on the squad.

When some of my grown daughters expressed sympathy for my unhappiness, their affection made me grateful to them but made me fear to burden them by occasion for more, remembering how my pity for my Mother's unhappiness had not increased my love for her. Elizabeth Barrett Browning put it well.

Scenes of parental protection or revenge for harms inflicted have struck responsive chords in me: Rigoletto's fierce resolve to do in the duke who had ruined his precious child. And William Tell, after his celebrated crossbow shot, asked by Gessler why he had withdrawn two arrows from his quiver, replying that if he had hit his son instead of the apple, "The second arrow was for you."

The Sienese poet Cecco Angiolieri said, "Florins are the best of kin." I never have believed this.

❖ ❖ ❖

Like most everyone, my emotional ship has sailed through sudden squalls and full scale storms, along with doldrums, pack ice, flat calm, roaring forties and lovely trade winds. Agitated moments ought not be under-rated. In *Howard's End*, E.M. Forster wrote:

> It is so easy to talk of "passing emotion," and to forget how vivid the emotion was ere it passed. Our impulse to sneer, to forget, is at root a good one. We recognize that emotion is not enough, and that men and women are personalities capable of sustained relations, not mere opportunities for an electrical discharge. Yet we rate the impulse too highly. We do not admit that by collisions of this trivial sort the doors of heaven may be shaken open.

For most of my life I looked forward to the prospect of some happy, loving union. For many years this was expected: an assumption that such felicity befalls every one; later it was anticipated with wistful hope. I longed for some close and enduring attachment to one

who would respond to me with warmth, not make me
feel as though I were living with a deaf nun; one ardent
yet satiable, so as not to make work of love; one who
would regard my eccentricities not as exasperating per-
versities but as endearing idiosyncrasies; one who would
interpret my housekeeping and household furnishings
as unpretentious individuality rather than slovenly indifference; one not so indifferent to my earnest dis-
course that she would interrupt me in mid-sentence, not
to comment or respond but to change the subject.

Friends have supposed me wary of those who
would try to use me to enrich themselves. But to spot
such characters—like some who appear both expensive
and cheap—soon enough to avoid risk or even inconve-
nience never has been hard. Rather, my fear has been of
one who would turn unfriendly after we were locked
together, a fear of becoming bound to one who would
make life miserable, whether by sullen indifference, icy
hostility, caustic sneers or whining complaints.

As I grew older, among those few whom I might
want, the chances that one would want me became ever
more remote. Surmising that if any would be willing to
marry me, her merit must be slight. I resigned myself to
permanent singlehood after sporadic sparks of hope had
smoldered, glowed and been stamped out.

My friends have meant much to me. More than
with any other non-relative, I played as a child with
Edward Ohata; a couple of years older, he was to be
looked up to for both maturity and size. His father had
immigrated from Japan and worked for many years as
grandfather's chauffeur. For a long time I regarded

"Skooky"—his nickname in childhood—as my best friend. In the middle of my forehead, a finger can feel a rough spot that recalls when we were throwing stones at each other on the Highlands beach, each ducking behind logs when the other threw. Out of phase, I bobbed up in time to be hit by Skooky's rock.

Edward, who had graduated from the University of Washington and earned a letter rowing on the light-weight crew, sought to join the armed service, applying, one by one, to those branches with the most exacting requirements for admission: Navy Air Corps, Army Air Corps, Marines, Navy. He passed all tests but was rejected. Finally, the Coast Guard offered to take him as a mess cook. I cried in shame for my country and pity for my friend. He joined the infantry and served in the Italian Campaign. Although he and I have seen little of each other in our adult lives, we have remained friends.

Unlike many men, I did not make many deep or lasting friendships during high school and college. One of the few remaining friends from those years, Homer Harris, was never a schoolmate. Hearing of his reputation as a great athlete and a superior man, I went to his doorstep and introduced myself to him. Most of my friendships were made in the first ten years after the War, with a few more accumulated since.

One factor in Jews' appeal to me has been that they seem to have a sense of justice, when compared with that of other ethnic groups, that is both stronger and more refined (despite a generation containing Stalinists, succeeded by a generation containing big-oted Zionists who regard fellow Semites who are not Jews as some of my ancestors regarded Indians).

After age fifty, although I kept most of my old friends, almost all the new ones came from younger generations. Not until late in life did any women become friends. This long delay owed to knowing few, to being a slow learner and to the changing times.

Although boxing meant much to me in other ways, friends did not come from this field, only some friendly acquaintances. On Leyte I spent some time with George Fitch from New Haven, where we had boxed together in the gym. The heavyweight champion of New Guinea, he had been a sparring partner for Joe Louis. After the War he became the country's first Black referee. His abilities were such that today they would take him to college, but then the limitations of his Army situation induced him to mention to me that he would prefer the Navy where, as a mess cook, he could wait on tables, serving white officers who had better manners than the ones to whom he was accustomed and where he could get out of the mud.

The one exception, who did become a friend, was Lonnie Austin, one of my Father's multitude of friends, who taught me to box and handled me as an amateur fighter. He told me of watching a hanging, of how the condemned man, who had killed several in the course of robberies, looked down malignantly from the platform as though he wished to execute the spectators. Once Lonnie took me to the county jail and introduced me to three teenage prisoners. One had beaten another boy to death, another had shot and killed a man for pay, and the third (to be released to join the Navy) was a little boy who had burned down the schoolhouse.

One fall evening, Lonnie's gallantry stirred me when he left my car at a street corner: a man almost sixty, without money, education, security or station, striding off through the drizzle as the night came down, his head high, shoulders back, arms swinging and back straight. Later, when a stroke had taken most of his powers, a visit to him was not an experience of human intercourse but a gesture of respect, like laying a wreath on his grave.

To define greatness eludes me as much as to define justice. However, Jon Goldmark struck me as a great man, the only such among those whom I have known, although a number of others achieved more success as most people measure it. Jon developed a philosophy, derived principles from it, and carved out his life according to them. In his later years, fate battered him hard, yet he maintained over himself a mastery that would have been repugnant were it not for his humanity, his humor and his ideals. Like his father's uncle Louis Brandeis, he was a truly free man. He lived life on his own terms. By contrast with his, my life to me has seemed like an unruly galloping horse on which my hold was thin and guidance uncertain.

A perfectionist as exacting as Toscanini or Ted Williams, ambitious, contentious and intense, he nonetheless was rational, temperate and just. I never saw him in his cups. He turned to farming in part to offset his competitive propensity to jump on any available squirrel wheel. Because his self control was warmed by passion and guided by principle he proceeded without either an opportunist's calculation or a moralist's rigidity. Although our bonds of friendship were long-sustained and strong, we did not share personal intimacies; my glimpses of his inner life were indirect, derived largely from our sharing fundamental values—probably more closely, except for my daughter Dorothy, than with any one else.

Many called him a "renaissance man." This is true in the current use of the term, as meaning excellence in diverse functions. But his interests did not include the fine arts (except for music), and he was about as far as one could get from that "unbridled subjectivity" (Burkhardts' phrase), the turbulent, passionate egotism of the Renaissance. He had more in common with some figures of two or twenty-two centuries ago: with *les grands seigneurs* of Mt. Vernon or Monticello, or with Epaminondas and the Scipios, than he did with members of the Sforza or Visconti clans.

When some balls of slime called him a traitor to our country, their charge was ironic as well as false. His sense of American tradition, belonging to it and having his part to play in it, was all of a piece with his U.S. Navy officer's sword above his fireplace, beside which, through the window, one could look across his wheat fields, his cattle grazing on the bunch grass of the Colville plateau, past his nearest neighbor's distant fence to the folded brown hills and the snow peaks beyond.

In my mind's eye, Alexander looks like him, exalted by the distant glories of Antiquity. Charlton Heston as Ben Hur reminded me of him. It is easy to think of Jon as Roland or Leonidas, taking his stand at the pass; making his tender farewell to wife and child before going out the city gates against Achilles; standing at the Tiber bridge, strapping his harness on his back and saying, "To every man upon this earth . . . "; as Regulus, boarding the ship for Carthage, to be taken to torture and to death; as Toshiro Mifune, facing fearful odds, hitching up his sword belt with a grunt as he lurches out into the rain; or as Bishop Latimer at the stake, turning his head to say: "Be of good comfort and play the man, John Ridley, for this day in England we have lit such a candle as will never be put out."

Hearing Giovanni Costigan speak was like attending a concert. Sometimes he spoke with such compelling force that one would feel in the presence not of the bold and masterly Don Giovanni, but of the Commendatore!—and he would do all this not with thunderous chords but in a soft and humble pianissimo.

Some of those whom I have enjoyed the most I have seen seldom because their brilliance made me hesitate to intrude myself on them. Adam Yarmolinsky is so keen and quick that no preliminary conversation is needed to bring him to the point. With Adam, one is always at the point. In Melbourne, on telling a girl about how I hesitated to speak in the presence of my bright friend (for three score years now) Dick Riddell for fear he might be bored, she sensibly commented that a companion's muteness bored. I accepted this lesson and ever since have chattered freely to him.

In business I had little friendship. Few of the personalities were congenial to mine, and the duty to act with impartial justice restricts friendship where one person can help or hurt the other in his career but the other cannot do the same.

To have friends for law partners has been my good fortune. Relationships within many law firms are impersonal, guarded and sometimes hostile, the members associated for exclusively career considerations. My partners have combined professional ability with personal quality and congeniality. While the mountains make me feel like a man and put me in tune with the earth, my partners' company makes me mellow and relaxed. In the years I worked primarily as a business executive, my children remarked that the only time Daddy came home cheerful was from the mountains and from the monthly partnership meeting. I admire my partners. To be among them gives me pleasure, and to be connected with them gives me pride. Although they are ambitious, forceful and competitive, they do not compete with each other, but treat each other with an easy and humorous generosity. Some of them underrate my abilities, but they do not fear or despise me, as I fear that some of my business colleagues have done. Nor do they try to use or manipulate me. If they do not understand something I have said, they ask me to explain it again rather than trying to read between the lines, guess or ask other people what is in my mind. None uses upon me the kind of flattery that insults by assuming that one may be expected to believe such oily stuff.

In recent years, since the firm has grown to tenfold what it was when I joined it, the atmosphere has become, perforce, impersonal and institutional, but many of my partners are nonetheless my friends.

For performing their difficult central function in society, with its insecurity, stresses and moral ambiguities, politicians have my admiration and sympathy for the conditions under which they must live. But my friends among them are few. Warren Magnuson was kind to me from my childhood. Even if we had known each other well, a close friendship with this most endearing man might have been made improbable by the inevitable effects on the personality of one who was a politician for almost all his active adult years. Too many politicians affect me as Gladstone did Queen Victoria, who complained, "He addresses me as though I were a public meeting." On the whole, though, friends, like gold, are where you find them, and in many places they can be found and made.

Fifteen friends gathered to celebrate with me my fiftieth birthday. We dined around a table set up in the yard. A couple of my children served the meal. As dusk fell, I stood with champagne glass in hand and made a toast to these friends, reciting something about my experience with each. For example:

> Jerry Berlin and I met twenty-six years ago through a couple of girls in Newport News. This may give the false impression that our experiences together were festive revelry; in fact, we have dealt with each other over the years almost wholly by thoughtful and elevated correspondence. We have felt drawn together as fellow gentlemen of the 18th century from which we feel displaced persons. He has reminded me of Joseph Conrad: Each man a Merchant Marine deck officer, a man of letters, an Anglophile. But those are superficial similarities. The deeper one is a stern, strong morality with emphasis on self-discipline. Bertrand Russell wrote of his friend, Conrad, what I can say of Jerry: "His intense and passionate nobility shines in my memory like a star seen from the bottom of a well. I wish I could make his light shine for others as it shone for me."

After an operation, Father was brought home, suffering from liver cancer. He was put in my bed, in which he died the following week. I had thought he had come home to get well. Early that April morning at my grandmother's house, where I was staying, I saw her climbing the stairs with weary tread, which gave me a foreboding of what I dared not admit to myself until a few minutes later, when I walked over to our house, walked upstairs where Mother came out the door. No express notice of the event then was needed.

He was fifty-five, and I was twelve. If you wish to

be immortalized as an image of perfection in your child's heart, do so before your human frailties have been observed, or at least assumed, as children assume about their parents when they grow up; yet do so after you have made a clear imprint on your child so that you are more than a name connected with a portrait on the table beside your widow(er)'s bed.

Although I have attended many funerals, most deaths of people I have known were of the old. For the survivors of those of us whose human assets are regarded as having been more or less amortized the sense of loss is rarely large.

Those whose deaths touched me included these. Two were family friends. Kitty Prince, a spirited achiever, lived as fully as she could while skin cancer wasted her. Once a week during her last month I sat beside her bed and read to her "The Tempest." She was moved and felt the fitness of the final language—the "cloud-capped towers . . . the great globe itself . . . this insubstantial pageant faded . . . our revels now are ended," Prospero breaking his wand and summing up.

Dorothy Block's energy and generosity that warmed without intimidating made her seem more alive than most people before a brain tumor cut her down in her thirties, leaving a crippled husband and six little children.

Another was John Kennedy. When Franklin Roosevelt died, people were moved, some perhaps more so than by JFK's death, but for a different cause. For twelve years, FDR had made a heavy and comprehensive impact on the conditions of our lives. He had shaped our history, and many felt him to be a sort of all-powerful father. In Melbourne the news of his death emptied the downtown buildings and filled the streets. Up the avenue where the consulates had their offices ran a line of flags, each at half mast. These Australians half way around the globe never had seen FDR, never had visited his country; few had ever heard his voice. Yet many wept on the sidewalk, many came up to us Americans in uniform, telling us, in tears, of their sympathy for our loss and that they felt it as their own. A short time later, when their own wartime leader, Prime Minister Curtin, died, less sorrow was displayed.

Mr. Roosevelt had cast long beams and shadows, and this older man's death made people deeply sad, sorry for themselves, but his family was not pitiful. By contrast, when John Kennedy was shot down, people's hearts were torn. They pitied gallant Jack, his wife and little children. Immersed in life, living at the top of the times, he had lost so much. Extending far ahead of him had been sunlit, flowered fields. In his career he resembled Charles James Fox, but the public impact of his death resembled that of Sir Philip Sidney's, of whom the crowds attending his funeral procession cried out, "Farewell, the friend, beloved of all, that had'st no foe but chance," or that of Rupert Brooke's, after whose premature death as a soldier in Greece during World War I Churchill wrote to *The London Times*:

> Joyous, fearless, versatile, deeply instructed, with classic symmetry of mind and body . . . he was all that one would wish England's noblest sons to be.

And the majesty of Jack's office increased the outrage of the monstrous act.

Although we never met, I felt drawn to Robert Kennedy, and admired him. A practicing, even believing, member of the Church that puts only slight emphasis on the Bible and prefers the New Testament at that, he nonetheless resembled in spirit a 17th century Puritan, more guided by the Old Testament than have been members of any other sect, probably including the Jews: intense, moralistic, believing in The Word, pursuing a clearcut vision with fierce resolve. Except for his sense of humor, he could have been one of Cromwell's Saints. In personality and style, he contrasted with his brother, John: casual, rational, a cryptoagnostic, accepting tradition, an upper-class British Whig. Robert's death shocked me more deeply than did the death of cool and elegant John. No one thought of Bob as a young god. His passionate righteousness, struggles, frustrations and frailties, made me and many others grieve his loss. We had felt his sympathies—whether for us or for those with whom we sympathized—and we cared for him. When he was killed, I had the TV stations sign off that night with a quote from Justice Holmes:

> We accept our destiny to work, to fight, to die for ideal aims. At the grave of a hero who has done these things, we end, not with sorrow at the inevitable loss, but with the contagion of his courage; and with a desperate joy we go back to the fight.

During Bob's funeral, the television zoom lens from high in St. Patrick's nave showed Lyndon Johnson standing in an alcove, looking at the somber multitude from all stations and sectors of our society and aware of the overflow in the street outside. Perhaps he was thinking to himself: "That little wart will never have the White House as his home as it has been mine, but I know for sure my death will not bring out a grieving throng the likes of this."

The funeral train, passing southward through mournful numbers of RFK's countrymen, paused at Baltimore, through which another train had passed, a hundred and three years before, bearing the corpse of another ambitious politician ("And the great star early droop'd in the western sky in the night"). The crowd joined hands and sang "The Battle Hymn of the Republic," that rhythmic chant that plucks deep chords in many of us, evoking our national past: the Union dead in our most terrible war, the theme of the Gettysburg Address, martial valor in support of principle and the sacrifices that men have made for the American Dream.

A surprisingly heavy impact was made by the telephone call that Dusan Jagersky had fallen while descending from the summit of an unnamed, hitherto unclimbed, peak in Alaska roped to Al Givler, a friendly acquaintance of mine. Their bodies remain, embedded in the avalanche cone at the foot of the mile-high cliff from which they fell. Dusan and I shared less background, experiences and interests, than I have shared with any other friend. We did not know each other long and had had only brief association (mainly climbing) but found a prompt affinity that made an affectionate bond. Uncomplicated and warm, he joyed in using his prodigious physical equipment. For long after his death (three weeks before we were to set forth on an expedition together) he came to mind often during pleasure, when I found myself thinking how what I was doing would have been enjoyed by him.

Henry King lamented his wife's death at twenty-four:

> Thou scarce had'st seen so many years
> As Day tells houres.

When my son Benjamin, at that age, drowned off Leschi one cold November night, he had been leading a life that I deplored. Wayward and self-indulgent, he blazed along in radiant vitality, disregarding the law and the truth, choosing not to "scorn delights, and live laborious days," but preferring "To sport with Amaryllis in the shade," and letting others do his share of work. At first his conduct gave me deep distress, which subsided to resignation when his course became fixed. He did not have my respect. Yet when the dark waters closed over that curly head, only one thing mattered: He was my little boy, and I loved him.

I mourned him not for his merits but from attachment to him and from regret that he could not play still more and that he had been denied the chance to put out what he had within himself. I grieved not for his having been a worthy achiever but because he was switched off before he had sung the repertory of his songs.

At Stevens Pass in the months that followed his drowning, my spirits floated on the chair lift. The ride up the hill does not exhilarate like the ski run down, but one's concentration is released. The winter serenity of the bowl, silent evergreens, blue sky above the sparkling snow, slopes animated by the young exerting themselves and exchanging cheerful yells, all made me rejoice to be alive. In turn, awareness of what Ben was missing made my eyes pour tears.

The truth of Bacon's aphorism that children are given as hostages to fortune I had known but had thought that it referred only to circumstantial limitations on free choice, such as impediments to work achievement and career advance. Then came awareness how, in truth, with each child a parent puts up collateral, pledging his heart.

Often people regard a young person's death as incomprehensibly senseless. But does any one die a sensible death? Is not death's mystery an aspect of life's incomprehensible meaning? Where a life has been cut off before its time, to remark on that life's intensity or productivity or good fortune as somehow softening the loss fails to touch what matters most: a missed chance to tackle more life. And that goes for every one. Ask the gallant lads who earned a posthumous Congressional Medal or V.C.; ask Schubert, Keats or Joan of Arc. The only point of mentioning the richness of a short past life is to suggest the likely rich future that was lost.

People have been consoled by the language for the burial of the dead from the Book of Common Prayer, that "Whosoever liveth and believeth in me shall never die." And people have been inspired by St. Paul's defiance when he declared his faith, "O death, where is thy sting, O grave, where is thy victory?" But to most of us, even those whom those words console or inspire, death stings.

Priscilla

Ben

Back Yard 6/62

6/84

Bill & Astri Baillargeon,
Harriet B. 6/89

Bill Sumner, Kay Bullitt 6/89

Patsy, Ashley 6/94

Margaret, Benj. Schmechel &
Aunt Dorothy

Jill, Harriet 6/94

David Riesman 1994

Homer Harris

Bagley Wright

Mike Roemer

Jim Wickwire, Bill Dwyer 6/89

Chapter | 3

BOOKS

Pray freely for thyself, and
Pray for all who long for larger life
    And heavenly cheer,
The truth will make thee free,
    And never fear.

—CHAUCER

The month sister Harriet was born, my parents put me in kindergarten at the Highlands School. Of the twenty-five students, a substantial number were related. Once we children were put through a pageant to the music of the Nutcracker Suite. My part was a mouse, and my only line a loud squeak, which entertained my cousins. On my walking in the School door three score years after leaving it, one whiff of its air brought back memories as vivid as those the madeleine evoked for Proust.

When I was age six, a nurse started to teach me to read. The lessons did not go far, and I disliked her, but the learning, remembered with a thrill, resembled sitting in the theater as the curtain starts to rise from the stage.

The summer I was nine, Mother employed a college student to tutor me and look after me in general, supplementing the supervision of the governess who would call me in from the yard to take my nap in the afternoon. He started to teach me to ride a bicycle. To it I attached signs for Father's candidacy for Governor and tried to campaign for him by riding on the seldom-traveled Highlands roads. About that year I started wearing glasses and ever since have worn them to read and write.

At eleven, my parents moved me to the 6th grade at Lakeside, a boy's private prep school that I attended for the next four years. On the first day, Latin began. Veo Small wrote on the blackboard:

> Amo
>
> Amas
>
> Amat
>
> Amamus
>
> Amatis
>
> Amant

Twenty-two years later this teacher subscribed to a right-wing attack on my patriotism, by way of opposing my candidacy.

Just before turning twelve, at school commencement I was given a copy of *Kim* as a prize for science, surprising this boy who had not excelled. Perhaps it came from having asked the teacher, Mr. Logan, after having read in the newspaper's Sunday supplement that the center of the universe had been discovered, how something could have a center when it had no finite limits. After this book, a high school diploma was the only academic award to come my way for the next fifty-seven years.

That summer I went to a secretarial school, learning to type, plus a smattering of bookkeeping. The typing has been useful ever since.

In the summer of '33, on turning fourteen, I toured Europe as the youngest in a troop of forty Boy Scouts from the Northwest. We attended the International Scout Jamboree outside Budapest; about thirty thousand were encamped. I admired, and hardly even presumed to envy, the other boys who were so much more grown up than I, their sophistication revealed by knowing hit tunes and songs whose very existence had been unknown to me. Remembered, this trip was an endless process of wearily climbing on and off buses and being led through cathedrals and past other objects of cultural or historic interest.

In Vienna, we were shocked to walk past well-dressed men kneeling on the sidewalk with their hands folded in prayer, begging because they were hungry and broke. Some people told us that they knew Hitler and the Nazis were evil but they hoped they would come. To tolerate the wickedness was a price they were willing to pay for something to eat.

The atmosphere in France struck me as pessimistic, languid and cynical, while Germany gave a tone of dynamic optimism, purpose and hope. Some members of a Nazi youth organization were presented to us as a counterpart of the Scouts. In Cologne, they told us that a few days before some of them had caught a Communist on the Cathedral steps and that he had fourteen knives in him before his body hit the steps.

At Heidelberg we were shown the university jail for students. Among the graffiti was a series of three or four cat silhouettes of descending size. This was explained to us as representing a katzenjammer—or hangover—and that each day it got smaller. Years passed before I came to grasp the magnitude of a hangover that would endure beyond a day.

Fifty-two years after the Jamboree, our troop had a reunion. We were a forestry professor, a Navy Rear Admiral, a radiologist, his brother, a judge—all four retired—joined by Dick Riddell and me, practicing law together. We had lunch and reported, speculated and reminisced about our comrades' fates and fortunes.

With adolescence and other disturbances, my concentration and diligence declined, and my grades reflected this on through the end of college.

Mother sent me east to prep school, much against my will. My parents had entered me at St. Paul's at birth, but after Mother concluded that St. Paul's and I were unsuited to each other, she allowed me to choose the school (on the basis of a trip on which she took me to visit several). My choice of Kent, in western Connecticut, for its comparative social democracy, was regretted later on my realizing that because the merit of social democracy was a lesson already learned, a school with higher scholastic standards and better teachers would have better met my needs.

At fifteen, my life at Kent started in the fourth form (sophomore year). The school had three hundred boys in five grades and was operated by the Episcopal monastic Order of the Holy Cross. Classes were six days a week. The school was headed, and truly led, by its founder, Father Sill. A substantial number of the boys (not including me) went to him to confession. Not a good administrator or diplomat but an impressive man. By his directness of purpose and force of character an institution was forged.

Math was both a pleasure and a success. Thrills came from discovering how nature is expressed in mathematical terms: how many natural forms and processes are represented by some simple mathematical formula that can be projected on a graph; the wonder of how a baseball knows it must make a parabola, planets know they must follow an ellipse, and a comet knows it must follow a hyperbolic path; the great number of natural distributions that fit a bell curve; and the Golden Section, such a dull-looking number (1.6180339) yet describing so many natural forms and also artificial proportions that appeal to some human eyes. All this charmed me as suggesting some kind of beautiful abstract unity in the world.

On the other hand, English composition baffled me; I was pen-tied and got low grades in English every year after childhood's end. The disparity in performance between math and English was such that my grades for one tended to be about one-half that of the other. At Kent my overall class rank ran around fiftieth out of seventy-five students.

Schoolmates, finding me inarticulate and without repartee, teased me a lot, mainly for social naiveté and unawareness (daydreaming, inattentive to surroundings). Not until some time later did it sink in that my standing with the other boys was better than I had thought. One thing that helped me win acceptance was a zest for slam-bang contact sports.

Homesickness bore me down. Letters home, especially the first year, were filled with complaints and self-pity, exaggerating the miseries and evils of the place. They often ended with words to the effect: "But don't worry about me." This recalls my censorship duties in the Pacific; Navy sailors wrote horror stories to provoke sympathy from their womenfolk.

At sixteen, a letter told of having "just finished reading *Les Miserables*. It is terribly good though it has pretty much history in it." Later, having read Plato's *Republic* on the train returning to school (a long journey in those days) I noted having been "impressed but thought it a bad form of government."

Another letter to Mother: "Father Sill said I would make a better gardener than a lawyer or something because I work harder on the yards than on any other thing." Three years later, she had me take vocational aptitude tests from a New York institute. The report warned against my seeking an occupation, such as law, that had much of a verbal component. It urged me instead to try to become something like an architect or an engineer.

Mother insisted on my going to Harvard, Yale, Princeton or Williams. My preference had been the University of Virginia, because it was big in boxing, or to stay home and attend the University of Washington. My internal screening process ruled out Harvard as snobbish, Williams as inferior, and Princeton because it seemed unfair to take advantage of my Father's reputation there, as others urged me to do. Yale was left, and to Yale then I went. I no more enjoyed being made to do this than one likes doing anything against one's will, yet in retrospect to have yielded to Mother's compulsion has left me grateful and gratified.

It was a thrill when the conductor entered the coach from New York that September morning and shouted: "Noo Haven!" Despite the years of prep school, freshman year still found me homesick, yet the new experience of college was exciting. The great University conveyed electricity even to students who were not learning much, and for those who came from conventional households or from boarding school, it was heady to live in a place that, by contrast, had *no rules* (although to some it may have resembled going to the Army from jail).

At Yale I lasted four years. I attended public lectures by Thomas Mann, Professor Kittridge (on *Lear*),

Charles A. Lindberg (urging isolation); Ray Kelly, National Commander of the American Legion ("I believe in free speech, but . . ."), Earl Browder, head of the Communist Party (a plodding fellow, he was heckled hard). I heard and met Carl Sandburg, a marvelous-looking man, and attended a composition class that Paul Hindemith was conducting for a few days as a guest at the Music School. What he taught surpassed my understanding, but he charmed me by his unpretentious manner, thick German accent and beaming smile.

Short of confidence, lacking purpose and reading slowly, I learned far less than most thinking people learn at college and acquired little culture, comprehension or mental discipline. Some of the time was spent boxing, in social exploration and at other play. Some time went into undirected reading, and much was frittered away in day-dreams. I failed to carry out assignments, often spending long periods staring at a page, brooding, unable to concentrate or to understand. Too shy to question the teacher when something baffled me, I would be unable to proceed, and the class would leave me behind. My courses were chosen on the basis of what I did poorly and therefore appeared to need rather than what excited my curiosity or was taught by teachers who might stimulate. After planning research on a project by collecting a vast bibliography, I would fail to read the books, much less write something derived from what had been read.

In the spring of 1941, James Grafton Rogers, Master of Timothy Dwight College, where I lived, rose at the end of dinner and spoke to us about the war in Europe, which filled our minds. He told us, "There's a bully abroad, and he's got to be stopped." Predicting that our country would be at war before long, he advised us to wait until we were drafted rather than enlisting. His direct language, without color or passion, made our proper course of duty seem simple to decide. His talk made a strong impact on me and, I think, on the others. Uncomplicated, gregarious and bluff, he was an able, sensible man. He did not appear to discern any merit in me—and had no reason to—but he was kind and friendly to me, and I remember him with warmth.

The following month, when my class graduated, my completed work had fallen far short of what was required for a degree. Before Commencement, after a few aimless days in New York, the train took me home, feeling worthless by comparison with my parents and schoolmates.

For part of my tour of duty at the San Diego Naval Training Station, I slept (away from the barracks) downtown in a shabby room in a shabby rooming house, to be near the courthouse library, where some free time was spent ineffectually trying to learn law by reading some law books. Although legal knowledge can be poured into a legally-trained mind in solitude, one cannot become trained as a lawyer without inquiry, argument and other kinds of verbal give and take. I commuted to the Station (about four miles) on a bicycle. Once while reading I rode it into a truck.

During lunch at the Chiefs' mess, a fellow chief came up behind the bench, saw my copy of *Crime and Punishment* on the table, and asked, "What's that, Russian law?"

While attending a Navy school on the Harvard campus, a treat was a "high table" at Lowell House, listening to a conversation between two Harvard professors: Gaetano Salvemini, who had been active in Italian politics, and Heinrich Bruening, who preceded Hitler as Chancellor of Germany. Reflecting aspects of their national cultures, one of them was fiery and the other learned and benign. They thought Roosevelt's foreign policy excessively expedient in a mistaken effort to avoid Wilson's mistakes. Salvemini said he hoped that Churchill would die on the armistice day.

Soon after, from the balcony at Sanders Theatre I watched Churchill receive an honorary degree from Harvard and then make a major speech. Seeing and hearing this great man's performance, I felt close to history being made. Using no prepared text, he spoke with the craftsmanship of a mason meticulously constructing a wall. Afterwards, we servicemen living on the Yard assembled in ranks, and he spoke a few words to us from the Chapel steps.

Gentlemen of the armed forces of the United States.

This is indeed an inspiring spectacle, and I am very glad that my hosts here today have not denied me the opportunity of meeting you here for a few moments, and of offering you a few words of salutation upon the work on which you are engaged.

We have reached a period in the war when many people are inclined to think the worst is over. In a certain sense, this may be true; that the issue—the final issue of the war—does not seem so much in doubt as it did some time ago.

I have no reason to suppose that the climax of the war has been reached. I have no reason to suppose that the heaviest sacrifices in blood and life do not lie before the armed forces of Britain and America.

I know of no reason for supposing that the climax of the war has been reached even in Europe, and certainly not in Asia.

The courses of instruction through which you are going are of the utmost value to those who will be charged with the responsibility of leading others in battle. If the troops have a good supply of thoroughly well-trained officers, then they get their tasks done with incomparably less loss of life. Therefore the work you are doing here is of the highest possible consequence. I bid you all good fortune and success, and I earnestly trust that when you find yourselves alongside our soldiers and sailors, you will feel that we are your worthy brothers-in-arms.

And you shall know that we will never tire nor weaken. We shall march with you into every quarter of the globe to establish a reign of justice and law among men.

Knowing my Father and grandfather had been lawyers probably was a factor in setting me on their course. To be a tenth generation member of an unbroken succession of American lawyers means something to my daughter Dorothy, so probably tradition or example would have put more weight on me had I known that Father had seven generations of American lawyers behind him.

While on terminal leave from the Navy, I entered the University of Washington Law School (my first attendance at a public school). My poor college record denied me admission except in the status of a special student, which permitted me to attend classes and take the tests, but not to graduate. In a hurry to finish, I attended school around the year, and finished in 1948 at summer's end. Most of the students had come from war service. The tone was one of sober diligence, the juvenile frivolity so often displayed by undergraduates having been left behind. Only four or five women attended the school—my class had none—and the circular letter informing applicants that they were to be admitted to the Bar from the January, 1949, examinations used the salutation, "Dear Sir."

The process of law study was a delight. The transition from comparative sloth to strenuous work and stimulating thought was a jolt, but made me feel like turning handsprings or bursting into song on the way to class. Among the regrets that hang in my sky like a cloud of demons, one of the lesser ones is failure to postpone my outside activities and concentrate on the law while at school.

From about six (on learning to read) to fifteen (sent away to prep school), I read a lot, taking books from the shelves of the family library as well as reading books that were given to me. Almost all were fiction: novels and tales, most of them adventure stories written for boys and some of them books for a general audience, like *Treasure Island*. I understood *Moby Dick* only as a whale-hunting story and as such considered it inferior to *The Cruise of the Cachelot* by Frank T. Bullen. The novels of Stewart Edward White and Rex Beach thrilled me—stories of young men whose strenuous and adventurous efforts in logging or commercial fishing took them to financial success and the girl of their dreams.

As a boy, I came to know examples of a now-vanished American type—the workman without formal education yet bright, well-read and sometimes even learned. They tended to have goofy ideas. If they had come to maturity today they would have gone to college, but back then the limitations of both the economy and the educational system sent them early off to work. Without formal education, they had read without guidance or discrimination, and their thinking had developed untested. Lonely among those who did not share their interests, these men were voluble when an ear was offered to their voice.

Despite my slowness, my reading continued. Most was self-indulgent, browsing, tasting, consuming what amused or interested me. Among my favorites were Sinclair Lewis's novels—his moral indignation and his loving eye for the American scene. Not until after college did my reading pursue a directed aim to become educated. The four Navy years allowed me to consume a considerable body of educational books, and to learn from them except those parts that without an explanation could not be understood. Although my reading has continued without a lapse, my slow speed has limited the number of books read. Some, read for education, have been so good that they spurred further education, lifting standards until they passed from reach again.

Many books have pleased me much. Gibbon wrote that on the night when he had written the final sentences of his History, which had consumed so much of his life and done so much to justify it, he went for a moonlight walk in his Lausanne garden. Deep satisfaction was followed by melancholy at the loss of his long-time companion. On finishing his great work, I felt a similar regret, wishing it would go on, a text without end.

In addition to pleasure and improving my mind, a purpose for reading has been to gratify curiosity. In

William Stafford's words, "The greatest ownership of all is to glance around and understand." Other motives have been information needed in the course of work, insecurity at being uneducated, obtaining grist for my own writing, using the pages of a book as a refuge from human contacts and fear of wasting time. The last two motives combined to set me in the lifelong habit of reading during meals—though not those "dangerous books qu'on ne lit que d'une main."

If offered a chance to do things over again I would learn more natural science, the physical world's uniformities, better to comprehend how it works, and perhaps what it means. Those glimpses revealed to me have been fascinating, such as the astonishing regularity of planetary motions and how the same temperature is shared by all of human kind.

This engrossment in books has been a form of human isolation but not a lonely one. Adventures among well-written words have been the opposite of lonely. Immersion in good books resembles an evening at a club of your betters who generously share their thoughts and feelings with you.

The books in my library are my most precious tangible possessions. Most are old friends and companions. Some belonged to my Father, to his parents or to my Mother's mother. Many passages I have marked because they are pleasing, impressive or true. On the margins I have written comments. In part, these books have become a collection of reference notes.

As for many other people, the sound of American place names has struck me: the musical charm of Alabama, Kentucky, Tennessee, Shenandoah, Yosemite, Santa Fe, Sierra; the harsh strength of Chicago, Fargo, Shuksan, Pittsburgh. For euphony, my favorite law firm

name is Chadwick, McMicken, Ramsey & Rupp—an
even meter, a heavy beat, easy diction, alliteration and
at the end a consonant that comes down hard. Another
good one would be the names of the chief tribes in what
became Dixieland: "Choctaw, Chickasaw, Cherokee and
Creek."

On a summer afternoon, after he had beaten me
at a game of badminton in his backyard, Ted Roethke,
the poet, went into the house cheerful and returned
disconsolate because his wife had scolded him. He sat
on the steps and would play no more. This childlike man
was touching in his sensitive openness and engaging in
his artless candor. He made the following draft of a
poem, which he did not refine so did not publish.

> Now why do I carry on like this,
> And freeze my soul to paralysis?
> Why, doctor, it's pure self-analysis
> — I really want to be him, be him
>   I really want to be him.
>
> The situation is sexual:
> With money I'm ineffectual;
> He's a real, I'm a fake intellectual
> — So I want to be like old Stim Stim
>   I want to be like dear Stim.
>
> Now get this straight: I'm no bigger lover
> I've always wanted a younger brother
> A home and a rich powerful mother
> — So I could be a little more like Stim,
>   like Stim
>   Just a <u>little</u> more like Stim.

> He isn't, like me, an aging lecher—
> Whom the Lord Himself wouldn't have
>   made dog-catcher
> With that first wife—may the Devil fetch
> And fling her to hell. And I'll bet you
> — We'll be calling him Senator Stim,
>   We'll be calling him Senator Stim.

My friend Professor Joan Webber, killed by rock-fall on Rainier, wrote a couple for me. The opening lines of one were:

> Believe in light. Translucent valor of the
>   setting sun,
> Blue ice, rain on the sea. Your eyes
> Say simplify.
> Forty, fifty years to get that down.

Near the War's end (after a few years of keeping a journal in an irregular way), I began a daily diary (combining with it the features of a scrap book, photograph album, journal and commonplace book), and have kept it ever since. Portions—refined and extended—became both *To Be a Politician* and this book. Over the years, both keeping the diary and having its record to review have influenced my life.

On a mistaken assumption, this was undertaken in part to become less inarticulate in speech. As in most learned skills, one learns best by doing the thing itself; one learns to speak by speaking. Writing may provide rewards, but the only skill that its practice produces is better writing and more orderly thought.

Never yet settled for me have been the main decisions that one must make for a diary: audience, discretion, volume and polish. Who shall be the intended audience? Is this written solely for my own backward glance? For my children? For publication? For some pedantic scholar a century hence?

As for discretion, even to disclose that one keeps a diary may tend to induce some of one's associates to show off or become overly discreet. Secrecy from those who share one's household is impossible to assure unless one takes the trouble to use a code. At one period, with this in mind, I wrote feelings that were unfelt, and thus falsified the record. Then, having concluded that a diarist should be forever candid in expressing what he chooses to include, I resumed the practice of putting down nothing that was not meant.

Tales one hesitates to tell should be omitted rather than distorted. Otherwise, a diary has no value to record one's life. Discretion itself is a form of revelation, and although omissions distort, they mislead the reader less if he realizes they are to be expected.

The right length for diary entries is hard to set. Dictating machines—and even word processors—encourage prolixity, language permissible to be spoken but that does not deserve to be preserved; and it makes sloppy expression harder to escape ("Writing maketh an exact man; speech a ready man").

Aside from grace of expression, rewriting is necessary for all but the most thoroughly organized minds to attain exactness of meaning. This justifies how much loss of spontaneity and consumption of time?

Reading the printed pages of others' diaries leads one to the puzzling and dismaying conclusion that in most cases publication is a mistake. The few diaries that

are worth reading in later years are those that combine
the author's gifts with the freshness of the moment (e.g.
Johnson's and Boswell's journey to the Hebrides), direct observation of people and events and recording of
immediate experience, without the film of memory that
overlays a distant backward look. That subject can be
the author himself if he is sufficiently interesting and
distinct.

Only a remarkable diarist can hold readers' attention. A few, in numbers too small to be considered a
class (Hammersköld), reflect on life's meaning, where
an able mind has long meditated the matters set down.
Incessant repetition of the first person singular joins
other limitations that tend to turn a reader off. Everyone will criticize, and few will read, daily entries by any
but those who took part in great events.

If the choice to publish was made by the diarist,
one wonders why a memoir was not produced instead.
Most diaries can be made more readable by transforma-
tion into a memoir. The only exception to this is the
rare diary best fitted for its form. One would not prefer
the memoirs of Pepys or Frank.

By definition a first draft, a diary's expression
can be improved by rewriting, by thorough editing and
by compression. The freshness of that rare diary that is
worth reading is an aspect of the rawness characteristic
of all diaries. The day's jottings of what happened that
afternoon beside the Pond were much reworked before
they became *Walden*. And a diary's substance can be
improved by the diarist's own later experience, perspective and reflection. A memoir is to a diary as a page of
history is to a newspaper page.

Whether the decision to publish is made by the

diarist or one (executor, descendant) responsible for protecting the diarist's reputation, one further wonders why diaries are published that will injure the author's name. Some show the diarist's worst side, perhaps make him look even worse than his worst.

Referring to biographies that recite behavior of a personal kind usually treated as private, Barbara Tuchman quoted Tennyson:

> What business has the public to know of Byron's wildnesses? He has given them fine work and they ought to be satisfied.

And she and he were right. One's private behavior is irrelevant to a measurement of the work one gives the world. But one who *presents* his frailties to the world does not deserve sympathy for invasion of his privacy; he is asking for disapproval. If he displays pompous boasts, caustic jibes and falsehoods verifiable as such, he exposes himself to criticism that does more harm, and more deserved, than what may be dug up by reporters with telephoto lenses and by interviews with soured ex-paramours.

A diarist has the prospect of holding readers' attention many years hence if he writes entertainingly of personal experience or if he describes interesting events clearly, without evaluating them. Yet many entries interpret events and make judgments of people on the basis of their behavior that day. And before the events have led to observed consequences followed by sustained reflection, even the most farseeing and wise among us cannot measure yesterday morning's place in history without someday being found far off the mark.

During the Civil War, the wise Henry Adams thought that the Southern people must be exterminated as the only means to peace; later, he would approve a peace so easy that it would admit recognition of the Confederacy.

Although editing by both diarist and editor may excise some judgments that hindsight could see to have been mistaken, nonetheless many may remain. Most readers, from their lofty perspective of a few decades, will not make allowances for errors made by a diarist who evaluated an event that took place the previous day. Such errors are to be expected and do not show the observer to have been a fool. But one may wonder at his public display of them a generation later.

The diaries of Harold Ickes, Lord Reith and Felix Frankfurter have been published. These men had distinguished careers and honored reputations. One was an effective, forceful Secretary of Interior, with a cantankerous integrity; one built the BBC and successfully performed other large-scale public administrative projects for his country; the third guided many gifted young men into public service and made a valuable contribution to American constitutional law. Each filled his diaries with petty spite. This can be reasonably explained. A busy man of affairs, compelled by the nature of his work to constant discretion and verbal restraint, may use a diary as an emotional trash can that does not truly represent all its author's aspects. Like drunken behavior, jottings in a secret book may offer glimpses of hidden traits, but also may less accurately reflect character than daily conduct over the years. However, reviews reasoned: Since the diaries were private, they were candid; since they were candid, they expressed the "true man;" therefore, the public career was a sham, and the man was to be despised. Yet these false and unfair conclusions, which gained wide acceptance, were only to be expected.

What these men wrote is understandable, even forgivable. But why did they allow (or perhaps carelessly fail to forbid) their executors to publish such self-injuring material in a "posthumous press release" (Thomas Mallon's phrase)? And why does a living man do this? Why did they not do as George Templeton Strong? A civilized and upright character, he nonetheless excoriated a multitude of human targets while in the closet with his pen and copy book. But his diaries were not published until three quarters of a century after his death.

Some diarists injure themselves with mean-spiritedness toward their colleagues, some with falsehoods, others with the truth.

A few take a twisted pleasure in confining their recitals to misdeeds, presenting a portrait that is not Cromwellian (the whole truth) because it is *all* warts. Before letting others see what he has written, why does the one who painted such a harsh likeness commit the folly of failing to balance it? (A small subset of this group, generally addressing an audience, disputes society's values and willingly incurs disapproval by making a defiant assertion of principle. One such glories in his wickedness, in an outlaw's derision toward respectable folk, e.g., Genet or Milton's Satan declaiming: "Evil be thou my good!")

Even honest folk who recite their past rarely go overboard in recounting sins and faults. Often they tell small ones, as Augustine confessed to poaching the neighbor's pears (though perhaps his moral standards were so high that to him this was a grave sin). Some endear themselves to the reader through their frailties that show their humanity, as when Augustine entreated his God to help him subdue his flesh, "but not yet."

Instead of reciting their misdeeds, other diarists claim perfection. By magnifying or inventing their virtues they show themselves to be braggarts and imply other warts as well. Although it is said that no man is a hero to his valet, some men unquestionably are heroes to their autobiographers. Likewise, many diaries are ongoing exercises in self-justification. Each day's entry portrays its author in a white hat, giving him a sympathy and moral approval that he was receiving from no one else. Such a harmless human private hobby calls for no blame. But publication fails to win applause or even vindicate. It persuades no one and invites ridicule. If read, it harms the author by disclosing his or her pathetic self-deception and by provoking others' disparagement. A reader may puzzle why the writer sent it forth.

Some admirable people's reputations are injured after death by the way their disciples and kin choose from the deceased's diaries and letters what the world is to be allowed to see. They may present an image of such moral perfection that it is disbelieved and taken for hypocrisy instead. Often this misfortune is suffered by the memory of one (e.g., Jane Austen) who has inspired such deep admiration among those responsible for his/her papers that they could not bear to see the person portrayed as not fully living by (or subscribing to) the highest accepted standards of the time.

The maxim that if you saw your own wood, it warms you twice can be applied to the satisfaction from writing: first the work and then the rewards of reaching an audience. When *To Be a Politician* was about to be published in 1959, it occurred to me that the work might have no more merit than Edmund in "King Lear;" but as his father, Gloucester, chortled, "There was good sport at his making."

Great luck was having to wait several years between sending the early crude typescript to publishers (twenty rejected it before it was accepted) and the last chance to alter the galley proofs. This delay allowed time for revision to improve the work. When it came out it made a splash. If issued in its form as first submitted, it would have sunk without a ripple. In three later editions, the same process applied.

Publishing the book and receiving critical acclaim from people whose judgment I respected gratified me more than any other piece of work that I have done. Richard Rovere wired me from New York, "It's simply magnificent," and Sidney Hyman, writing a review for *The New York Times,* called and asked, "Say, who are you?" As proof of my first substantial success of any kind (law review articles, previously published, had been satisfying but not important), it helped to make up, in part, for scholastic failures and to show people I was not as dumb as they may have thought.

To thank or compliment a judge on a decision that favors oneself is not courtesy but insult, by suggesting that the decision had been an act not of justice but of generosity, mercy or friendship. Although the same principle should apply to critics, I could not forebear to tell a few of those who had reviewed my book the pleasure received from their approving words.

Although the book is organized around the central core of the politician's role, it concerns politics only a little more than *Don Quixote* concerns chivalry or *The Magic Mountain* concerns tuberculosis sanatoria.

Some readers have found the book sad in tone. To me, it expressed the reality of life's river: sometimes dark, sometimes bright. But if their interpretation is correct, the tone is not that of Henry Adams, but of *Ecclesiastes*; a sadness not about politics, but about life, "the still, sad music of humanity." It is not a bookish, fastidious man's peevish disgust at his fellow citizens who are such Philistines that they fail to entrust to him their civic affairs (perhaps my subconscious says this, but it does not authorize me to speak for it). Rather, the book approaches that outlook (which I do not fully embrace) that analysis tends to refine away the significance of our actions until not much remains but reflexes and appetites.

Scratching paper is such a somber battle. There are no witnesses, no one else in your corner, no passion. And all the while, waiting outside, are your blue spring, the cries of your peacocks, and the fragrance of the air.

—COLETTE

Among the ways books are written, one is to take up a pen, write steadily from beginning to end in a blank bound book, then hand it to the printer to be set in type. In this enviable method, one spins out his story as a spider extrudes its thread. Another way is to make a series of blueprints. First a general scheme for the whole book, succeeded in turn by other outlines, each more detailed than the one before it, until at last one has little left to do except to fill the interstices as a child rubs crayons within the contours of a coloring book.

My own methods for writing something, whether a brief or a book, are more laborious and complex, and are taken in a series of steps: Clarify a particular thought (often a motive in the writing is to unravel some puzzle in my mind), clarify expression of each thought, put the separate thoughts in logical sequence and, last, refine the language by which the reader may be caught and held.

The work is organized by parallel attention to outline and text, back and forth, revising each and conforming the order of each to the other. For a long text, where no theme has yet come to mind, a process of accretion is followed, with organization at a late stage. It is composed as though one were making a mosaic, assembling a picture puzzle or picking up scraps of string and winding each into a growing ball. Then one day one unravels the ball and ties the bits of string end to end until they form one long strand. In this way, disjointed observations and ideas gradually are developed, and a connected theme is discovered near the completion of the work.

Not until the final, revised version of *To Be a Politician* was done did I realize that it had an underlying theme and that this theme was freedom, primarily personal free choice as a member of society. The kinds of choice ranged all the way from a politician's need for an alternative trade and the need for citizens to tolerate a politician's nonconformity to speculation about free will and whether freedom exists at all. The book assumed the merit of a free society and speculated about how to increase free choice for all.

In time, writing things that never reached an

audience frustrated me less, as awareness came that skill with language depends on practice as much as does mastery of a musical instrument or a sport, something forgotten by aspiring authors who regard as a total waste a typescript that gets rejection slips. And writing for an audience of one may profit a man much. Half a century of reflective correspondence, ranging deep and wide, between friend Jerry Berlin and me, each stretching his mind from respect for the other, has been useful practice at putting words to paper, although a wholly incidental benefit from our intercourse that gave us mutual delight.

Ford Madox Ford wrote that people do not think ill of one who declares that long ago he had written well, because "[F]ew are so envious as to censure the complacencies of an extinct volcano." But except for those whose powers have departed, a writer may fear that such a boast would remind others that he had not improved. In his *Autobiography*, Gibbon tells how, when in old age, he discovered an essay he had written in his late teens, he was humbled by its high quality. He was reminded of a similar reaction by Sir Joshua Reynolds who, after a lifetime of application, came upon some canvases he had painted as a youth. Likewise, Swift looked back with admiration at the skill that had gone into his *Tale of a Tub*. That form of discouragement was spared me on looking over papers written long before at Kent. However, they expressed values and interests that had remained unchanged. For example, a concern for justice and for a free society, a preference for decentralized organization (in contrast to a monolith or a multitude of fragments); a puzzlement over what is freedom and how does one get it or enable it.

To reach another's mind one must try not only

to say what is true but also to say it well. Every writer forgets at his peril that he is, in part, a Scheherazade. Artistic gifts of expression have brought a number of thinkers' ideas even more credit than they deserved, e.g., Plato, Rousseau, Bergson, Freud. Another cause for excessive credit given to some of these people may be that the distinction of each in his field has made him a symbol for a certain sector of achievement. As such, his name has been used to simplify a mass of complex information in our past. After Leonardo had read the manuscripts of obscure predecessors who had described devices they had conceived, he drew designs of them on the basis of which he later received credit for their invention.

Our changing technology has lost us many useful figures of speech. Some images are obsolete, like the stone arch, the sword, the single-furrow plough and the blacksmith's tools and work. Others have swiftly disappeared, along with clothespins, hatpins and buttonhooks. Even railroad imagery means little to most. Pillars in a big room may not bear the ceiling. Walls may be built of poured cement rather than joined bricks. Much of the new technology, more molecular and less molar than before, lacks the mechanical or structural relationships that many may comprehend. The phrase "to dovetail" has less force to illuminate a thought now, when items are more often joined by welding or glue, or where what used to be a structure of jointed items now is a single seamless piece.

I admire Milton's and Joyce's mastery of language and Jane Austen's pure English, but my style models have been: Bertrand Russell, Aldous Huxley and several French writers for clarity; Caesar and Grant for simplicity; Tacitus and Bacon for succinctness; Gibbon for elegance and wit; and the King James Version and Book of Common Prayer for music. A style, or general approach, that repels me is the excess and coarse exaggeration of Rabelais, Sade and Céline, who aim to scandalize and shock. The cold-blooded craftsmen de Maupassant and Maugham, turn me off. Toscanini, Nabokov and Hugo Black all looked to the author's precise expression, in interpreting which they followed with strict fidelity. The purity and humility of this approach attracts me without persuading me of its soundness as a method.

Gibbon concluded that the best criticism of his work was his own, as he of all people had the fullest knowledge of his subject and gave it the most attention. He probably was right, but constructive advice is nonetheless needed. This is hard to get. Nonprofessional criticism can furnish most help at the stage of an early draft. Yet unless you are either an important person or established as a writer, few friends will even read a rough typescript thrust upon them. Some, fearing to hurt your feelings (or because they really did not read much), offer undiscriminating praise, which does not even reassure, much less enlighten. Others feed their vanity by attacking your work. Few judge a rough draft by fitting standards. Instead of measuring the substance, the most important thing at that stage, they are put off by the crude form. Having consumed your store of grace with these friends, you cannot seek their comments on a better draft when the work has been refined.

A good time or place to write is hard to find. At the office during the working day, I am distracted from writing by interruptions, importunities and awareness of other work that may have less ultimate importance but that reflects a certain and immediate need. The office at night or on Sunday is dull and lonely, a place of work with other workers off at rest or play, making me sorry for myself and often woozy and fatigued. No better is a back yard table on a summer day, with sunlight filtering through the leaves, quiet except for buzzing bees; the impulse to lean back and savor well-being resists the purpose to haul my wits together and push the pencil on its way.

Writing on the job is convenient, if the job permits it. Trollope, Melville (also Hawthorne) and Stendhal each wrote while supporting himself at an undemanding job for the governments, respectively, of England, the United States and France, which in this way subsidized art. However, a writer with a sinecure pays with diminished experience and stimulation for his free time to write.

A varied law practice gives a writer wide observation of human problems and experience. A lawyer gets a look at all elements of life in which deep feelings are involved—children, health, pain, liberty, money, property, reputation and love. One's work gives practice in written expression and allows flexibility in allocating time to writing but it makes heavy demands on energy and time. It helps to make one's verbal expression orderly and accurate about meanings. It encourages fluency but not lucidity or grace. And it puts precision above clarity. Some lawyers with able minds write like Hegel: propositions of uncertain validity advanced with strong logic through opaque language. On the whole, the profession neither attracts nor develops creative gifts.

The conditions of politics encourage bad writing. Like a lawsuit, a campaign is an adversary proceeding in which language that offers nouns and verbs—that is, statements of verifiable fact—had better be true because it will be scrutinized by keen and hostile eyes ready to refute it. Yet contestants may safely use (or allow or employ others to do so) adjectives and adverbs—no matter how improbable—that favor their cause. Thus the faults of exaggeration and excessive use of modifiers are compounded.

In proportion to the small numbers who engage in the addictive sport of climbing, many write books about it. Some describe absorbing scenes and events; others tell dramatic tales. But when the writers address why they and others climb, as a "religious philosophy of mountains," mystic vapors fill the text. The better books address causes, not their inner meaning.

Most prizefight fiction is not good. Although professional fighting is a sordid business, the authors are naive cynics thinking themselves realists when they portray it as exclusively materialistic. For fighters, it still is more a sport than a business (even business is more romantic than some of its practitioners admit or its critics believe). A prizefighter's motives include several that rival money: popularity, excitement, achievement and sport. A top fighter would rather box than anything else, just as the best musicians care less for money than music. Since novelists do not write for money alone, their assuming fighters to be concerned with nothing else displays a mistaken disdain.

No writing can help but embody what others have written. This inevitability is not confined to the general subject of humankind in society. It covers all writing, even poetry and mathematics. The use of language itself rests on a vast web of others' past thoughts.

Our work, like ourselves, is derived from the past; we do no more than twist or bend what we inherit. Nothing is wholly original.

When W. H. Auden, in a poem, used the phrase "ironic points of light," which Melville had written a century before, he neared, but did not cross, the line that bounds plagiarism. Unless a writer learns from reading his betters' works, he is ill equipped to add to others' knowledge, understanding or pleasure. Yet to learn is to incorporate in oneself. Each of us can—must—say with Ulysses, "I am a part of all that I have met." None of us is like Captain Ahab, who "stood still like an anvil, receiving every shock, but without the least quivering of his own." We plagiarize if we echo another's voice. When we use another's beam we plagiarize not when we alter it as a prism but only if we become a mirror that reflects.

In examining a writer, critics err if they forget that they are interpreting an interpreter. Some regard a writer's expressed ideas as meaningless by supposing him no more than the helpless mouthpiece of the conditions that shaped him. To dismiss Pascal's work as the product of pernicious mystical doctrines, horrid fears and bad health is to miss out on a contribution to human thought. Other critics mistakenly examine a work in an historical vacuum, without regard to the circumstances that influenced the writer. Yet to disregard the surrounding context leaves one missing ironies and liable to think that Swift favored eating Irish babies and that Gibbon revered the Church. Without awareness that life expectancy was about thirty years, one might think irrational the early Christian thinkers' absorption by the possibility of life transcending death.

People are mistaken when they disparage work

of merit because its author's original motive—and perhaps the only discernible one—was not exalted. *Oedipus in Colonnus* appears to have been prompted by the author's troubles with his sons. *Areopagiticus* was set under way by the author's frustration with the narrow grounds for divorce. Franklin is thought to have opposed oppressive authority because his older brother had beaten him. Repeated beatings by his brutal mother induced Turgenev's sympathy for Russian serfs. And innumerable works of genius have been created by craftsmen to earn a living, each masterpiece turned out for one more paycheck.

When we try to convey our thoughts to others, and their incomprehension or hostile response discourages us, we may be consoled to remember how our thoughts may harmonize with those of respected names from long ago. In illiterate societies, how lonely and easily crushed independent thinkers must have been when they could turn to no one but neighbors!

Some lonely folk are led to write by hope of reaching others' minds. Montaigne has been thought to have written the self-portrait of his *Essays* in the hope of finding some reader who would become his friend, to replace the great attachment of his life (along with his father), Etienne La Boétie, who had died when they were young men. Whitman longed to immerse his soul in everybody and everything. Of course, the loneliness may be intensified by the solitude that writing compels.

As others have done, I turned to writing, without social confidence and ready wit, frustrated with attempts to expound expansively in social conversation, and lacking both aptitude and taste for salon epigrams or cocktail party wisecracks. In conversation, my groping, tentatively presented uncommon thoughts provoked a demeanor in others that often may have expressed an amused and sympathetic interest. But to me it was scorn, which spurred me to go home and write.

In my early forties, my interchange of thoughts and feelings with others shrank. Despite my wish for the refreshment of human touch and give and take, my social inadequacy let me find few that suited me. My children helped but were not enough. In this increasing isolation, often my principal companion would be a typescript that became, as described by Churchill, "successively a master, a mistress and a monster," and also, for me, my teddy bear.

Writing a legal brief takes effort, but one knows that it will be read by the appropriate people (court and opposing counsel), and one expects to be paid for it. The same goes for a journalist's work. But to write a book without assurance that it will be published is harder. To the mental effort is added the moral effort of overcoming the fear that the work may go for naught, as though splitting kindling for the stove without assurance that the wood will burn. The lonely process of writing original thought was described by Holmes:

> No man has earned the right to intellectual ambition until he has learned to lay his course by a star which he has never seen—to dig by the divining rod for springs which he may never reach. In saying this, I point to that which will make your study heroic. For I say to you in all sadness of conviction, that to think great thoughts you must be heroes as well as idealists. Only when you have worked alone—when you have felt around you a black gulf of solitude more isolating than that which surrounds the dying man, and in hope and in despair have trusted to your own unshaken will—

then only will you have achieved. Thus only can you gain the secret isolated joy of the thinker, who knows that, a hundred years after he is dead and forgotten, men who never heard of him will be moving to the measure of his thought—the subtle rapture of a postponed power, which the world knows not because it has no external trappings, but which to his prophetic vision is more real than that which commands an army.

And elsewhere he wrote, concerning praise for a dead master of some field of thought:

> [T]here is pleasure in bearing one's testimony even at that late time, and thus in justifying the imagination of posthumous power on which all idealists and men not seeking the immediate rewards of success must live.

One has to try to generate a continuing presumption that some people will think the product worth reading. Neither refreshing originality nor a pioneering extension of knowledge is proved by independent thinking alone. Marguerite Yourcenar had her Hadrian write to his adoptive grandson that "It takes more than audacity of mind to free us of banality." Unconventionality of subject deprives it of a measuring stick, yet does not show that it contributes to the thought of humankind.

The detachment essential to good work augments the loneliness from the physical solitude.

> A certain degree of isolation both in space and time is essential to generate the independence required for the most important work; there must be something

which is felt to be of more importance than the admiration of the contemporary crowd.

—BERTRAND RUSSELL

Enough assurance to sustain the effort may distort one's judgment and thereby impair the work. Yet if you fear you may be writing trash (unpublishable trash) or something that has meaning only to you, even stubborn determination may not suffice to offset the doubt that saps your effort. On the other hand, as in many vocations, you are carried along by finding pleasure in the process of your work.

Office Desk

Chapter | 4

OUTDOORS

Sing, O heavens; and
be joyful, O earth; and
break forth into singing, O mountains

—ISAIAH

From the frozen ledge on Mt. Rainier, I jumped and waved to catch the pilot's eye. Without a sign of recognition, the search plane grew smaller until it disappeared into the blue sky. In the past, some occasions had made me think that the odds on surviving were poor. At other times, I had realized that death had just passed me by—such as during the War or a near miss at an intersection—but these moments had come and gone without time for thought and were considered only in retrospect.

To last a couple of days was my guess. No notion of survival remained, even one fathered by hope, as hope was gone. This awareness did not affect my general beliefs: philosophy, theology, cosmology. My mind did not turn to questions of God, an afterlife, divine punishment or reward, the relation of humankind to the universe. My wits enjoyed none of that concentration that Doctor Johnson said awareness of impending execution induced. They felt only their habitual need to reduce vaporous ruminations to clearly defined thoughts, the only kind that have worth. My reaction was sodden despondency, sullen dejection, a grunted monosyllabic obscenity. No pangs, tears or sobs, not even effort to contain them.

What to do? A short time allowance commonly prescribes pursuit of immediate pleasure. Its unavailability compelled resort to what one does in books: The condemned prisoner looks up at his barred window. The moon and stars remind him of the last time he walked in the garden with his beloved. The memory of this and other joy sends him to the table. He takes up the quill and dips it in the inkwell (the stories have the cell contain these writing materials). He writes to his near and dear (kin, friends, lover and followers, if he has them) a few pages of noble thought, lyrically expressed.

Seated on Mike's rock helmet, which he had left behind, I wrote two letters. The writing took effort. Weakness augmented the sense that nothing mattered any more. Of course, in part, it did matter—hence the letters. They comprised two sets of requests to sister Priscilla, who I knew would carry them out. One concerned items of business, e.g., "My will is in the bottom drawer. . . . Find my wallet in my pants, which are in the back of the car. . . . Turn over to my partner _____ the file on _____." The other one recited farewells to family members and friends, e.g., "Tell _____ that I am proud of him and love him." That done, I could think of nothing more either to fulfill duty or seek pleasure.

On May Day, 1979, four of us had set out on the climb. Though none of us had done this route, finding our way was not hard. We seldom faced a choice. At the second uneventful day's end the sky darkened and a storm began, first graupel, rolling down the slope like ball bearings, then a steady fall of wet snow. At 12,900 feet we shoveled a platform into the knife-edged Liberty Ridge and lay down in our bivouac sacks. We could not keep out the snow; three feet fell during the night.

It wet our clothes and sleeping bags. The next morning we dug snow and hacked ice until we reached rock, making a cave in which we could not sit up straight and from which our feet stuck out. My son Ben, my friend Eric, the climb leader, and I occupied it, while Eric's friend, Mike, tied to a rope anchored on our six-by-eight foot platform, went down the side of the Ridge a few feet, dug himself a hole and crept in.

After sixty-two hours, the storm abated, then ended, and the sun came out. During this time we lay next to each other, damp from the first night there, and tried to keep from shivering. We were entertained by thundering rumbles of avalanches as they poured over the ice cliffs to our east and west. A few times we heard one coming down upon us from above, where the Ridge was broad. As though we were lying on the track before an oncoming train, we could feel the ground trembling beneath us, and we would tremble too. Before reaching us, each avalanche would spill most of its contents over the sides; the rest would pile a load on the porch in front of our cave, covering our feet. One of us would kick loose, wriggle out, shovel off the load of snow, and return to his sack. We lay hoping that the next would not bury us too deep for escape.

Day by day we reduced the portions of food that we consumed until it was gone. When our stove fuel ran out, we no longer could melt snow, so we ceased to drink. Ben and Eric suffered more from the cold than did the other two of us because their down sleeping bags had become sodden. Most of the time we alternately shivered and shoveled.

The immediate cause of being caught on our icy perch was the storm. In turn, we exposed ourselves to this plight by judgment error and bad luck. An interme-

diate cause—the decision to start up Rainier—was enjoyment of mountain climbing.

At first our concern was slight. During the storm,
Ben, age twenty-two, threw a tantrum when he remembered his two tickets to the Supersonics basketball team
playoff game that night. After the first clear day he lost
his $5 bet with me that a search plane would come by
next day. We were aware that passing time was tilting
the odds on survival further against us. After two days of
clear weather (a cloud bank below us at 10,000 feet, but
sun above) with no one having come to look for us, we
thought we had been forsaken. As he lay beside me, Ben
hit me on the chest a couple of times with his undirected
fist, bending his arm at the elbow, and saying, "I don't
want to die, and I don't want you to die. I love you,
Daddy, and I want to spend a lot more years with you."

During our sojourn on the Ridge the party's
members conducted themselves well: no panic, bicker-
ing, recriminations, fighting over food, overreactions
or outbursts.

Later conversation among us, looking back on
this time together, brought out that our dream lives
there had been more active than at any time before. Our
sleep was fitful and brief but it churned out dreams.
They were not nightmares and they had little plot, but
tended to be kaleidoscopic.

We concluded that the avalanche risk created by
travel upon the six feet of new snow had become outweighed by the risk of dying where we were. The other
three set out. Weaker than these lads, fearing to slow
them too much or to collapse on the snow and freeze
that night, I stayed behind, seeing them off with trepi-
dation and hope. I continued to hibernate, conserving
energy and heat and enjoying the luxury of lying

crossways in the now-roomy cave, my feet under the roof. My companions sought to pass over the summit and down the easier standard route, but chest-deep snow turned them back, and they headed down the Ridge that we had climbed. We expected them to make it out by that night and that next morning their summoned help would come.

I ate my last piece of food, a caramel, and washed it down with the last swallow from my water bottle. All next day the sky was clear above the cloud bank, except for a six-inch snowfall at midday. I kept sticking my head out the cave, looking at the sky for help. In late morning, that small plane came in sight, cruising back and forth across the Mountain's north side, in a systematic search pattern that indicated my companions had not made it out. If they had, the plane would have known where to go. Presumably, an avalanche had covered them. The plane's departure showed the search abandoned.

I sat hunched like a glum bump. . . .Late in the afternoon, a sound broke in on my gloomy musings. A plane was heading straight for me; it turned, then dipped its wings as it flew past. It circled back and repeated the signal. This notice that death had been generously postponed provoked a surge of feeling: first, elation at knowing I would live, then grief at the loss of Ben and my buddies (forgetting that only they could have directed the plane to our ledge). I wept over my little boy, down the Ridge beneath a load of wet snow. A few hours earlier, thinking my own time was up, I had felt no distress at the others' ill fate.

Before long, an Army helicopter came. In haste, I scooped my gear out of the cave and started to stuff my pack. The rotor blades' blast swept off my sleeping bag and made me drop to my knees to avoid going with it. Unable to land, the helicopter lowered a sack of emergency supplies. As it passed across my porch, I snatched the sack and took out a two-way radio. Eager for marching orders for a liftoff from the chopper hovering nearby, I examined the radio for operating instructions. The only words were a warning that "Any unauthorized use of this constitutes a violation of the Federal Communications Act" and a recital of threatened punishment. Switching on the receiver, I heard: "Holy smoke, we've just blown off some guy in his sleeping bag, over the Willis Wall! We've got to be careful."

To pluck me from the ledge, the helicopter let down a board seat on the end of a slender cable and maneuvered overhead to bring the seat within my reach. I had envisioned taking pictures while hanging on the wire. In the event, however, camera forgotten, I threw on my pack, grabbed the board, threw my legs over it and took the straddled cable in one hand; then leaned back, looked up with a grin, and with the other hand gave a debonair wave like a pilot about to take off in a World War I movie. Both arms were thrown around the wire as it whisked me out over the abyss. Under other circumstances, this would have been detestably terrifying, but here the alternative made it easily tolerable. The seat began to spin, reminding me of childhood, when a playground swing would be wound tight and allowed to unwind; on dismounting, the dizzy and nauseated rider would stagger and fall, to the spectators' amusement. My clutch became desperate. Standing over the open hatch, the soldiers cranked in the wire until I was sprawled on the floor like a landed fish.

In a few minutes the helicopter set down on a gravel bar in the Carbon River. Walking down the ramp, I greeted a friend in the Mountain Rescue Council and asked him, "What word of my boy?" He replied, "They made it out." Releasing a sob of relief, I stepped forward into a crowd. After answering a few questions before microphones and TV cameras, I entered my car (parked, by chance, a few yards up the River bank), thinking how one climbs successfully and uneventfully for years without acclaim, then by one mistake becomes an object of embarrassing attention. When I took off my parka for the first time in six days, the sweater worn beneath it looked as though I had been sleeping with chickens.

After reaching Seattle and helping Ben and Eric settle in adjoining hospital beds for treatment of frostbitten feet (Ben lost parts of his toes), I drove to my apartment, turned up the heat, ate heartily from the refrigerator and went to bed. On the Mountain, alone, I had felt no loneliness. On return, I felt a touch of self-pity for the lack of one with whom to share this recent experience. But awareness of being alive and warm overshadowed this and all else.

Adventure novels read as a boy suggested the choice to start a chapter in a tight spot. In the opening paragraph a rifle shot rings out, an elephant falls to earth, and a hunter steps into the jungle glade. By action, the reader's attention is caught.

From childhood, the uncultivated outdoors—water, woods and mountains—has appealed to me.

> Where rose the mountains, there to him
> were friends,
> The desert—forest—cavern—

Were unto him companionship.
—CHILDE HAROLD

The attraction started with play on the beach and on
nearby uncleared land—a forest to a child. After my
taste had been established, stories of adventure on the
sea, bold exploration of new lands and stalwart pioneers
excited my imagination and gratified my curiosity.

At seventeen, I wrote that it was permissible to
exhaust energy resources because energy cannot be
destroyed but natural beauties, once lost, are forever
gone and asserted the high value that one can derive
from natural beauties, quoting Bryant:

> For his gayer hours,
> She has a voice of gladness, and a smile,
> And eloquence of beauty and she glides
> Into his darker musings with a mild
> And healing sympathy that steals away
> Their sharpness ere he is aware.

And a letter home: "I think about the woods and mountains all the time."

My first glimpses of the wilderness came to me in
old men's fireside tales. At age ten, the real thing was
introduced when the Joseph Black family and ours took
a packhorse trip in the north Cascades west of the north
half of Lake Chelan. As they have ever since, the camp-
fires enchanted me: the flames, the warmth, watching
sparks fly upward, disappearing in the dark. One day as
Father and I sat together above a narrow bridge across
a gorge, a deer crossed the bridge and bounded past us
up the slope.

Some of the men told me a tenderfoot story of

"ice worms," which were supposed to lurk in the glacier ice. (Forty-nine years later, Harriet's magazine published an article about just such worms that do exist.) Later, the jokers offered me proof in the form of a mason jar full of water and spaghetti, allegedly found below the Lyman Glacier. The guide whispered to me to reverse the joke by putting the ice worms in a grown-up's sleeping bag. So I did. That evening, the young man, having discovered this, dried his bag in front of the fire, pretending to be bitten when he reached inside. The bewildering subtleties of which practical jokes are funny and which are beastly dismayed me when my parents rebuked me for having removed the jar top and poured the contents into the bag.

We camped at Lyman Lake, visited so seldom that no harm was done when one of the men felled a small pine, its boughs providing us with beds. In those days, neither protecting the environment nor conserving the wilderness touched public awareness, much less provoked concern. Like the stars in the sky, no value was put on keeping it because it was not threatened. Forty-five years later, when my daughter Jill and I walked along the shore, signs forbade camping within two hundred feet of the Lake because the turf had been trampled into mud. Down the valley, during this intervening period a copper mine had been dug and worked until nothing worth taking was left, and the village of Holden had been built beside it and occupied until it was vacated when the mine was shut down.

My first mountain hike was taken at thirteen, four days in the Olympics with Edward Ohata, my cousin David, and my grandmother's German gardener, Paul Stenneberg. Under my Trapper Nelson packboard, burdened with baked beans and other canned goods, I tired soon, and each step was arduous up the Dosewallips River trail. I winced when Mr. Stenneberg contrasted me as a soft rich boy with some of the hearty lads who breezed along without staggering. On the Anderson Glacier we came upon a pond; responding to mutual dares, we undressed, slid down the snow and swam across as fast as we could, the water feeling like a hot wire around our necks.

In my mid-thirties, after many urban years, leaving town only to do something like attend a political picnic or look at a tract of land with other men for a business deal, I began the practice, continued ever since, of going into the mountains in both summer and winter. For about thirteen years, these excursions were undertaken exclusively with my children. In the winter we skied, and in the summer we hiked and camped.

Margaret once remarked: "Daddy, remember the time I fell and broke a ski on the Lucky Shot run at Crystal Mountain? When you stopped beside me, you taught me a new word." "What was it?" I asked apprehensively. Sure enough, it was a four-letter word: "Alas."

My daughters Ashley, Jill and Dorothy and my nephew Jock huddled closer to our campfire by Lake Constance when they heard me read aloud to them Jack London's story, "To Build A Fire." While we had been hauling ourselves up the steep trail to the Lake, I feared meeting a social worker who might charge me as an unfit parent and take Dorothy. Not yet five, she had insisted on carrying her own tiny pack (containing a handkerchief); one hand was in mine, and the other held her thumb in her mouth.

When Ben and I were climbing toward Frosty Pass, and he was too small to carry a share of the load, he addressed a stream of questions at me. For example,

"If you were an octopus, could you hold each of the things in the pack?" On my eventual gasp, "Daddy's too tired to talk!" he replied, "Then how can you say it?" The next morning I felt myself a negligent father when he climbed out of his sleeping bag in his muddy boots.

On another hike, from Stevens Pass down Icicle Creek, with sons, nephews and brother-in-law, we camped under a carpet of stars. When a storm came over during the night, some of us hunched against a pine, our legs extended as spokes from a wheel. At dawn, the rain still falling, I went over to check on Ben, then age four. He lay in a depression that had become a puddle. His fingers were wrinkled. When I picked him up in his sleeping bag, water cascaded from it as though he had been sleeping in a jug.

When he grew older, we skied together until his rising line on the skill graph crossed my declining line, and he left me behind. When he became a ski racer, I would take him to his races. Recruited as a gatekeeper, I would shout encouragement to him. After one race he implored me, "Daddy, when I come past, don't call me Benjamin Bunny" (my pet name for him).

To join the game soon seemed more fun than to stand shivering on a hillside. My limited skill made racing a harsh apprenticeship. For some time, a race course was something to be survived rather than raced, as much moral as physical exercise. Time after time I would drive alone to a ski area, practice hard, fall hard, and feel like a beginner—or worse, an ender. My hardest skiing falls have been taken on practice runs of downhill courses. The discomfort did not bother me, as bruises and bumps had long been familiar, but they drained my limited confidence. After some years I began to get the hang of it and had good times. Also, the racers came to know each other, and some companionships led to friendships.

The best score I ever made was second place for men aged forty-eight and over in the downhill event in the National Championship for "seniors." To receive a chintzy medal advertising Big Sky instead of a displayable trophy was annoying. The race occasion that gave most pleasure was the "Bellingham Annual Ski-to-Sea Marathon," a relay race. I gathered a team consisting of a kayak racer to paddle the Nooksack River, a bike racer (David Rudo, my dentist) for twenty miles down the road, and a runner (Jock Collins, my nephew) for the seven-mile final lap, while I did the ski-race leg. We placed third out of more than a hundred teams, and each of us received a big, garish trophy. At the end of this happy blend of athletic competition and spring fun in the sun, all gathered by the river in a field to drink beer and dance to rock bands while waiting for the race results.

At thirteen, cousin David and I, with a Scout leader, paddled a canoe down the length of Sammamish Slough, as my Mother had done around the turn of the century. At about fifteen, I sailed across the Sound with Edward Ohata in his canoe, without paddles. To return, we used as paddles a couple of pieces of driftwood we found on the beach. A strong wind arose, and the seas were swamping us when a motor cruiser came alongside and took us aboard. Emptied of water, the canoe was towed behind as the yacht went in to Indianola and anchored. Wet and hungry, we paddled ashore where we came upon a friend from the Scouts who put us up for the night. Next morning we and the canoe returned on the ferry, where grim mothers and grinning younger sisters met us at the Seattle dock. One night three score years later, a full gale in the Straits of Gibraltar made a trying adventure of sailing—and trying to command—a thirty-six foot sloop, with two greenhorn friends and one staunch comrade who from time to time forgot he was not captain.

Mother employed a carpenter to build a fourteen-foot catboat for me in our backyard. She named it the *Whitecap*. She and a family friend sailed it across the sound, with me riding in it as a passenger, frustrated at not being allowed to take part in what she had said was mine. For the two years before the War, I owned and sailed the *Hanko*, a Six-Meter boat. Good times included stirring struggles with wind and wave and one moonlit summer night, going down the Sound before a gentle breeze, my three buddies asleep below and the radio playing Tchaikowsky's "Andante Cantabile."

Once I sailed across the Straits of Juan de Fuca with the rail under most of the time. The little craft rising and falling among the whitecapped waves, the wind and recurrent spray in my face and the journey's challenge evoked manic yells. On reaching the partial shelter of Port Townsend, when I undertook to drop the sails and cast anchor, the main halyard jammed, so the big sail stayed up, and the anchor dragged. Soon the waves began to slam and grind the hull against the pilings of a dock. The outboard motor declined to start. With no one either to help me or to tell me what to do, this plight put me at my wits' end, when from the darkness appeared a Coast Guard boat which threw me a line and towed the sloop to a refuge safe and snug.

I sailed the *Outer Space* from Marbella to Fort Lauderdale and did not regret the voyage but prefer to sail no further from home than Olympia and Desolation Sound.

Harriet and I had many good times on the water and in the hills. We hiked for a week through the Pasayten Wilderness, seeing no one. One quiet afternoon and evening we paddled kayaks around Decatur Island in the San Juans. Assisted by the tides (and opposed when we mistimed them), taking in the scenes around us at our leisure, like the Thoreau brothers on the Merrimack, we slipped past overhanging mossy boulders and sometimes idly drifted as gentle ripples passed us on their way to stroke the shore.

Although I had enjoyed hiking and camping since childhood, I had not climbed, regarding such pursuit as an infatuated quest by sturdy cranks. At about age forty-eight, out of curiosity and in the absence of some human object for passion, challenge, diversion and solace, I tackled small and easy peaks as a casual experiment, and then progressed to harder and higher ones with an appetite that grew from the feeding. The skills came from doing, books and companions' tips. My most technically difficult rock climbs were not done until after turning seventy-two.

The novel experience of climbing a rock "chimney" recalled an incident from about age ten, when I tried to climb the laundry chute from our basement. After an upward struggle of a few feet, my grip slipped. A rod that had been standing in the shaft jammed up my left nostril, making it bleed freely and later leaving a mark.

At first, having steeled my nerves to reach a summit, I would go down promptly to end the strain of anticipating the descent. In time, with confidence, the top—if warm—became a place to loaf and bask. Everything in the mountains became a pleasure save the discomforts: exhaustion, cold, a blistered foot, a Procrustean bed.

Few climbs have given me trouble or anxiety except where a wrong route was taken or where a companion imposed a risk on me. Ben and I enjoyed a number of climbs together, but not Bonanza Peak. Leaving the glacier, we traversed to the north face. Here all was shaded, slippery, damp and steep. Nothing in this dismal scene fitted the written route description, which I had misconstrued. A series of gullies bore-patches of snow and ice, but we mainly climbed on rotten rock. Recurrent showers came down on us, volleys and thunders of big ones and little ones, whizzing and clunking, while we would sprawl against the gully wall like kittens trying to escape from the bathtub when the water is turned on. One chunk dented my hard hat; another sliced our rope in half. On reaching the ridge, we saw the summit a few yards off. But a tower between, unclimbable by us, made us retrace our steps. This was no more a father-son playful outing than was the excursion to the mountains in the Moriah territory that Abraham and Isaac took.

On another day, on the northeast buttress of Chair Peak, unable to find holds above me and starting to retreat a bit in order to try to one side, I peered between my legs to see where to put my feet. Expecting, in fantasy, to see clouds floating past and maybe an airplane, I saw my climbing partner, a high school senior, who had been belaying me.* Impatient with my slow progress, he had abandoned his anchored stance and started climbing. This was a shock, but under the

---

* and who, fifteen years later, married my youngest child

circumstances I dared not raise my voice. Later, because it no longer mattered, I did not remonstrate but was reminded of an incident from long ago. When Thomas Bullitt, elder brother of my ancestor Cuthbert Bullitt, was leading a party to survey the land by the Falls of the Ohio (where Louisville is now), another exploring group that had accompanied them went up the Kentucky River where they left their canoes and walked to a salt lick:

> A large herd of buffalo being in the lick, Samuel Adams was tempted to fire his gun at one of them, when the whole herd in terrible alarm, ran directly towards the spot where Adams and James McAfee stood. Adams instantly sprang up a leaning tree, but James McAfee, being less active, was compelled to take shelter behind a tree barely large enough to cover his body. In this condition, the whole herd passed them—the horns of the buffalo scraping off the bark on both sides of the tree behind which McAfee was standing, drawn up to his smallest dimensions. After all had passed, Adams crawled down, and McAfee mildly said: "My good boy, you must not venture that again."

Drudgery inheres in this sport. In few places does one step out of the car and start up fascinating granite. In the Cascades the drudgery is great. One often first must trudge up tedious miles of rising forest trail, then penetrate almost impenetrable defenses: Slog through swamp choked with thorns, clamber over and under fallen logs crisscrossed and wet, struggle through phalanxes of entangled brush with its interlaced prongs pointed down the nearly vertical slope like ranks of pikemen defending a redoubt, stumble among the loose boulders of a stream bed, creep up grass and heather slick with dew and ascend a treadmill of scree before the battlements of ice and rock are reached.

These outer defense works have the merit of reducing the crowds. For some, they increase the eventual pleasure. St. Augustine wrote:

> The price which we pay for those very pleasures of life are the difficulties which we must overcome, difficulties which are neither unsought nor unwelcome, but intended and desired....The greater joys are always ushered in by greater suffering.

However, such a wilderness passage gives me no moral satisfaction; nor does coming out at the far side give me aesthetic pleasure, but only relief.

I had supposed that dragging a sled (bearing most of my 130-pound load) up the Kahiltna Glacier would be an effortless glide, letting me feel like a Venetian gondolier on an idle moonlit paddle, singing languorous arias. But when it came to be done, the appropriate song, if one had breath to sing, was not "'O So le Mio" but "The Volga Boatmen." One understands why Jack London's Buck left the dog team to go live with wolves.

An expedition to a distant mountain that is high, stormy and cold resembles drilling for oil deep underground or taking the plaintiff's side in a contingent fee trial where damages are large and the defendant is solvent but unwilling to settle and puts up a stiff defense. The required investment is large, the potential payoff big but uncertain, and the enterprise justified only by success.

Frequent wilderness journeys cannot be made without some discomfort at times. In late September, after two days' tranquil, solitary climb of Buck Mountain, I glissaded too fast down a snow slope and took a tumble. I shook the snow out of my clothes, picked up my wristwatch and entered the woods under a steady, gently-falling rain that barely could be heard. My direction became uncertain when darkness fell. Before long the sopping brush had soaked my clothes and pack. Sliding down creek banks and creeping up the far side, tripping over unseen objects, altering course, I concluded that reaching the road that evening was less likely than getting hurt. To prepare for the night meant coming to a stop when the slope underfoot felt not so steep as to need holding on to stay put.

My sleeping bag held some warmth, even though each move would sound a squulch. (Dana wrote: "[F]or genuine discomfort, give me rain with freezing weather.") Impatiently waiting for the day during this exceedingly long night, I began thinking that perhaps there was truth in Velikovsky's notion that some concatenation of heavenly bodies had halted the earth for a while (helpfully rolling back the waters of the Red Sea at a critical moment). At last, gray light filled the sky, and with ease I hiked out.

Once on Forbidden Peak, benighted on a ledge, alternately dozing and shivering, I hunched on my pack, my back against the cliff. Whenever my eyes would open, my two climbing partners, visiting Lithuanians, could be discerned in the darkness: One (who died on Dhaulaghiri the next year) lying on the mosaic of stones he had placed on the snow, the other doing calisthenics.

Some people think climbers to be crazy folk, reckless toward themselves. Most may be eccentric by some definitions, but few are self-destructive. Although climbers as a group derive enough pleasure from mountaineering to compensate them for the discomfort and pain—and a few actually mind them less than some other people do—I know none who like pain or who (under given circumstances) prefer discomfort to comfort.

When several days' exertions have sapped a climber's energy and strength, an ascetic might succumb to the longing to slump to the rain-soaked ground. A hedonist, however, may be driven on, sustained by a dream that he will sit in a sun-dappled perfumed garden outside Aix en Provence, reading the phosphorescent sentences of Flaubert's *Sentimental Education* and eating what a fastidious Frenchman would consider to be adequate food. In order to reach the far-off car or camp, hunger for ease and comfort (as well as the impulse to survive) can supply that ruthless fixity of purpose required to maintain attack on seemingly endless dripping cliffs fortified by vine maple, padded with soggy moss and studded with rocks dislodged at a touch.

The journey to the wilderness used to take at least as long as it does today. The woods were closer to town, but cars were slower and the roads poor. One winter Sunday our family went to Snoqualmie Pass for a picnic, a full day's excursion. Snow lay on the ground, but its depth had not yet closed the winding gravel road that not until 1931 was kept open through the winter. Ours was the only car parked up there. Where we were sitting in the snow, I was given a cup of hot cocoa, set it down and then cried when the cup disappeared.

Now, one still can escape the crowd but at the price of hiking several uphill miles. No longer can one reach solitude at the point one leaves the road. The wilderness realm and the number of unspoiled beauty spots have shrunk, but travel on foot, the way that least impairs the wilderness, is far less difficult. Except the water in the bottle, everything one puts upon his back and feet has less weight. Many items have less bulk, tents are waterproof, and stoves work.

Nearing the end of an arduous climb, on the final miles down a trail, often my afterburners turn on. Although nothing diminishes the fatigue, my dragging feet take wing like those of the horse that smells the barn.

Sometimes, after days in the mountains, coming out to the head of the logging road, footsore and weary, looking through the trees for a glimpse of car, one is reminded of why, before we rode machines, to steal someone's horse was a serious crime. Only once was a familiar car at the trailhead anything but a welcome sight. Its presence told us that our companion, who had undertaken to hike out before us (from our bivouac below Nooksack Tower), had failed to arrive. A week later, Rimas's body was found below the cliff from which he fell when he had strayed from the descent route in the dark.

Some people think that a mountain hike resembles a visit to the zoo. In fact, except for deer, one rarely sees a large animal: bear, wolf, cougar, wildcat, martin or fox.

Assuming that the mountains' tranquil beauty would inspire deep reflection, people sometimes ask what interesting thoughts have developed in my mind out there. Camping may evoke this, but on a climb such thoughts are meager. While one toils uphill beneath a load, his thoughts are no more wide-ranging than when pushing a stalled car. During a technical climb, one concentrates on the task at hand. This may offer interesting complexity, as on a rock face, working out a route and holds. Or it may be monotonous, as on a long, steep icy slope where, to avoid a fatal misstep, constant effort must be taken not to let your attention stray from the white patch at your hands and feet. But none of this thinking is consciously productive beyond the process of the moment. Likewise, one thinks of little worth repeating while descending fast, dull with fatigue, trying to keep from stumbling by attending where to step.

The mountains have drawn me to them from mixed motives: some healthy, some regrettable, some natural though not commendable. These include pleasure from the beauties of nature, harmony with the wilderness, the sense of permanence and continuity with the past ("the everlasting hills"), escape to simplicity from the problems of "real life" (work and human relations in the city) and a respite from the human race. Sometimes, warm companionship as well.

Appealing wilderness must contain solitude, nature and beauty. For solitude, one may lock the bathroom door. For exposure to nature, one may look at the sea and sky from aboard a ship or plane. Solitude plus nature can be found in polar wastes, tropic jungle or the Sinai Peninsula. For nature and beauty, one can have the Zugspitze, Lake Louise or the slopes at Aspen. Only where all three elements combine does the magic work. Outside of some mountain ranges in the middle latitudes (and sometimes on a sailboat in the tropics) few such places remain.

Most mountain scenes attract the eye, if not other senses as well, with some exceptions. Glacial moraines, for example, resemble abandoned strip mines. One may enjoy varied charms: distant vistas, cozy glades, fantastic rock formations such as those west of Silver Star Peak, the "splendid silent sun" gleaming on the seracs, ice palisades and other glacial shapes, and Marlowe's "rocks of pearl that shine as bright As all the lamps that beautify the sky."

> The scenery of the snows, the winds' free
>   orchestra,
> The Stretching light-hung roof of clouds,
>   the clear cerulean and the silvery fringes,
> The high dilating stars, the placid beckoning
>   stars...
>   —WHITMAN

Best is the alpine zone just above the timber line: snow fields, meadows, heather, boulders, clumps of trees, rock outcroppings, waterfalls, flowers and cliffs. Enhancing the spell is quiet, prevailing more often in fall and winter, when the bugs are gone, the streams low and travellers few. As for those who have pursued certain women, a spectacle that mingles mystery and beauty exerts a magnetism on some of us.

> When you stand in a wild country, looking at a
> jagged line of unknown peaks, cut like steel against
> the sky, the desire to go to them is well-nigh
> irresistible.
>   —BELMORE BROWNE

The mountains give joy from a vibrant awareness of your surroundings, absorbed by your senses, up high where "life is a flag unfurled." Tocqueville wrote of having visited places in the Alps where nature "deploys, even to the point of horror, a grandeur that transports and impassions the soul." Describing how the zest of the effort may lift one's feelings, that reserved Victorian Tilman put it:

> [A]s the demands of the climbing became more insistent, grievances seemed less real, and that life was still worth living was a proposition that might conceivably be entertained.

One is repeatedly blessed, not merely by fine moments but by long stretches of good time. Lounging on a heather bench, you may lift up your eyes unto the hills and a slanting snow-lined ridge below horizontal scarlet ribbons in the sky. The gentle harmonies of an enchanted evening contrast with the hush of dawn, breathing fresh perfumes, the early morning light touching the spires above, your lungs filled with high-octane fuel that floats you along, yet lets you keep in touch with the earth beneath your feet, and sometimes hands, as you discover what lies ahead. Other occasions—as on a stony plateau, in chill, silent moonlight, under a high dome of glinting stars, a stark escarpment rising beyond—infuse you with melancholy, like the bleak isolation of Paul Morel in the closing lines of D. H. Lawrence's *Sons and Lovers*.

Francis Parkman wrote of his beloved wilderness:

> There are few so imbruted by vice, so perverted by art and luxury, as to dwell in the closest presence of Nature, deaf to her voice of melody and power, untouched by the ennobling influences which mould and penetrate the heart that has not hardened itself against them. Into the spirit of such a one the

mountain wind breathes its own freshness, and the midsummer tempest, as it rends the forest, pours its own fierce energy. . . . [I]t is the grand and heroic in the hearts of men which finds its worthiest symbol and noblest inspiration amid these desert realms,—in the mountain, rearing its savage head through clouds and sleet, or basking its majestic strength in the radiance of the sinking sun; in the interminable forest, the thunder booming over its lonely waste, the whirlwind tearing through its inmost depths, or the sun at length setting in gorgeous majesty beyond its waves of verdure. To the sick, the wearied, or the sated spirit, nature opens a theatre of boundless life, and holds forth a cup brimming with redundant pleasure. In the other joys of existence, fear is balanced against hope, and satiety against delight; but here one may fearlessly drink, gaining, with every draught, new vigor and a heightened zest, and finding no dregs of bitterness at the bottom.

Mountain scenes and spectacles not only remind one of associated experiences—past and prospective—that please or satisfy. Giving pleasure in themselves, such scenes can cheer, console or soothe. In 1853, seeing Rainier from Naches Pass, Theodore Winthrop remarked that it answered his need for a "visual image that can be a symbol to us of the grandeur or sweetness of repose."

Gleaming memories of the mountains include some times alone: the night on Glacier Peak; hiking up Phelps Creek in the quiet summer darkness; the fall silence on a crag of Custer, musing on how many surrounding mountain miles contained not another human soul; a like reflection one January evening on Esmeralda;

the descent from Copper Peak, plunging down the snow slope with the triumphant theme of Beethoven's Emperor Concerto clanging through my head.

And some in company with others: the bivouac on the ledge of Katsuk; scrambling up the Fisher Chimneys in the darkness; descending Cowlitz Ridge with three children, as boiling storm clouds chased us down to Indian Bar; with my nephew-godson, our chins on a ridge-crest, peering through the hole in a rainbow that formed a perfect circle, hanging below us like a smoke ring; roaming through the meadows above the Royal Basin and across the slopes above Spray Park; reaching Canadian summits never before climbed; a merry gallop down St. Helens behind two spirited children; smelling the pine forest on Tahquitz Rock; on the way out of the Pickett Range, striding along sunlit Easy Ridge while listening (from a friend's borrowed earphones) to "These Enchanted Halls" from *The Magic Flute*, this baritone aria that has enraptured me more than any other song.

And a thunderstorm one summer morning. Standing with my daughter, Margaret, twelve, on the rock outcropping where we had made our camp, we looked across the heather from a shoulder of Sahalee Arm to Johannesburg's forbidding, black north face as forked lightning bolts from the dark sky repeatedly struck down upon the jagged summit ridge.

A life without adventure is likely to be unsatisfying, but a life in which adventure is allowed to take whatever form it will is sure to be short.

—BERTRAND RUSSELL

My appetite for adventure and hardship has not been a lifelong craving like that of Wilfrid Thesiger but has applied to occasional short periods, varying a life of comparative predictability and comfort. Sometimes as a child I would help men try to pull apart big dogs (setters and police dogs) that were fighting. These episodes frightened and upset me, but some adventures frighten yet satisfy and thrill.

Climbing offers danger of two kinds. One is composed of risks that effort or skill cannot avoid: falling rocks or ice, avalanches, some high altitude storms and (remote risk) lightning and equipment failure. If taken, these risks can be minimized by prudence but wholly escaped only by luck.

The other kind of danger penalizes a lapse of attention or a judgment error. In the latter, one may go beyond one's margin of strength, skill or endurance under conditions that demand it for survival. Or one may miscalculate the odds on the kind of risk that effort or skill cannot avoid, so that one accepts odds worse than one wishes to take. Such accidents commonly begin with a blunder and end with a thud.

According to the risk to which they expose themselves, climbers may be classified along a range. Over the years, I have sensed in myself passage through—or a visit to—each of the following described chambers, except the "obsession" and "single big climb" syndromes. At one end of the range are suicidal men who take climbing as a lethal device, as some people take long-sustained consumption of alcohol. Next come those sunk in despair (sometimes men shocked by disappointment in love), who climb either for oblivion through exhaustion or to put themselves out on the high risk edge to recover their sense of power or worth. Indifferent to living, they are indifferent to risk. A few youths, whose high spirits and innocence make them assume immortality, fail to recognize risks for what they are. Their climbing careers are short.

Then comes a large proportion of those who are obsessed, driven by an incessant compulsion to climb one route or summit after another, never satisfied by what they have done. Among these, however, some couple obsession with caution that keeps them from taking high risks, e.g., Fred Beckey, the celebrated pioneer of Northwest summits.

A small group whose members often take high risks is composed of those who make only one big climb in their lives. They are inexperienced, the climb for them is important, and they do not plan to undertake another. Making this summit today matters more to them than to one who, knowing he will have another day to try again, turns back at wet rock, unstable snow, severe fatigue, oncoming night or conditions that foretell an avalanche or storm.

Next come the competitors. Mountaineering success serves as a self-testing device and—a less direct means of satisfaction—earns recognition from peers. The competitors seek to score by collecting routes or summits the way some people collect baseball cards, Ming porcelain or autographed photographs and other people seek to win at sports. Those in this sector of the spectrum do not seek risk in itself and they are not indifferent to risk. They treat risk as a tradeoff for achievement, part of the price paid for the reward of self-esteem. Extreme examples of this competitor breed—some of them Japanese—seem to regard themselves as infantrymen and the summit as a hill to be taken forthwith and at all costs. Non-climbers, of course, may feel that to climb the side of something and then climb back down is not a pearl entitled to such a great price.

A few aim to prove manhood by proving to themselves that they are not cowards—somehow, one proof is not enough. A variant impulse denies—or defies—the loss of youth, and perhaps expresses a residual wish to make up for failure to earn a letter in a high school sport.

The safe end of this range is occupied by those whose climbing looks to a non-climber more dangerous than it is because they try to confine themselves to risks that threaten only a climber who slackens his vigilance or effort. Rather than resembling one who faces a wholly random possibility, like one who risks his money on a roulette wheel or his life by driving on New Year's Eve or joining the Marines, most climbers of this kind resemble one who goes up a ladder or who speeds on skis or a galloping horse. He has chosen to go where his safety depends on how he handles himself. He can protect himself against much of the danger that he allows himself to skirt.

Such a climber is prompted by the reverse of a suicidal impulse. His appetite for life makes him want to live forever. He exults in using his body to the full and without knowing into what experience it will lead him. This intensity and acceptance of uncertainty come not from desperation but from zest. He prefers to measure the quality of experience and level of achievement by difficulty rather than by uncontrollable danger. An episode in which the latter intrudes itself provokes disgust rather than exhilaration; it impairs rather than enhances a climb. The risks taken are not ends in themselves, but incidental consequences of full engagement, living on the cutting edge. To be sure, the risks taken by the obsessives and competitors are likewise incidental consequences, but those who love life give the risks more heed.

Some risks are undertaken both as means and as end. When an avalanche caught my friend Jim Wickwire and me, Jim held us fast, and after the flow of soft snow had passed on down, we were left with our shoulders at the surface, able to struggle free. We resumed our downward journey, undisturbed, taking this as part of the day's play near the Arctic Circle at 15,500 feet.

Starting to climb late in life made finding companions difficult, especially at first. Members of my generation climb no longer, while among those few younger climbers whom I know, not many care to tolerate my slower pace. One early climb was undertaken with a fellow who had responded to my note on a mountaineers' bulletin board. Off route, groping in mist, unroped on muddy rock above a gully on the south side of Mt. Garfield, we saw below us a stream that entered a snow tunnel. On my remark that to be swept under would be a dreadful way to go, he commented that how you go matters not, so long as you are ready to Meet Your Maker. My reaction was to think: "Not being ready, I wish not to climb with one who is." Nor does one want a climbing partner who regards this endeavor not as outdoor fun but as an exercise in machismo, because the latter outlook puts *your* neck at risk. After attending the funeral for one of my five friends who have been killed climbing, my reaction was not fear to climb but rather the reminder that in this sport one must take care.

✧ ✧ ✧

In the mountains no glory is attained. The only sense in which that word may relate to one's days and nights up there is a sense of the glory that can be felt in being alive, a sense one may derive from a piece of music.

When friends have commented that mountain climbing takes courage, their characterization seems mistaken and their admiration misplaced. Whatever motives induce one to climb, whether they are single or multiple, conscious or unconscious, healthy or sick, they have one thing in common: They are for oneself. That is, they are selfish. Fund solicitors for an expedition to Central Asia sometimes speak as though one is being asked to buy a pair of spurs for a Crusader who is setting forth to recover the Holy Sepulchre from the infidel, when a more apt analogy might be to buy balls for tennis-playing friends.

The only way that climbing risks can merit the term "courageous" is where the motive for taking them is *not* selfish. That is, where they are undergone to rescue or otherwise help another person. Arguably, bullfighting is less selfish than high-risk climbing because El Toreador's performances help support Señora Toreador and the kiddies, please the blood-thirsty spectators and propel the national economy. Suppose the rules of golf were amended to permit games to be played only during thunderstorms. Should we admire for courage those whose addiction/fanaticism put them on the links, their life insurance policies written only by Lloyds, and at rates comparable to those on tankers during war?

To stretch the meaning of "courage" to include strenuous and risky efforts to surmount features of geography in order to satisfy oneself is to blur the term by broadening it to a range more fitting for the language of those savages whose mathematics are expressed by "one, two, three and many." How can this selfish practice be called "courageous" without debasing the language, romanticizing recklessness and trivializing the meaning of this noble human quality? The label that fits is "nerve."

Errands into the wilderness and on the sea have been for me a major challenge, diversion, consolation and delight. Mastery of self in nature has been a long and, on the whole, gratifying pursuit.

Sometimes a low mood has driven me into the mountains alone. Often I would go not with the enthusiasm of Winthrop, who "flung [himself] again alone upon the torrent of adventure," but grimly, to prove something self-justifying. However, I usually have had a fine time. The motives for setting forth may have been deplorable, but the process itself invigorated me, giving me a sense of strength and freedom and sending me home buoyant. Although I was immersed in solitude, did nothing productive and emerged tottering with fatigue, the experience somehow would relieve me of the sense, that had sent me there, of being lonely, worthless and weak. And always I have come back.

On these solitary excursions, I have climbed about fifty summits and roamed many a hill and dale. A few of the most gratifying climbs have been deep in the mountains when the nights are long.

Some attempts have failed. After my numb fingers let go at the top of a lay-back crack near the top of the "Overexposure" route on Liberty Bell, I slipped and fell on the last hard move. By luck, the fall chastened but did not injure; it sent me back down the hill in silent darkness, breathing the cool October air, the exhilaration of the venture tempered by the sober relief of the escape. At seventy-three, I went back to complete this unfinished business. Improved skill and more strength let me climb with confident ease until an absent-minded mistake with my rope rig caused me to peel off no more than six feet below the point from which I had fallen twelve years before. Punishment for this error, perhaps compensating for the previous charity of fate, included broken ribs and a punctured lung. A year later I went back and made it. Although success was satisfying, an inner struggle denied pleasure in the process. My vow not to be defeated pushed me upward, while my shaken nerve pulled me back.

When climbing alone, the danger of reduced protection or none if you fall and no help if you become sick, hurt, lost or stuck is offset in part by your exemption from the social pressure to follow companions on a route where the reach may exceed your grasp. Thucydides wrote, "Many, though seeing well the perils ahead, are forced along by fear of dishonor, as the world calls it." One may be further guarded by the care that awareness of the risk makes you take for every place you put a hand or foot. In Whymper's words: "When one has no arms to help and no head to guide him except his own, he must needs take note even of small things, for he cannot afford to throw away a chance."

Icicle Creek Irrigation Ditch

Liberty Ridge 5/8/79

On Denali, 6/81

Shelby Scates, Bill Sumner 7/81

Harriet B. 10/84

Alex Bertulis

Above BellaCoola 8/88

Joshua Tree 5/90

Mt. Patullo 7/85

Chapter | 5

CIVIC

> The secret of happiness is liberty,
> And the secret of liberty is a brave heart.
>
> —PERICLES

In the summer of 1932, when I turned thirteen, Mother took me to the Democratic National Convention in Chicago. The atmosphere on the convention floor was exciting the night FDR was nominated. One evening there she took me to a delegates' dinner at which the speakers were Robert Hutchins and Will Rogers; the latter explained he had eaten his dinner before he came, so he was free to say what he pleased.

A year later, she took my cousin and me to Hyde Park for lunch with the Roosevelts. Mrs. R. sat me between Vincent Astor and my Father's cousin, Bill Bullitt, to whom the President introduced me by calling down the table, "Say, Bill, that's Scott's son you are sitting beside." When he had been wheeled into the room in his wheelchair and said, "Hello, boys," with a friendly wave of his hand, his presence was blithe and commanding. If you were told that one among a crowd of strangers was the President of the United States, you would pick him. This contrasts with an experience nineteen years later, walking through a campaign train in Snohomish County. Where the corridor of the Pullman car narrowed and turned a corner I squeezed past a man going the other way. Of slight build, he wore steel-rimmed glasses and a black suit with a vest. For a moment I took him for the conductor, then realized he was the President.

A week or two after Hyde Park, Mother took me down to Washington, where she attended a White House conference. Declining the chance to go along, I walked through the City to the ball park; Washington lost to the White Sox.

My low draft number forecast that the authorities would not call me "up" (as the phrase went) for a long time, but when our entry in the war seemed near at hand, I enlisted in the Navy to get on with it. The Pearl Harbor attack a week later brought things on sooner than I had expected. Late in the month my train left for Norfolk Naval Training Station. For the first six months, my monthly pay was $99. During the four war years, I allotted part of my pay to be sent home to two social agencies: the Ryther Child Center and the Family Society.

In those early wartime days, at this, the Western Hemisphere's biggest Naval base, the atmosphere was tense. Wary eyes scanned the eastern sky for formations of Messerschmidts.

Distressed by the evacuation of Japanese-Americans from the Pacific Coast, I typed the following letter to each of our state's Congressional delegation:

I urge you to use your efforts and influence to have the Nisei members of our Army sent to whatever fighting fronts there are or may be to the east of us.

The problem of resettlement of the coast evacuees would be made much easier. The public knowledge that Nisei boys were risking and giving their lives, fighting for the same ends next to our Caucasian-

American sons, husbands, etc., would be more effective than anything else in easing the friction here. While public comment and attention is focused on the evacuation itself, I imagine Congress and the Government are mainly perplexed with the places and manner in which they will be situated and the relations to their neighbors.

When the war is over, if such a change has not been brought about, we will be confronted by a problem very difficult to solve.

On the European or African fronts there is not the personal bitterness against the Japanese as in the Pacific. They would be regarded more as fellow soldiers rather than with resentment and suspicion.

In the minds of many of us there is a question as to the extent of their loyalty. Why not prove it conclusively by this means rather than making guesses with no factual basis? If we continue to prevent them, in effect, from taking any voluntary action, they will continue to be the unknown quantity that they are now.

The Nisei soldiers, now stationed in the several camps and forts in the central part of the country, are doing nothing and becoming embittered and discouraged at being prevented from fighting for their own country and forbidden a chance to show their loyalty to it.

Their performance in action may be expected to be courageous. They are aware of being in the spotlight and that they stand or fall by their own behavior. Most of them feel that as the situation stands now, life has little to offer them—that there is little to live for unless they change conditions by their own fighting.

It is the one chance for the Japanese-American group as a whole to establish itself in the public eye as an integral part of this their country.

This move should help to clear up a confused condition as well as meliorating a difficult political situation, the future as well as the present.

I am convinced of its necessity and feel that the future of the Japanese-Americans will be decided by the course taken with the members in the Army.

Having made many mistakes, I was gratified when events showed this recommended course to have been right.

Applying for sea duty, I was assigned to the U.S.S. *Bogue*, a newly commissioned escort carrier. The night before we sailed from Bremerton, one of the sailors shot a hole through his foot to escape going to sea. Assigned to be the athletic director, I was given little work—standing security watches, doing odd jobs and leading calisthenics on the flight deck from the bridge. Among the chiefs, my name was "Muscles." Half derisive, half friendly, this term related to my duty assignment rather than to my bodily structure.

On a weekend liberty in New York, I went to a "Labor Unity for Victory" rally. Blue sky, lush green turf, music and fluttering flags around the Yankee Stadium rim made a striking spectacle. An enthusiastic crowd of 50,000 cheered the speakers who foresaw victory and enduring peace with a new day dawning for a Henry Wallace world. Paul Robeson (who sang "Peat Bog Soldiers" and "Ballad for Americans") and Mayor Fiorello LaGuardia received the biggest hands among the speakers (Congressmen Vito Marcantonio, Claude Pepper et al.) as they walked out to the pitcher's box.

The Communists apparently had organized the affair, but their irritating tone of spitefulness overlaid by unction failed to spoil the gladness it inspired.

Next week, I went to the "I Am An American" Day rally in Central Park and enjoyed the afternoon despite the self-congratulatory program. A big crowd listened to songs and to speeches by Vice President Wallace (who spoke well), Governor Lehman, Rabbi Wise, Frank Sinatra and Nathan Milstein. The theme was, "Aren't we proud of ourselves to be Americans." If people are to congregate and proclaim pride, it should be in something other than themselves.

On liberty in Boston, I attended a program at Symphony Hall contrived to strengthen Soviet-American friendship. Alternate speakers eulogized the others' country. Although I was ashamed to be the only Navy representative who chose to come, the affair seemed useless; nothing constructive was said, nor did the right people attend. They were Soviet-lovers, there not for instruction, but to be indulged.

In San Francisco, previously having been commissioned ensign on my 24th birthday, I boarded the U.S.S. *Monticello* with 7,000 troops and sailed to New Caledonia, a three-week voyage.

A small attack transport ship took me north to Guadalcanal: Uncomfortable, ugly and remote—some of the men wanted the Japanese to be made to live there after the War. Then I served four months in the communications center at the Naval Advanced Base on Green Island in the Solomons. On duty at the airfield there, unknown to me, was an air cargo officer, Lt. j.g. Richard M. Nixon.

After volunteering for sea duty with the 7th Fleet, I volunteered for a mobile communication unit to be used as a landing party. The group formed at Hollandia, the base in northern New Guinea. We stayed at Fleet Headquarters on the hill above Lake Sentani while helping to prepare the twenty-three-man unit. Although my place was second in command, my responsibilities were not large.

In Humboldt Bay on the New Guinea coast, where part of the invasion fleet was gathered in the fall of 1944, we boarded LST 452 after splashing in the surf all morning, as we spread a footing of sandbags for our trucks to reach the ramp. We weighed anchor with the convoy on Friday, the 13th. About our destination we knew only that we were headed for the enemy up north. Ships proceeding together, day by day, carpeted the sea to the horizon. After a hot and uneventful trip across the Equator, we approached Leyte Gulf. There a like fleet joined ours from the east. An aspect of American genius was demonstrated to us by the sight of history's second greatest concentration of ships, coming from vast distances and with coordinated purpose, as they converged upon that wooded shore.

The ship was packed, with little room to do anything but stand. As one looked forward from the bridge, the long deck filled with vehicles resembled a street filled with stalled traffic. An Army photographer on board, in later years a Hollywood director, told me that the generals were gracious to the cameramen so that when pictures were taken they would not be left out.

The landing* was the most grand and awesome spectacle I have ever seen. Before dawn on D-day (October 20) we peered through the gloom at the ships near

---

* invasion of the Philippines

us. In the distance ahead we could hear the beginning of the shore bombardment, and see an occasional flash. The sea was smooth and the air hushed. As light began to fill the sky, a lone plane appeared, a two-engined Betty (Japanese) heading for us. Ack ack broke the silence. To avoid the spouting red fountains of tracers the pilot sheered off and cut across the convoy, staying high. Each ship opened up as soon as the plane approached the range of its most optimistic gun crew. A bomb finally dropped in the water, missing a destroyer escort. At last, after these dull, tame years in the service, we had heard a shot fired in anger, we had joined the War.

We approached and passed first our battleships, then, further in, our cruisers, which were pounding several miles of coast. These magnificent, formidable ships filled us with confidence and pride. For a moment the picture crossed my mind of a quiet summer morning in childhood. From our balcony we watched a battleship come down the Sound, the crew arrayed on the after deck in white uniforms, as a band played "Stars and Stripes Forever."

About an hour later, when we could make out the beach and the forested hillside that bordered it, the transports slowed to a halt, and nets were hung over the side. The troops clambered down and tumbled into the waiting boats, which formed a long line abreast, each packed with soldiers, rifle in hand, in the bow two sailors machine-gunning the beach, and fluttering in the stern the little flag—our flag. One boat returned close by us, without having reached shore. A mortar shell had landed in it; the only visible survivor was the coxswain, who was crying as he sat in a welter of bloody meat.

I stood on the bridge and leaned against the starboard rail. All was quiet on board, the only sounds faint in the distance. On glassy water, garbage and a broken crate drifted by the hull. Heading the column of LSTs, we saw a few futile splashes well ahead of us, near a buoyed flag that a launch earlier had set to guide our course to land. Things were happening all around us. The scene was a complex entertainment; one wanted to watch repeated performances to catch what might have been missed.

We began to hear firing on shore.

A loud bang and puff of smoke on the deck among the trucks up forward was followed almost immediately by another farther aft that sent debris high in the air, with a man's lifejacket slowly turning on top of the cloud. Those splashes had been from an enemy "75" getting the range on the path we were taking. The shore battery had used the buoyed flag as a reference point, as General Beauregard had done for Fort Sumter against the Union ironclads.

During my dash aft for shelter, before a dive among others who were sprawled behind the deck house, a piece of shrapnel struck me. The size of a quarter, it remains in my right shoulder. Negligible as an injury, this wound gave me pride as a symbol of military gallantry. Since the period when some of my more distant forebears were killed by Indians, my grandfather Tom Bullitt was my only ancestor wounded in combat.

We hugged the deck, trying to crawl under each other, while successive shells hit the ship and exploded. Hearing a shout that a wounded man was nearby, I peeped around the corner where a soldier lay near the rail in a puddle of blood. Pulling him to his feet and finding he had a number of what appeared to be small wounds, I put one of his arms over my shoulder and helped him below to the battle sickbay, made from the officers' mess compartment. The surgeons would look at each man brought in; if he looked as though they could save him, he was put on a table to wait his turn; if not, a blanket was put over him, and he was laid on the deck outside.

On the way to the sickbay with the soldier, we stepped into the wheelhouse and closed the door behind us. A shell had pierced the bulkhead and exploded. Everything was smashed. The dust hanging in the air and the quiet from a momentary lapse of bombardment, for an instant recalling childhood play in my grandparents' attic, gave the sense that this had been a quick bad dream, now ended. Then my glance took in the teen-aged helmsman, to whom the photographer had given a water color a couple of hours before. In the corner, on his hands and knees, he was covered with dust, his head gone.

At H hour plus l, the first LST, we landed on Red Beach a few steps from where General MacArthur later waded ashore. The engine room telegraph having been broken, the unsteered ship ran aground without slackening speed, but no one noticed the bump. The next LST behind us drew alongside with fire in her deck ammunition that sent 20 mm shells flying in all directions. Below, the members of our unit found each other. Breathing the sharp smell of cordite, we cast the deck chains from our two trucks.

As the ramp was lowered, two soldiers stepped out on it. A bullet hit one, and he lurched against the other man, sending both overboard into the deeper water at the side. Laden by packs on their backs, they did not come up.

Along the beach soldiers crouched behind trees and hummocks. They would fire and then run forward, crouched low, to another bit of cover. Here and there some lay still where they were.

We drove our trucks ashore, the first Navy men to have landed in the Philippines, and hastily dug in to avoid the sniper and machine gun fire that zipped past. The soldiers went on.

At night we slept in our two-man foxholes. It got dark at seven, and to be safe you stayed in your hole. If you got out and moved around, some nervous man might shoot at you. The first night we discovered our holes were too short. Artillery on the beach fired at the enemy positions. Before the hills had stopped echoing one report, another cannon would shoot.

Corpses were a feature of the beachhead landscape. American bodies were brought in on litters and laid in a row under blankets before they were buried in cemeteries that the chaplains laid out. The helmsman in the wheelhouse had been the first dead body that I ever had seen.

After a couple of days I walked through the woods toward Palo, where the fighting continued. Stinking bodies of the Imperial Marines were scattered along the road and around their shattered concrete pill boxes. Big men for Japanese, they lay bloated in the sun until a bulldozer could bury them.

Over the radio circuits that our MC unit monitored, we listened to intense conversations between men engaged in history's largest sea battle, nearby but out of sight.

After four days on the beach we went up to Tacloban (Imelda Marcos's home town) on an LCT ("landing craft, tank"). We camped for a few days beside the dock to which was moored a Liberty ship with a cargo of aviation gasoline. On the grass inshore from us were several truckloads of dynamite. The ship attracted air attacks. It was never hit, but the surroundings were. Each day our tents and trucks were patched to cover holes that bomb fragments and strafing bullets made. One morning, when a flight of enemy torpedo bombers came over, one plane, its engine stopped by fire from our side, headed for the dock on a steep glide and tried to hit the ship. It did not quite make it and splashed into the water alongside. As the plane sank the pilot climbed out and started to swim ashore, but the gunners on the ship's deck gave a burst of fire that cut him in half. When his body drifted to the dock, souvenir hunters collected his ears.

For my wound, an order came for me to be awarded the Purple Heart "with appropriate ceremonies." The members of our unit put on their black shoes and stood in one place to spare them from the mud. The commanding officer displayed the medal to the others, then handed it to me, saying that if I were wearing a shirt he would pin it on me. Later, some one told me of a Marine who had received the Purple Heart for a wound sustained when he went into a cave on Saipan and brought out an eight-year-old boy who bit him in the stomach.

Once as a bomber dove, I raced for a dugout (feeling that the pilot was aiming at my back) and stumbled while crossing a road. Because to return to my feet for such a short distance seemed a waste of vital time, the rest of the flight was taken on my knees, gashing one. Its effects eventually laid me up for five days in an Army field hospital before returning to my unit. Most of the patients were bomb casualties. During the air raids each night those who could move would hustle outside and crawl into a trench.

One day several men were brought in; flaming gasoline had covered them when a kamikaze crashed his plane into the bridge of their ship. From beside a dugout I had watched men jumping overboard to escape the heat. Bandaged from head to foot, these casualties looked like snow men. Holes had been cut over their eyes, noses and mouths. That night, their breathing became hoarse and labored, loud in the silence. One by one, their breaths became shorter and finally stopped. The corpsman on duty would determine the right cot, and a couple of litter bearers would grope their way in, bumping their knees against the cots in the dark. One of them would say, "Let's get moving, Pete, and take this one out of here before the next raid begins."

Behind the hospital was a tent with wounded prisoners lying under it. Many patients voiced the wish, not shared by me, to go out and run bayonets through them.

One evening when no alert was on, engineers close behind us set off an overcharge of dynamite, showering rocks on the tin roof and nearby tents. Men over a large area leaped from their cots and into fox holes half filled with water from the typhoon the day before.

Some of the patients were delirious, reminding me of the dying sailor in the movie "For Which We Serve" who called for his captain, the tender and understanding Noel Coward (playing the character based on Lord Mountbatten). When these men called for anyone, it was for Mama. None was heard to groan, "I want my Colonel."

One patient, a soldier, had been standing out in

a field, shaving. Some Zeros swooped in low, and an excited anti-aircraft gunner, swinging his muzzle below the horizon, shot the man through the back. The unexploded 20 mm shell rested at an angle, and its point could be seen bulging under the skin of his chest, as he sat in a chair. The doctor assigned to operate walked in circles while he waited for the demolition squad. Then he barely touched the man's chest with his knife, and the shell jumped out into his hands. (This I was told, having retreated when the operation was to start.) A couple of days later a news story was broadcast to the States by one of the correspondents. It began, "A strange accident occurred here. A Japanese plane was strafing, and one of its cannon shells . . ."

We moved to a field next to the air strip, where dive bombing was replaced by high level bombing. A dive bomber pilot would release his bomb low enough for it to be fairly accurate; the misses were what worried us. Also, when you heard a plane go into its dive you could tell whether it was coming near you or not, and if not you relaxed. In high level bombing, the planes would circle in the sky, off and on, throughout the night. When a bomb started whistling down you could not tell where it would hit.

When a bomb exploded nearby at night, stretcher bearers and companions of those who had been hurt went to look for them. The rest stayed in their foxholes in case another might be coming soon. In daytime, one climbed out of his hole after the explosion and joined the knots of men who gathered around the casualties lying on the ground near the hole the bomb had made.

The air fights were exciting, though one-sided. Often only a lone Japanese bomber would appear. One of our fighter planes would attack. As its machine guns fired, you could see the twinkling flashes along the leading edge of its wings. If hit, the bomber often would burst into a ball of fire and take a long, fast arc to earth.

Ten days after the Leyte landing the rains came, and deep mud prevailed for almost five months. By and by, I moved to a tent that had a board floor. My work schedule was six hours on and twelve off.

During these fall and winter months the arrival that pleased us most was that of the first ground-based fighter planes. A flight of P-48s came over low, and everybody cheered. Next in pleasure was a load of long-accumulated mail.

In my childhood, men enthralled me with tales about their experiences in the Alaskan Gold Rush. Having forgotten most of them has given me regret, just as I now regret having forgotten some of the stories heard during the War of others' adventures: stirring, fantastic and vivid.

During the Battle of the Java Sea, when a member of a destroyer's gun crew climbed through the hatch from below with a shell in his arms, he found himself looking down the barrel of the six-inch deck gun, which had reversed its direction when the ship had taken a 180 degree turn during his trip to the magazine. Startled, he lurched backward just as the gun went off over his head, and he fell overboard. In his alarm, he forgot to let go of the heavy shell until he had plunged deep, thereby letting the destroyer's propellers pass over him. Bobbing to the surface, he swam ashore (as Admiral Imamura did a day or so later), grateful that the sharks had spared him, made his way to Batavia (now Djakarta) and reported for duty at the temporary Allied Headquarters, soon to be withdrawn further to Brisbane, where he was assigned to the *Houston*. To soothe his nerves, he reclined on a bale in a warehouse and drank a bottle of gin. When he emerged, the cruiser had sailed without him and next day was sunk, losing most of those aboard including Captain Rooks, whose son later practiced law a block from my office.

A shipmate told of when his aircraft carrier came within range of a Japanese battleship. Its big guns were loaded with armor-piercing shells, an error when its target was a thin-skinned carrier. He was startled to see what appeared to be pairs of newly-made portholes appearing in the hull simultaneously on opposite sides of the vast hangar deck.

One of my tent mates had served in a guerrilla unit on Japanese-occupied Mindanao: a furtive, desperate life in the jungle, constantly on the move. A Russian who worked for him had been a crew member on a Russian destroyer that came to the Pacific during the Revolution. When their side lost they had no home port, so the admiral aboard sold the ship to the Philippine government. The money was treated like the proceeds from a fishing boat catch; each man took his share and went his way. Some Australian guerillas who had escaped from Singapore, would use their time off to go down from the hills and look for Japanese soldiers, at whom they would take a few shots.

Except for stories about my grandfather and one of his brothers in the Civil War, my knowledge of POWs is limited to tales of long ago, like Churchill in the Boer War and Richard I hearing Blondel, the troubadour, from his castle cell, and to stories heard in World War II. A British paratrooper told me about having been sold by an Italian to the Germans for

50,000 lira and spending a year as a prisoner. He told of a Scot shot down in France who knew no French but roamed the countryside for a year. Whenever a German spoke to him, he would respond in Gaelic.

Returned from a German prison camp, an Australian told me how the prisoners got their news. From their hidden radio, three men would take down the news program in shorthand each day as it was broadcast in English, French or German. (Another POW told me they hid their radio in a medicine ball.) They would make copies, and twelve men would read them throughout the camp. Then the papers would be destroyed. When someone asked him how it had been, he said it wasn't bad, that he had been arrested once and had been in jail for six months and that that had been lonely. Asked if that was solitary confinement, he replied that it was.

When he and his colleagues rode west toward France after their release, they ran into a battle. This frightened him less than his ride with the Americans. They were crammed into a three-ton truck, going at a fast clip. Another truck pulled alongside, an arm stuck out, holding a bottle of champagne, the driver of this man's truck took the bottle, rested his elbows against the wheel and drained it. From then on, the Australian said the ride got so exciting that they noticed nothing smaller than "88" shells.

VJ Day in Melbourne provoked an outburst of feeling even more intense than in the United States. The threat had been greater because the enemy was closer and relatively more powerful. Life had been more disrupted. Because the country lacked war industries and admired virility and sport (to many, war was a kind of sport), almost all able-bodied men had gone to war. And their war had lasted almost twice as long as ours. In the downtown streets about a quarter of a million people turned out, shouting, singing, blowing horns, waving flags, throwing fish and other things, linking arms with strangers and skipping down the street, kissing each other (the plainer sort of teenage girls taking an avid part), climbing up on things, playing or just blowing musical instruments, carrying signs, throwing paper out of windows, lighting firecrackers and rockets, chalking "PEACE" (some scholars wrote "PAX") and "VP" on the trolley cars, lighting fires with wastepaper, knocking people's hats off, dancing the hokey-pokey, bothering policemen and lots more. The fact that scant grog was flowing contributed to the comparative decorum. The next day the streets filled again, but with a less exuberant crowd.

During the War, it seemed to me necessary to think through my own war aims and to list their reasons, in descending order of importance: Protect immediate family and friends; enable our nation's people to retain the privilege of shaping its destiny; prevent the Axis powers from oppressing conquered lands and minorities in their own countries; enable an enduring peace to be established; forestall the necessity, should we lose, to prepare for, and ultimately fight, another war as soon as we are able; insure our country's wealth by retaining control of its own material resources and access to foreign ones; and get it over with sooner to let me go home.

On return to the States after the War's end, I met, disliked and scorned some conscientious objectors. Some of these were rosy-cheeked, strapping lads in sports jackets and others pallid intellectuals; all enjoyed possession of their lives and the freedom, peace and comfort derived from others' selfless gift. Sneering bohemians would say, "I wouldn't have any vulgar sergeant push *me* around." They regarded soldiers as suckers and war as a plebeian racket. Conversations with them and other pacifists in later years provoked me to resent the attitude sometimes expressed that all soldiers have been either brutes or dupes. On the other hand, one cannot but admire some older people, often Quakers (like Art Barnett, a lawyer who stood up for the rights of the American Japanese), although disagreeing with their belief in the sanctity of life, for their willingness to make sacrifices for their principled stand against violence of every kind.

In hindsight, faced with the 1941 decision, my choice would be the same. Duty as a citizen sent me off to this just war. But as to the value of this experience, a different question, the effects were mixed. Much of those four years I disliked; all of them I grudged, preferring something else: pursuing pleasure, service, success, ideals other than the one pursued at war. Yet in many ways they broadened and enriched my life, taught me things about the world and myself that I never would have learned without having gone. A young man who lived through World War II without taking part failed to share fully in "the action and passion of the time." While in uniform, I envied those who stayed home, but not in later years.

Before resuming civilian clothes, I plunged into civic affairs and politics. My political activity during those years was mainly in the liberal wing of the Democratic Party and in the liberal movement outside of that Party. My main subjects of attention were international cooperation, responsive and responsible governmental structure, housing and municipal planning, and racial justice, emphasizing jobs. Curious about government, I attended sessions of Congress, the Washington Legislature, the Seattle City Council, the King County Board of Commissioners and, earlier, the Victoria Parliament in Melbourne.

My civic outlook contained a tincture of the classical Greek and Roman civic ideal—pure, generous, upright—that from the mid 18th to the mid 20th centuries was absorbed in school by members of the British male upper class. To take part in public affairs seemed called for by common sense, reflected by the Greek root of the word "idiot" as meaning a private person, and my Father had given the impression that to take part was not a burden but a natural process, less a moral duty than a satisfying and essential part of life.

Three causes propelled me into public life. Father had done this. It was one of the central functions of society and a path for ambition. And for a young man who owed much to Fortune, which cannot be repaid, public affairs offered a chance to keep the gifts from going for naught. Our family now has started its second century in Seattle, and for almost four hundred years on both sides some of its members have been taking part in the public life of what has become this country.

My political outlook was not a conversion but a process that extended from childhood into maturity. If my outlook must be labeled it is as a liberal, yet aspects of conservatism appeal to me, both the emphasis that European conservatives put on organic institutions and historic continuity and the emphasis my conservative countrymen put on personal responsibility. Insofar as my liberalism was derived from a parent, it came largely from experience of Father and memories of him, although in later years others attributed it to Mother. My outlook concerned social justice and equal opportunity for talent. It involved less faith in the merits of affirmative action by the national government than scorn for those who abhorred such action. It contained sympathy for the poor and others denied a chance to show what they had in them. It regarded the Republican party as one of selfish materialists and snobs.

A large feature of those days was a series of struggles with the Communists in the Democratic Party and other political organizations. Some of this was exciting, some just nasty; lots of long night meetings in stuffy halls where shouting, bombast and hurried caucuses combined with endless parliamentary maneuvers. I shared some of the Communists' ends, such as better treatment of the poor and correction of racial injustice (during my time in college, *The Daily Worker* was the only periodical to criticize Blacks' exclusion from professional baseball). Their ruthlessness did not repel me, but I detested their dishonesty and their contempt for democracy, an arrogant paternalism. After fighting the Communists for years came a period of defending myself against charges of being one.

A group of young men (hardly any women), most of whom had taken part in the War, associated loosely as civic and political colleagues. We had energy, ambition and ideals, and together we had a good time. During this period, I came to know many of those who were to be my friends and associates during the following three decades, plus some whose sons in later years became my companions and friends.

Our activity in those first five post-war years embodied more civic hope than at any time since. (One evening some of us met to discuss measures to establish the United Nations Headquarters in Seattle.) Our ideals were high and seemed worth pursuing. We did not know the difficulties in making a happier world. Also, opportunity offered itself to help humankind through U.S. action. Our country then had so much more power than any other that it seemed able to accomplish a lot in whatever direction it chose. The Marshall Plan pleased us, but we wanted more good deeds.

Seen in retrospect, much of that thinking on public policy seems unsophisticated or blind to what was important. Our successors probably will think likewise of contemporary civic thought. Back then, some of those who thought in ideological terms advanced notions almost as silly as those Chinese Communist fanatics who felt that the color red expressed such symbolic merit that they proposed the traffic be made to go when the light turned red. Some believed that most of our social and economic problems could be solved by asking the Federal Government to solve them. Others were consumed by an intense religious faith in anti-Communism, appearing to assume that most of the governments and populations between East Berlin and Canton must be intimidated or converted to abandon their wickedness—and likewise for the multitude of traitors by which our own society was infested. Another unrealistic plan to which many intelligent people subscribed was world government, but its utopianism—an approach to government that seems socially desirable—tended to redeem its impracticality.

In the '40s, perhaps ideology was too heavily stressed for reality to be best understood. Now, perhaps, it is not given enough emphasis, confining our sources of direction to our unconscious premises formed by long tradition of self-government.

Among the civic gatherings of various viewpoints that I attended in the immediate postwar years was a Progressive Party rally, at which Henry Wallace and others spoke, in the spring of 1949. The main theme was "Down With the Atlantic Pact" (NATO). Above the stage hung a truculent banner showing a giant woman stevedore who brandished another banner in a heavy outthrust fist and clutched a baby with the other arm. Even the baby had powerful muscles, and it was shaking its fists at a fat American who was wearing a dollar sign. The banner's caption: "Enforce Peace."

At dinner one evening, James Farley, who had been Roosevelt's campaign manager and Postmaster General, recalled the past to my Mother and me. Some of his remarks:

When Chief Justice Hughes walked home from the Court the day he retired, he told a newspaperman walking with him that he thought Black would go down in history as one of our greatest judges and Murphy as one of the poorest.

FDR delayed appointing Frankfurter until Brandeis retired so there would not be two Jews on the Court at the same time.

In the Court-packing fight, FDR assured Senator Robinson that he would be one of the two new justices appointed if the plan passed. That assurance won the support of much of Congress. When Robinson died, support was lost because members felt that the promise went with Robinson, so his death had much to do with the failure of the plan, and FDR should not have been so down on Garner, who was not to blame for being unable to put it across.

The nominating speech for Al Smith in 1928 was written by Judge Joe Proskauer, and FDR wanted to delete the phrase "the happy warrior" before delivering it.

When Al Smith and FDR first met after the 1932 nomination, FDR said, "Glad to see you, Al. That comes from the heart, too." Smith shifted his cigar and grunted, "Glad to see you, too, Frank." FDR was on Farley's arm, and no one else on the platform was near enough to hear what was said. A wire service reporter named Sturm, who had been at the edge of the platform, remembering Smith's past use of the phrase, "Hello, you old potato," wrote it down on a guess and put it on the wire. The remark swept the country, gathering votes for FDR by pleasing Smith supporters that Al's feeling for FDR should be so warm.

When Churchill was walking out of Commons, he looked over to the seven Liberal Party members sitting together and said, "So few; and so futile." Farley asked, "What's Joe (Stalin) like?" Churchill replied, "He is a murderin' bastard." Farley asked Churchill how Truman enjoyed Churchill's Fulton speech, and Churchill replied, "I saw the motion pictures of my speech, and he seemed to be enjoying it." Farley said that he, Henry Wallace, Frances Perkins and Garner were the only Cabinet members who, in disagreement with FDR, would stand up to him.

At thirty-one, I was elected to the fifteen-member King County Charter Commission, the only Democrat, and received the second highest vote among the ninety-six candidates. For two years, meeting on the

ninth floor of the Courthouse, we drafted a reorganiza-
tion plan for the County government. The voters rejected this proposed charter, which in substance was
adopted about twenty years later. Our work was important, and the project was sound, but the group's medio-
cre average ability made the process dull.

At thirty-three, pursuing a long-held ambition, I
ran for Congress. The seat for Seattle and Kitsap County
had become vacant when the incumbent ran for Governor. I won the Democratic nomination but lost in the
general election.

On a number of early mornings that summer and
fall, I campaigned at plant gates with the Congressman
from Everett who was running for the Senate. We had
known each other slightly for eleven years and got on
well, although in 1942 we had sharply disagreed in
correspondence about the proper treatment of the Japanese-Americans. For the next thirty years, my relations
with Henry Jackson were sometimes strained. We disagreed on arms control and Vietnam. He was angered at
me when a *Seattle Magazine* piece quoted him on a tour
through Okanogan County as telling the driver not to
digress to the Indian Reservation, because "They don't
vote." He touched me with a note of sympathy when my
son was drowned. We were not friends, but he had my
admiration for some impressive qualities, and always my
full respect.

Now, my age more than doubled, I still would be
willing to advance most of my 1952 platform. Items
included strengthening the U.N., reducing tariffs, un-
dertaking a Point-4 Program, reorganizing the bureaucracy and tax structure, extending social security, and
establishing a national FEPC (Fair Employment Practices Commission). However, one radio speech, dis-

cussing the need for regional economic diversification beyond Boeing and the Navy Yard, contained these words: "For example, I'd like to see a ski tow all the way to Camp Muir." Looking back long after, I wrote in the margin of the typescript, "Good God, I'm glad I lost!"

Two years later I ran again. Early one morning, while campaigning along the Waterfront, I accosted a man who was standing on the sidewalk with a broom and apron in front of a seafood restaurant. He asked me to step inside, took down a couple of chairs from a table, poured coffee, asked some thoughtful questions, then wrote out a check for a substantial campaign contribution. Ivar Haglund became well known as a businessman and local character.

My prior loss by a 1-1/2 percent margin in a Republican landslide made me think my prospects for this campaign were good, but a major figure in the State proved me wrong. Profiting by the lessons learned the last time, I campaigned well, but he beat me two to one (then went on to lose to the incumbent in the general election). The one-sidedness of the vote was a shock. Just before the election, the self-deceiving optimism of a candidate had led me to believe my hopes were possibilities. In defeat I felt as I would a quarter century later, after two failed assaults on McKinley: disappointed but, knowing the good fight had been fought, neither frustrated nor ashamed. After writing longhand letters of thanks to about a hundred supporters, I stored the records.

That race for office was my last. Even after being relieved of hostages to fortune composed of large debts and small children, and even though continuing to regard politics as one of the most important fields of human endeavor and one that I understood, I was not even tempted. Experience had shown my lack of both aptitude and taste for the function. To be a politician had ceased to be my wish.

Soon my spirits revived with rest, the passage of time, and consoling thoughts about my living conditions that I came to realize I enjoyed more than I would the life of a Congressman: law practice, privacy, the beauties of nature and pleasure with my children and friends. After about fifteen years of civic and political activity, frustrated by the ineffectiveness of both the groups and myself and impatient with inaction and endless circular talk, I became unwilling any longer to take a large part in civic work. Since then, the skepticism produced by observing intelligent efforts to do the right thing achieve little public good has not dimmed my public concerns.

In later years, having come to realize I could perform better as an appellate court judge than in any of the occupations I have undertaken (practicing lawyer, business executive, entrepreneur, politician, teacher, writer and Navy enlisted man and officer), I sought appointment to vacancies, but in vain.

Although many conscientious citizens now feel strongly indignant at injustice in American society, my indignation does not now often burn. Although injustice abounds, and we are threatened by risks of harm to us all, such as the weapons of mass destruction and some decline in our wealth, the present seems less unfair than the recent old days. The society's wealth-producing capacity has multiplied several times over what had been developed throughout the previous history of the human race; Blacks' and women's chances for dignity and fulfillment have vastly improved; unskilled workers no longer endure grinding toil and the risk of destitution; and isolated old folk watch TV instead of looking out the window by day and staring at the wall when the sun goes down.

During my boyhood, a man would consider himself liberal when he relaxed his practice and accepted a Catholic in his firm; and when a man declared himself to be without race prejudice, he was taken to mean that he bore Negroes no ill will, not that he questioned their separate condition and subordinate station. Well-bred people did not speak of sheenies and shines, jigs and kikes, dagoes, chinks and micks, but when they heard such words they did not take offense.

Here is an example of how things were worse. During my last year at college, an acquaintance asked my help in seeking an elementary school teaching job in Seattle. In response to my letter in her behalf, the Superintendent of Schools (Worth McClure, after whom a junior high school since was named) wrote me that the Seattle school system did not hire Negroes (this although Lucille was well-mannered, well-groomed and had earned her Master's degree from Yale).

In political campaigns, the standards of morality and taste are no worse. In the '30s, many people amused one another and expressed their political preferences for President by exchanging dirty jokes about the President's wife. In 1952, at a League of Women Voters meeting to hear the candidates in Seattle, a major party nominee for the U.S. Senate told a joke the point of which was Mrs. Franklin Roosevelt being drowned. Eleven years later, on November 22, some people gave parties to celebrate their civic joy.

✧ ✧ ✧

In 1966 I wrote the following editorial, delivered it over television and radio and had it published in the papers.

Greetings. Until now I've never broadcast an opinion for this Company, but the war and its treatment in the news compel one to speak out. The intensity of our military action should be stepped down, and we should stop bombing North Vietnam.

Sometimes a war may be justified, an essential means for a people to preserve its liberties or its life. In the case at hand, will this war's return to us equal its rising price, price in the broadest sense? Let us consider the cost and what we get for it in this long-continued and expanding war.

Part is the sacrifice of our young men: for some their lives; for others, their precious, youthful years. Part is the money which could be spent in other ways. The rest is what we do to those whom we attack, whom we cripple and kill, some of them brave soldiers, some unarmed civilians, innocent children. Of course it's nonsense to suggest waging a precise war, confining slaughter to the wicked strong, since the war-making process by its nature is not only cruel but crude. War always poses the question whether the purpose justifies the whole cost. In World War II, it did. In this war I submit that it does not.

On the contrary, it increases the risk of loosing an exchange of nuclear rockets, those fiery swords which would destroy us all and make the face of the earth look like the surface of the moon. It provokes other major powers, China and Russia, to join the Vietnam war. And it further stretches that distrust and antagonism which impede the measures needed to suppress those rockets before the day they enter reckless hands. Pearl Harbor's 25th anniversary reminds us that leaders of even an industrially advanced nation can be utterly reckless.

We must also acknowledge a fact repulsive to American ideals: Our intense warfare fails to enable construction of a just and stable society in Vietnam. It fails because it disrupts the society, tends to degrade and corrupt large elements of it, and makes ever more enemies by war's inevitable mistakes—where hitting the wrong target leaves embittered survivors.

Perhaps our hopes could be realized were the fight to be carried on somewhere else, leaving tranquil a Vietnam whose folk might then proceed to govern themselves, and with some help from us, to develop their country. But our destructive course now spirals downward. The more we claw the place into a plowed field populated by refugees, prostitutes and hostile guerrillas, the less we can achieve at helping them build the kind of society we would like.

Our war is repelling other countries, appalling them, turning them against us. Yet on this planet we cannot make out alone. The success of every country's foreign policy, even ours with all our might, depends on respect and cooperation abroad. Furthermore, the weight of opinion against us throughout the world ought to give us pause, and hint that the rest of the world may be right.

So let us lower the fighting's intensity, narrow its extent and stop the air strikes on the North, while for now we maintain our military presence, our strategic hold, letting the deliberative body in Saigon move toward a government which is constitutional and, later on we can hope, representative, as it ought to be. At the start, at least, we can expect more northern enemy troops, relieved from bombing, to march south, but their threat to us is slight.

And our new direction can assist us: first, to reduce the bloodshed—ours and theirs; second, to cool the overheated atmosphere of that miserable country as a step to enabling its inhabitants to make peace with each other; and last, to raise our standing among the nations and relax the tension between the great powers until they can suppress those instruments which can, and may, wipe out the human race.

My daughter, Margaret, then five, listened to the broadcast indifferently until the line about "hostile guerrillas," at which she jumped to her feet with shining eyes and shouted "Gorillas!"

This speech (made before Martin Luther King, Jr. spoke out against the War) evoked a passionate outburst of response from many people, some in support and others opposed. Among those who favored it, many letters and telegrams declared that the author had thought he held his opinion alone and was heartened to find it shared.

Four years later I gave a similar editorial, criticizing the concealed Cambodian invasion. Compared to the earlier one, the responses were neither numerous nor intense. During the decade in charge at King, I limited my words spoken on the air to these two editorials, for combined reasons: self-effacement, wanting not to presume on my authority and, a lesser cause, not finding many appropriate issues important enough to justify the long time that writing an editorial would take.

With a relish that might have been malicious if he had not been squalid, I learned of having been put on President Nixon's "enemies list." By degrading American public life and soiling the reputation of the democratic process, Nixon ranked himself high among those in our history who have done the most harm, despite the merit of some of his public measures and policies. The eventual magnitude of those others' harm owes to the extended operation of the causal process that they started long ago. The shortness of the period during which the effects of this man's acts have made their way through our society has been more than offset by the enormity of his deeds to enlarge their pernicious impact.

The scandals arising from the Nixon and Reagan administrations, stemming from their leaders' character, did not surprise me. But even though some of them could be understood if not predicted, most events and many trends have surprised me. Examples are the leftward shift among Catholics, the rightward shift among Jews, the growth of ardent belief in evangelical Christianity, the appeal to some counterculture members of an obscure sect of Japanese Buddhism, and the maintenance by Spanish and Portuguese of democratic government despite scant experience in that complex art.

The best orator I ever heard was Churchill, the most dynamic voice (based on radio only) was Hitler's, and the best at charming anecdotes in speeches was Alben Barkley. The most pleasingly graceful, among those who had something to say, was Adlai Stevenson, a friendly acquaintance and distant cousin (descended from great grandmother Bullitt's brother).

Stevenson once took me over to the U.N. from

his apartment and showed me to the gallery for a session of the Security Council, which he then joined. The Council was considering charges that shots had been fired at Israeli fishing boats upon the Sea of Galilee. He wrote on a pad, then handed what he had written (perhaps of historic import, it looked to me) to an attendant, who soon handed me his note, asking me to come by for a drink. That evening in his living room as I sat with one leg resting on the other's knee, a hole in my shoe sole recalled a celebrated news photo of Stevenson in 1952, sitting with a hole visible in his shoe. This provoked an amused remark. Shifting my legs in a nervous reaction provoked laughter when my other shoe showed another hole.

After a later visit to Stevenson, on the way down in the elevator, which also was occupied by Walter Lippman, the hotel manager entered at an intermediate floor. He gave me a friendly greeting, recalling a business discussion in Seattle once with him, his boss, Conrad Hilton and Bagley Wright. Lippman looked miffed, as he was accustomed to being recognized. A wish to learn how to live like this more of the time was stirred by these experiences, which were fun for this country mouse.

Once Norman Thomas asked me up for tea with him and his wife at their apartment. They were a gracious couple, and I enjoyed them. He was a broad-gauged, high-minded old gentleman. Their son had been a Kent schoolmate of mine, a fellow of good quality but without his father's concern for social reform.

During senior year in college, I was flattered by friendly attention from a prominent classmate named Jim Angleton, a soccer star, founder of a poetry magazine and a bright and imaginative scholar of literature.

He told me I was the only individualist produced by Yale since Sinclair Lewis. When we got together years later, he was head of counterintelligence for the CIA and known to others in the Agency as the "Prince of Darkness." This man, who never had visited the Soviet Union and knew no language spoken there, told me that the long-apparent hostility between the Soviet Union and China was a deception to conceal the program conducted from the Kremlin to propagate the faith of Communism world wide and to extirpate all heretics. He also told me his preferred choice for President of the United States was Robert B. Anderson, a lawyer, business executive, lobbyist for Rev. Moon's Church and Eisenhower cabinet member, who later was convicted of income tax evasion and operating an illegal offshore bank, for which he served a prison term and was disbarred. Such blindness in a man so powerful as Jim appalled me, and his later fall into disgrace made me sad.

Since my becoming eligible to vote, my only failures to vote in all available elections for public office or public measures were two. One was the general election in 1944, when the absentee ballot did not reach Leyte in time. The other was a generation later. On a municipal election day, I drove home from work in the rain, put on my nightshirt, fried and ate some hamburger, read for a while and turned in, before remembering my neglect.

Most students of government decry passionate idealism in public affairs because of the harms it often has done. But it has its uses. Some competent historians think that the French Revolution achieved little of social value, and perhaps they are right. But a good performance of the Marseillaise cannot help but tell us what that Revolution has meant to many French and people of other lands who yearned for social justice. It inspired such hope and effort. And the Rising Sun: How many Japanese hearts has it stirred, for better or worse?

The basis of my preferred social policy toward sinners and ethics, criminals and crime, is utilitarian: what will work to make our treatment of each other more tolerable. An aspect of this is the need for codes of both law (as to which most agree) and morals (as to which some do not). This reflects our human frailty, our need for uniform standards and the large degree to which justice depends on certainty.

My utilitarian approach to ethics is modified by an outlook that gives special weight to those particular kinds of happiness favored by idealists. As to government, I concur with only those utilitarians who define pleasure to include liberty, so that the latter can be rated higher than comfort.

Those people annoy me who find most public policy questions easy and think their answers easy to apply: Raise teachers' pay, tax the other folk more, call out the National Guard, send criminals to counseling, balance the budget by reducing waste, make the Germans behave. Whatever they may have been in past ages, these questions, to any thoughtful mind, cannot help but perplex.

To me a central civic aim has been to guide or build toward a society that offers us all the chance to realize our potential and then put it to use.

> So, then, to every man his chance—to every man, regardless of his birth, his shining golden opportunity—to every man the right to live, to work, to be himself, and to become whatever thing his manhood

and his vision can combine to make him—this, seeker,
is the promise of America.

—THOMAS WOLFE

We should make our society's paramount aim to enable
us all: To live long, in good health, to develop and exercise the best we have within ourselves and to pass on
something of worth to those who come after us. For
this to be done requires not only establishing and protecting individual rights but also performing civic duties to make an effective community that can enable
those rights.

Some people throw away their potential from
laziness or lack of self discipline. Others choose to give
up some development or exercise of their potential out
of idealism, loyalty or moral principle, such as the poor
Jew who becomes a door-to-door salesman after high
school, enabling his younger brother to go to college
and head for medical school, or the young woman who,
to care for her parents, goes without much pleasure with
a man. But most choose to try to fulfill what is in them.
In the past, society's greatest limitation was failure to
enable full development of potential. Now we may be
entering on a condition in which some people may be
under-employed because although they took advantage
of the opportunity given them to develop their potential, they are not enabled to put it to use.

But more is needed. One is to formulate as a
corporate goal a conception of the good life and then
pursue it. Another is a concern for posterity. Without
citizens and leaders looking to serve those who come
after them we are doomed to a future that is bleak. Even
the young should plant trees beneath which they will
never sit.

Almost all citizens know that a public leader in a democracy has a duty to seek what her constituents want. Many also know she has the complementary duty to seek what, in her own judgment, as colored by her values, is the public good. But few citizens seem to see the politician's central function—less a duty than a necessity—to reconcile these obviously conflicting duties by perpetual compromise: External, among her constituents' interests, and internal, between constituents' conflicting wishes and her own judgment. Many citizens often consider that by such compromises their own principles or interests have been betrayed.

Those who do not acknowledge the public leader's role to include something of herself in her policies and perforce regard her proper role as that of a poll-reading errand runner, tend to the short run above the long. Like Esau, preferring present advantage to permanent rights, or like impatient shareholders who look for quick profits and oppose a management that is concerned with the risks that pursuit of quick profit imposes on long run prospects for gain, these citizens' demands emphasize benefits that are prompt. Giving posterity scant heed, unwilling to defer gratifying their wishes for the benefit of the unborn, they fault the politician who does. And by and by, the politician who does either gets their message and acts as though she has ceased to care about the unborn or is replaced by another politician, who obeys.

Among those citizens who do not serve in public office, with its mixed but nonetheless real satisfactions, most active citizens make their efforts for an aspect of the public good during only a short period in their lives. Before and after that, they devote themselves to survival, to heaping up riches, to an art or craft, to pleasure-seeking of some kind or, for interests that extend no further than their families, to other wholly private pursuits. Only a rare few sustain their civic efforts for long because to do so is so hard. And few among these few contribute to the public good. Most who continue for many years do so on inner supports that distort their values or their judgment. They cannot plough through decades of civic effort to do good deeds without motives or disposition that impair the quality of their deeds: career opportunism, egomania, hatred or a well-displayed sense of moral superiority. Few can plug away for long at a principled civic life as neither a fanatic nor a dilettante. Examples of such people remain listed in my memory, but few readers would recognize their names.

Who has been America's greatest private citizen? Depending on one's point of view, different names suggest themselves—Benjamin Franklin, Horace Mann, Susan B. Anthony, Joshua Chamberlain, Charles C. Burlingame, Louis Brandeis (before becoming a public official), Eleanor Roosevelt, Martin Luther King, Jr., I. F. Stone and so on. In the American experience over almost four hundred years, more significant than the altitude of stature displayed by the all-time best have been the myriad outside formal government who have done a constructive part.

Those public leaders willing to serve in a low station after they had occupied a high one, with no sense that this demeans their dignity, deserve to be admired. Such were John Quincy Adams, who served in the House of Representatives in his later years, and Epaminondas who served in the Theban army as a common soldier after he had earned, as a general, everlasting renown.

From the beginning of government until modern times, the ideal of a leader serving the public good meant the public welfare as distinguished from the leader's private gain for himself or his family or perhaps his class. Eunuchs and celibate priests were favored as advisors and administrators because the ruler knew they would not be feathering their children's nests. But since flagrant self-preference no longer is widely practiced, it has ceased to be an issue.

Now the problem has shifted. The old meaning of the "public good" did not address the multiplicity of interests and interest groups that now compose the public. How to reconcile these toward the overall public benefit perplexes all.

Many people used to bless things as they were, to say that what is is right, because they did not think there was anything they could do about it. This acceptance, this unwillingness to question the inscrutable ways of God, Job's passive attribution of all things to God's will, was used as a consolation under hardship and as an argument to resist reform and other social change. Later, many came to accept the reformist's hopeful expectation that things can and will be improved.

Swift refused to accept as good the evil facts of life, yet expected no improvement. If this is realism, it is brave; if not, it is pessimism and a cowardly defeatism masking itself as pride at rejecting the vanity of human life. Swift assailed not only its vanity but its value as well, yet did not feel it futile to write a book. Does this mean he only pretended his despair as a technique of shocking people into improving themselves? Or did he write out of anger and malice to rebuke mankind? Probably a blend of both.

Since growing up, I have thought that although the theory that every day our world improves and only needs assistance of good-willed people to speed the process may be true, the weight of evidence rebutting it makes its use as a basis for conduct fatuous optimism. However, I never have ceased to think that, as a means for improving the justice and conditions of our lives, the political process not only is not futile but is the best.

One feels gratitude to those people—almost always young—who believe that they, with others of like mind, can remake the world. Their illusion sustains them in efforts that do make their part of the world a better place.

3/30

San Diego NTS 9/42

Leyte 12/44

7/54

1962

Chapter | 6

LIVING PRACTICES

> That which before us lies in daily life,
> Is the prime wisdom; what is more is fume
>
> —MILTON

> ...life consists not of a series of illustrious actions, or elegant enjoyments; the greater part of our time passes in compliance with necessities, in the performance of daily duties, in the removal of small inconveniences, in the procurement of petty pleasures; and we are well or ill at ease, as the main stream of life glides on smoothly, or is ruffled by small obstacles and frequent interruption.
>
> —SAMUEL JOHNSON

When we were children, our only swimming for a number of years was in Puget Sound. After swimming pools came upon the scene, few ever again swam in the Sound unless they had fallen overboard.

Three times I bought a piece of land, had an architect design a house and had the house built. A vacation and weekend cabin on Squak Mountain, a few miles east of town, was destroyed by vandals because it remained unoccupied after my then wife had said, after a visit during construction, that it made her want to cut her throat. The land on which it was built (590 acres) I gave to my older children, who gave it to the State for a wilderness park. The second, on one and one-half acres on Capitol Hill, I lived in with the family for twenty-one years, and gave to the City of Seattle for a park, reserving a life interest in my second wife. The third, and best, was my home on the shore in West Seattle, built on a forty-degree, tree-covered slope a hundred feet above the beach. Its windows look westward across the Sound to the wooded ridges and beyond them the Olympics, over which one sees the setting sun—a view almost the same as that seen from our childhood home. This place, of three and two-thirds acres, I gave to my City, reserving a life interest in myself.

Since the passing of childhood fears of "things that go bump in the night," I have felt safe indoors, with a couple of exceptions. At fourteen, while I lay on my stomach on the floor of a Montana garage, with my feet in the freight elevator cage, Art Robbins, who was standing nearby, warned me that the elevator was dropping, so I hastily withdrew my legs before the roof sheared them off. At thirty, on the top floor of 1411-Fourth Avenue, I hastened to the staircase as an earthquake made the building swing and sway.

In school dormitories, my roommates ranged in number from one to seven. For a time in San Francisco I lived in a room with five beds and two radios. Returning from Sydney to the States across the Pacific on the S.S. *Lurline*, with about sixteen thousand troops and close to a thousand war brides and babies aboard, fifteen of us shared a cabin; we lived in comfort except that the fresh water supply was short. About twenty-five of us lads occupied a long tent at the work camp off Chinook Pass. At Noumea, thirty of us were housed in a Quonset hut.

On the *Bogue* was the chiefs' compartment, usually dimly lit, in which we thirty-five chief petty officers slept. My battle station was nearby, with a damage control (about which I knew nothing) party. On Christmas night in Panama, after I had climbed into my bunk, some of the chiefs in the adjoining mess compartment had a drunken and bloody fight.

At boot camp, our barracks hall held eighty of us recruits. On some nights, to shut out the incessant racket of happy shouting, singing, swearing, arguing, crap shooting and blaring radios, I hung from under the mattress of the bunk above me blankets that served as curtains around my own bunk.

For the last nineteen years I have lived alone.

For interior decor, my preferences apply more to items than to any single style. For tone, I prefer spare furnishings, simplicity and absence of clutter. For many years I have slept on a mattress on the floor. This answers every need for comfort and convenience except for having to sit down low to put on shoes. For decorations and furnishings, my favorites are hand-me-downs: grandfather's easy chair; grandmother's etchings, forks and blue china; framed letters to family members from Andrew Jackson, J. Q. Adams, John Marshall et al., a trivet carved by Uncle Jim (as well as a wooden chain carved by me—a sign of a misspent youth); a patterned quilt made by my maternal grandmother's maternal grandmother, and so forth. On my office desk, holding pencils, is my Father's Ivy Club mug, on the pewter surface of which his brethren had scratched their names.

I always wanted to play the role of host, an expansive paterfamilias, talking freely and enjoying children and friendly guests. For long, I did not succeed in this, feeling a sojourner in the house where I lived. I usually found myself performing the functions of butler rather than host and longed wistfully for my Father's capacity for charming social intercourse, bringing people together and amusing them (in addition to his freedom from the butler/busboy role). In recent years, living alone, I have entertained often and well, enjoying the sense of belonging there as host.

When my children were small, Christmas gave me pleasure because it gave them such pleasure, even though the preparations were tiring. But except for those years, Christmas has evoked mixed feelings. What draws me toward it is what appeals to all: the spirit of extended family ingathering, gemütlicht warmth, reconciliation, generosity, carols, greens, wood fires, the reassurance of repeating a happy tradition and the feeling that "The hopes and fears of all the years are met in Thee tonight." On the other hand came the melancholy sense of being out of it. I would identify, as well as sympathize, with the people going nowhere on the street downtown on Christmas morning.

Condorcet, that optimistic philosopher, had been condemned to death for criticizing Robespierre. When hunger drove him out of hiding and to a tavern where he ordered an omelet, he was asked: "How many eggs?" This deeply learned man knew much but was not up on making omelets. His random answer of "twelve" (maybe biased by his appetite), provoked notice. When he was asked for his papers, he was found to be carrying only the Epistles of Horace, so he was taken away, identified and put in prison, where he died. My knowledge of cooking only marginally exceeds Condorcet's. I have learned little more than boiling, broiling, frying, toasting, unwrapping and uncorking. Cooking to me never has been more than drudgery, a necessity for feeding myself or guests.

Good meals give me pleasure, however, from the food, the company and the surrounding conditions. These should enable social intercourse that is felicitous and complete. The place should be well lit to let the diners see each other and likewise be seen. The meal should be served with unobtrusive courtesy, marred by neither the pretended familiarity practiced in some places that aspire to style nor the rudeness often endured in big cities. (In an expensive New York restaurant, on a cart left beside the wall, a chafing dish stove lit the drapes. When no one acted and the flames began to shoot upward, I skipped across and smothered the fire by twisting and patting the drapes. When dinner was done, I paid the check, and our party left. No member of the restaurant staff expressed anything but some sour looks.)

And last, so that one can hear one's companions and be heard, the place should be quiet, without the clatter of dishes or even music. In explaining his Court's decision, which involved music provided by a restaurant, Holmes wrote:

> The object is a repast in surroundings that to people having limited powers of conversation or disliking the rival noise give a luxurious pleasure not to be had from eating a silent meal.

Referring to some ancients as authorities, Montaigne wrote:

> [I]t is a practice of vulgar men to call in instrumentalists and singers to their feasts for lack of the good talk and enjoyable remarks with which intelligent men know how to entertain each other.

Our practices at the table have changed over my years. In childhood, the nurses emphasized sanitation and eating vegetables. Prohibition was in force until I turned fourteen. Having seen no drinking (except as a small child, unaware of alcohol, watching my grandfather zestfully shake cocktails and pour them), I was shocked to walk into our living room at, maybe, age eleven to find Father and a neighbor, Mr. Ballinger, with glasses of sherry beside them. Then, after several adult decades when a social dinner concentrated on alcohol and meat, with a high place given to the ritual steak, there came a shift toward more healthful and refined food and drink.

For forty years most of my breakfasts have been eaten alone, and many other meals as well. This practice has led to the habit of reading while eating. It is better than nothing, but I would prefer good conversation, my favorite form of social entertainment. Madame de Stael, mistress of the subject, wrote:

> ...that first of pleasures, a conversation, in which there reigns the most perfect harmony in all that is felt, with all that is expressed.

Conversation that takes the form of sharp dispute, if conducted with civility, gives me pleasure and often instruction. When several take part, my contribution to such free argument is meager, however, and furnishes little sport. My slowness to put new thoughts into words often makes me miss a chance to respond.

A Frenchman wrote that to one who feels, life is a tragedy; to one who thinks, life is a comedy. Like others who both feel and think, I have seen it as both. An example was the forlorn climber who had brought to an end his party's expedition far from home when he carelessly let his pack slip from his back, dropping it into the mist-veiled void.

Seeing life as a comedy has meant much to me.

Enjoying humor in conversation, amusing others and being amused by them, I prefer the company of humorous people and become impatient with those who are not. Sometimes from carelessness or to entertain or elude a string of sad facts, I have committed the fault of those tedious folk who turn everything into a joke.

People who answer questions responsively make better company than those who do not. Lawyers interrogating witnesses often have to ask a question repeatedly before the witness will answer it responsively, even where the witness wishes to cooperate with the lawyer, and sometimes when the witness is the client; often the witness does not listen, thinks the question is something else. In a social conversation, to repeat a question risks giving offense, and without the engine of the judicial system to compel answers, you may receive no more if you have given offense.

A minor conversational annoyance is to hear some one say, "Honestly, I tell you..." or one of its variations. This form of speech carelessly implies that in absence of that preface the speaker is not telling the truth; also, any assertion about one's own truthfulness is logically meaningless. One's truthfulness can be measured only by one's conduct or reputation (others' observations of his conduct). If someone says he is generous, rude or punctual, the listener may accept the statement as a fact if he regards the speaker as truthful. But if he says, "I tell the truth," he communicates no information, and if he says, "I lie," he creates a paradox to boot.

Most lawyers' speech is fluent, some are delightful in conversation, but many talk too much, arguing to gratify their vanity or sense of workmanship or for the fun of the game. Some hairs need splitting, but others do not, and some lawyers insist on splitting them all.

I always have begrudged time and attention given to clothes, shopping for them infrequently and in haste, although not always as abruptly as on one warm summer day while working as a bank messenger. After lunch at the end of a dock, I took off my clothes above my waist and sunbathed on the stringpiece. A breeze blew my shirt and tie into the Bay, and they drifted out of range of two boys who sought to hook them with their fishing lines. In a waterfront shop, replacement garments (including a weird necktie) were acquired and put on before my return to work.

Within my hearing, my parents never discussed clothes or even mentioned fashion. During college, a shoeshine boy gave me a ticket to a football game in the Yale Bowl because my clothing made him think me poor. (Later, having taken the ticket made me feel ashamed.) For a long time my dress was shabby, partly from thinking clothes unimportant, but also from a reaction to those schoolmates who made much of clothes. This was one respect in which I did not try to emulate Father. My sisters and I have apparently taken after Mother in our comparative indifference to dress.

In later years my practices improved but, owing to habit and a sense of going unnoticed, not a lot. My pants have not ceased to look as though I was about to jump. I have bought for myself no jewelry and have worn none but my Father's ring. When one of my daughters gave me a broad brimmed felt hat, of a kind that she had heard me mention liking, I put it on, strode to a mirror and struck a pose. Instead of the dashing bullfighter expected, the mirror displayed a grizzled prospector, tugging at his reluctant burro as he shuffled through the dusty hills.

For their socially constructive value, I prefer on occasion some formality and ceremony in architecture, manners, language, dress: certain oaths, institutions, landmarks in life and in relations, such as a courtroom, where authority is needed and power is absent. But most of the time I prefer a style of unpretentious informality.

Athletes composed my recruit company in boot camp. Some were major league baseball and football players, some former All Americans. Most were from Texas and the Carolinas, physical education majors from small colleges, agreeable, hearty fellows, and we got along. An atypical member of the group, Joe Stone, a former prizefighter, thoughtful and educated, became a longtime friend.

My temporary assignment of cleaning latrines did not make me keen on a career of that sort, but the training program was not difficult, and the living conditions were not uncomfortable. Having lived away from home during the preceding seven years made the transition to boot camp easier than it was for many. Some, especially those from a close family circle, were homesick. The food was about as good as that at Yale, although served in a less refined manner and without napkins. Never before had my hair been cut so fast.

When our transport ship approached the Equator, I asked a navigator to point out the Southern Cross which, according to tales of the tropics, was always "blazing overhead." To find it just another constellation rather than the theater marquee of my boyhood imagination could not but disappoint. On the beach at

Noumea, I saw Admiral Halsey, who had an anchor tattooed on his arm, and his aide, Harold Stassen, go for a dip.

In some respects Green Island in the Solomons resembled a second-rate summer resort on the Gulf Coast in the 1930s. With a couple of other men, I shared a tent about sixteen feet square. We slept under mosquito netting rigged on a frame so that our cots looked like four-poster beds with gauze draperies. To resist malaria, we took atabrine pills each day. We bathed from a bucket. For face-washing, shaving and brushing teeth, we put a horizontal board between two trees, sawed holes in it, put our helmets in the holes and water in the helmets. We were issued two gallons a day.

The daily temperature was 85 to 95 degrees, and the annual rainfall was about 140 inches. When my clothes had almost dried, rain would fall. The dampness rotted most cloth and leather (such as watch bands). We sometimes had to do without fresh water for washing, but the absence of hot water for bathing was more strongly missed.

We walked through deep, black mud until truck loads of coral sand and gravel eventually covered it. My costume was a pair of heavy green pants like those used in Army fatigue uniforms, a khaki shirt, a pair of high shoes, and a cardboard sun helmet like the one I used to wear doing farm work on Icicle Creek. Some of my companions called me "professor."* This revealed something about both me and them.

At our camp in New Guinea, the moderate temperature (from the altitude) and the steep, green hills

---

* When my age, Darwin on the Beagle was called "Philos".

suggested western Virginia, and one could imagine bridle trails in the forest. Down below, the repulsive shore was hot, swampy, malarial, under a dark and brooding sky. At the port, a cluster of shacks in the mud, no one whistled or sang, laughed or smiled. The effort to snarl limited open rudeness. Men plodded through their duties with impassive faces and springless steps.

On Leyte, the Americans fascinated the locals. This visit by rich, generous, exotic men who arrived in great ships and rode big, noisy, intriguing machines was a wondrous show to country folk who never had seen anything but rice fields, bamboo trees and swamps.

Some of the toughest faces I have ever seen were worn by Filipino guerrillas who slipped in and out of the forest. Stories were told of how they would catch a solitary Japanese soldier, kneel on him and, to obtain the gold fillings, pull his teeth.

The Solomons, New Guinea and Leyte, although far from home and alien in many ways, had familiar aspects. Instead of exotic insects, we met our old companions: the house fly, mosquito, gnat, beetle and earwig. Wash hung on clothes lines; one heard the sound of gasoline engines and saw the same sun, moon and sky. Most of the stars were different, but they looked the same.

The natural surroundings contributed to the monotony, with neither change nor contrast. Everything remained the same: temperature, landscape, length of days and nights. Green is the profuse jungle's only color and all that one could see. There were no smells and only one sight. The heat was spongy and enveloping, rather than the prairie's withering blast.

When the sun appeared, the sky switched from dark to light without intervening twilight. Twelve hours later the light went out. Conversations lacked the stimulation afforded by both sexes taking part. You consumed some energy overcoming inertia from heat and monotony and the rest of it in work. You vegetated in the tent. The drum of raindrops, alternating with the buzz of bugs, dulled us all.

The work, weather and companions limited the life. The jobs for most were petty, routine tasks that stupefied, gave us no benefit and seemed to give our side little help. The tone did not differ far from that of a boarding school that assigned the boys to classes five years behind where they belonged. Play was negligible, and one's powers atrophied from lack of use in work. Two processes offset each other: The tedium became harder to endure, while improving conditions provided more comfort.

World and national affairs, and even the War (for most people, most of the time) were so remote, and we heard so little about them, that not much distracted our attention from our personal lives. The big issues were the immediate animal comforts. Complaints of the present (the chirping frogs outside the tent are too loud) and speculation on the future (maybe better chow), joined with yearnings for stateside life: nostalgia, plans and when those go-home orders will come through.

With no women and the few men all from a narrow age range, human association lacked the variety of a village. Much like shipboard duty, you had time to yourself, but conditions prevented you from using it to advantage. The time was spent in the sack (in reverie conjuring up vicarious experience, pretending to be somewhere else—anywhere would do), in puttering around the tent or in endless and useless talk of going home.

The following verses expressed feelings shared by many out there during those years.

South Sea Lament
(written in idle hours at Tolosa)

The yellow tinge of atabrine discolors all our skin
It's rumored that we'll cease to be completely
     masculine

Your eyes and mouth are full of dust, and mud
     comes to your knees
The sweat pours off you in a flood, you never feel
     a breeze

At first what we expected was a sort of lotus-land
Where men forget their troubles on an isolated
     strand

A haven and a heaven where it's always afternoon
A happy, peaceful place to loaf beside a blue
     lagoon

The magic spell of tropic night beneath the
     twinkling stars
The sound of lilting music from the strumming of
     guitars

With coconuts and alcohol and soft sea breezes
     there
You live in languid idleness, just like a millionaire

On cool screened-in verandas you relax and take
     your ease

The mornings in a hammock that you've slung
    between the trees

And ready for the Yankees' disregard for all taboo
Are pretty Sadie Thompsons quite adept at
    pitching woo

Reposing in a grassy glade, indulging in amour
Like on a set in Hollywood with Dorothy Lamour

You spend the days upon your back just lolling in
    the shade
And swizzle with a swizzle stick your glass of
    lemonade

You while away the evenings with a group of
    chosen friends
Consuming your mint juleps or some other
    mellow blends

Relating while reclining on a custom built settee
Interminable stories of adventure on the sea

I've stood and watched the Red Cross girls with
    gold braid in a jeep
To try to make the time go by I've hit the sack in
    sleep

To mitigate the harshness of this regimen austere
I've stood all afternoon in line to get a can of beer

I've guzzled tuba on Samar and tried to hold it
    down
I've strolled along Tacloban's dock, seen all that
    crummy town

I've written many letters and I sometimes get a few
But most of them go elsewhere, and I never get my
due

I've made some necklaces with shells, and built
some furniture
But therapy from handicraft just doesn't seem to
cure

Enough of sleep beneath a net upon a sagging cot
Of looking at your shipmates when you'd really
rather not

Of getting stuck with splinters from the edges of
latrines
Of never reading anything but last year's
magazines

I hate to have to do without the better things of
life
I want to live in comfort far away from scenes of
strife

I want to do my sleeping in a bed that's not a sack
I want to do my living in a house that's not a shack

To come back to your home each night instead of
wait for mail
To use a hanger for your clothes instead of just a
nail

A piece of steak beside a fork, a highball in your
hand
A torrid number on your lap and music from a
band

The stimulating contrasts on the earth you
    understand
The brown and rolling furrowed hills of cultivated
    land

We're sitting on a sandbar, getting old and
    taciturn
The golden days of youth fly past and never will
    return.

When the Navy sent me south to Melbourne, the day I arrived from the islands and rode out St. Kilda Road on the trolley car, the leaves were turning brown. The orderly houses and gardens, giving the settled tone of residential streets in Swarthmore and Haverford, and, above all, the bracing fall air, made us feel as though we had been liberated.

In childhood years, we drove to town down Greenwood Avenue, across the Fremont Bridge, and along the west shore of Lake Union, passing Cousin Cully's mill at the south end. Except for a few on a dock, partings and returns by travelers took place at the two railroad stations. At seventeen stories, the Hoge Building, exceeded by only one other in the Northwest, itself rose above the rest.

In the downtown streets cars were few, most of them rattled, none had trouble parking on the street. On the sidewalk were few women, Blacks or people who worked for government. One saw more establishment men (who did not, as now, go straight from office to a car in their building's garage or occupy offices out of downtown). A new phenomenon is the lost souls: scav-

engers, fugitives, waifs, demented (growling or shouting at unseen foes), beggars, drunkards and addicts.

As a youth I would saunter along First Avenue,
looking at the street life. The men were mainly young
loggers and sailors, in from the woods and the sea.
Tanned, energetic, rough and strong, they had money
to spend. Forty years later, one could see the same
string of taverns, but the whorehouses had been replaced by porno shops. The scene had become pallid,
filled with pathetic figures, enfeebled by life's limitations or its blows. In time, a series of real estate undertakings by me and others transformed this street.

Some travel I have enjoyed, but its prospect
never has pulled at me. Throughout school and college
years I crossed the country by train, arriving on the
fourth day. Not until age twenty did I take a plane ride
and did not use planes for regular travel until after the
War. (When we were children, people would run out of
their houses when a plane came overhead, to look up at
the sky.) Riding Pullman cars west of the Mississippi,
before the War, was the most enchanting travel in
which I ever have engaged.

To return to Seattle from a farm job in the
Wenatchee Valley before going back to college at
summer's end, I walked out to the county road and down
it, hitchhiked to Peshastin, then hopped a freight. I
boarded a flatcar after first walking along the tracks
looking under the cars for the "rods" on which people
rode in the stories I had read. Through the Cascades
that cold night, I donned all the clothes in my suitcase,
my pajamas last, and walked up and down the flatcar,

swinging my arms and trying to keep from falling down (or off). When the train passed under the Dravus Street bridge, slowing as it entered the yard, I jumped onto the sloping bank and rolled in the cinders. Then followed a long walk, trying to hitchhike and feeling disappointed that no one gave me a ride. Someone later pointed out what had not occurred to me—that drivers might hesitate to pick up someone who was wearing dirty pajamas and walking backward in the dark.

In June, after sophomore year, I bought a well-used Indian* motorcycle for forty dollars and, never having ridden a motorcycle before, set out from New Haven for Seattle. Here are some excerpts from diary entries:

> On second day, put on sailor hat which soon blew off. On making U-turn to go after it, got too near fence, and, flustered, went into it and tipped over, catching right leg underneath, bruising it and punching hole in shin with something, although did not know it at time. Went through Albany and headed for Niagara Falls on Route 20. In early afternoon, started losing power, catching and going in spurts. Stopped for advice at garage where mechanic discovered clogged jet and blew it out.
>
> Everyone seemed to be nice to a motorcycle rider, and the riders themselves seem to compose a fraternity, like boat owners or motoring in the old days. Many riders in Canada who were passing would stop and turn around and come back to catch up and talk. About 10:30 I got so tired I just stopped in the dark beside the road not caring what was there. Climbed

---

* then a competitor of Harley Davidson

off the machine, fell into the ditch and climbed out on the other side and spread out quilt and lay down. Was so sleepy I got the quilt sideways so my feet stuck out a foot at the bottom. It felt like a yogi spike bed and had bugs and caterpillars besides. Next morning it turned out to be a pasture. In the night a couple of policemen scared me shining a flash light down and wondering what was going on. Went 420 miles.

Saturday. My hands were blistered by the sun (later most of the skin came off the backs). Started out early, stiff and sore. Rode motorcycle more easily, not gripping the handles as if it were a bull in a rodeo. Later in morning it started to rain and did so off and on all day. While turning a corner at an intersection in London, took a spill on slippery pavement and rolled across the street but did not get hurt.

Saw 2 deer. Decided to stop for night on reaching Roscommon, Michigan. Weather was threatening so was going to sleep in a lumber shed but was invited home to bed by one of the little boys whom I had been taking for rides. Accepted immediately but, when I saw the house, only politeness kept me from returning to the shed.

The rest of the one room shack contrasted with the new Frigidaire and the radio, with no electricity to run them, and the new car in addition to the father's truck. The new mother, whom the father had recently married, looked deranged with her mouth hanging open, as she well might be to go to a place like that. (The previous mother had died the month before.)

The family slept in the garage because, the boy first said, the bedbugs were so bad in the house, though when he wanted me to sleep there he recanted his statement and explained that it was because of the house smelling so bad (excellent reason) due to the recent death (he did not explain). I spent an uneasy night.

Sunday. I had expected to be proof against any possible rain with high shoes and tin pants [waterproofed—used by loggers], but the wind pressed the pants against my legs and the water ran down them and drained into the shoes. After a few miles on the Upper Peninsula, the road became dirt, or rather mud, as it had been raining for 24 hours. It was necessary to go about 20 to keep from skidding and even then was difficult riding. Saw a banked turn ahead so, for fun, went around it without slowing up but, on coming around the corner saw the road immediately make another turn flat to the left. Knowing it impossible to make it, went straight and off the road, into the ditch, out of it, through some brush and back into the ditch. Fortunately, as I would have had a hard time getting it out alone, a car came along just behind and viewed the incident with shouts of "Ride 'em, cowboy!" It stopped, and the boys in it, wearing baseball uniforms, helped pull it out.

Reached Escanaba at dark. After inquiry went to Coney Island restaurant, open all night. A waitress there was nice and let me wash up in the kitchen and brought me an extra cup of coffee on the house. On hearing where I was coming from she asked if I ate goldfish. Slept at a hotel next to the restaurant for 50 cents.

Monday. At a gas station I talked with a man who had gone from Iowa to Spokane in 1900 with a wagon and team. At Duluth, wet and cold, I was allowed by a hotel man, for a quarter, to spread out my roll on a bed and mattress in a lightwell used as a storeroom. Interesting sounds came from the windows letting out on the well.

A few dull days followed, occupied by engine trouble, breakdowns and repairs, with only a short distance traveled. As time went on, my money ran short. Hunger and cold never pressed enough to make me beg because so many people were kind to me, offering and giving me meals, lodging, mechanical advice and parts.

One morning in Minnesota, I turned an unfamiliar lever, hoping this would cure the faltering engine; instead, it shut off the flow of oil, so the engine heated until it "froze." I bade farewell to the corpse, made a pack of my bedroll and walked down the road until blisters made me flag a bus to Moorhead. There a man on a truck invited me to work in a circus. Overwhelmed to be offered a job for the first time (in contrast to acceptance of my requests), and in a circus besides, I immediately accepted and jumped on the truck. But soon, aware that Mother's worries at my absence would be intensified by prolonging it, I sadly tendered my resignation.

The night was spent at the police station in a large jail cell. We transients were allowed to sleep there, on a board platform a couple of inches above the concrete floor. Bright lights protected each from the rest. The diary entries resume next morning, my twentieth birthday, boarding a freight train:

Took a transfer back to Dilworth where a through freight was making up. Sat in the dark in a reefer compartment while waiting and talked with a boy who was going the other way and seemed kind of crazy.

No empties on the train, so three other fellows and I climbed onto a gondola car full of machinery. We packed close as it was cold and raining. Did not see what the other boys looked like till next morning. Then we got in an empty half-full of sawdust, which was pure luxury and the best conveyance I rode the whole trip.

When we stopped at Mandan we each put in a dime and sent two of the boys up to town to get some food. Two yard bulls came and arrested us, and the others when they returned; one told us that if we didn't have the fare ($4) from Fargo we would have to work 20 days on the road gang. He added that "they" would aim at you a device that would discover any hidden money. His words shocked me, so I did not think about there not being such a thing [road gang or hidden money spy] there, so I paid in the station, one of the bulls taking the ticket and putting it in his pocket (one can imagine what he later did with it). The others had said they were broke. I then went off around town to the jails to try to get some of that food but found the boys had just been put back on the train which had left, with the next one 24 hours later.

I hung around town all day in a restaurant or under a bridge that crossed the tracks or in an empty with some young southern bums. In the evening, I sat furtively in the corner of the hotel lobby, until they kicked me out as I looked the part of what I then was, a hobo. There was a hard thunderstorm. Slept in an empty which had had coal in it with an old colored man who left during the night to catch an eastbound train.

Boarded the train as it was pulling out. Rode on top for a while then moved back to a flat car when we stopped, to sun my leg to try to heal it. Later moved to an empty with 2 or 3 men in it when the weather started to threaten and stayed there the rest of the day. One of them was an old windbag, aggravating with his misinformation and "so he says to me and I says to him."

When we reached Glendive, a division point, about 6:00 I left my pack in the car and went for some dinner, during which one of the men brought it in saying they were moving to another car, which was very nice of him. Came back and got in another ex coal-carrying empty which successfully kept everyone else away.

Had good sleep, though cold. Came into Laurel, the division point a little beyond Billings where we stayed til 4:00. Walked up to town with a nice Englishman named Michael Collins who had come all the way from Boston and still had his suit clean. He bummed himself a meal, while I sat in the store and drank malted milks and read the papers.

On leaving we got in a gondola full of iron girders and ladders painted orange that came off. There were about 15 others on too, several Negroes and one smart man dressed as a brakeman. One of them offered me some alcohol for my leg and said that you could get free medical treatment for it.

The cinders got in our eyes too much, so we [Collins] went back and stood behind an oil tank car. When we stopped we arranged that we would walk back along the train on opposite sides to look for an empty in case one would have only one door open. I walked to the end unsuccessfully and looked on the other side for him but he was not there, and I never saw him again.

When we started I climbed on top and walked along till we began going fast, then descended into a reefer compartment where I stayed until reaching

Livingston where I got a fine dinner for 25 cents in a Japanese restaurant which I liked.

Got in an empty with several men and spent the evening talking with a nice fellow from Los Angeles who could have married a girl worth half a million but unfortunately married her poor aunt instead. [In the tone of a cosmopolitan traversing the provinces, another hobo remarked rhetorically: "Montana girls" as we passed a herd of sheep.]

At Bozeman the conductor from the way car or caboose just behind stuck a lantern and a shotgun (its muzzle looked a foot across) in the door and kicked out all the young fellows from a combination of personal orneriness and the fact that Bozeman needed men for the haying then and the young ones cause most of the trouble on the trains. I walked up the tracks and then got down in the ditch and hid there among the weeds and got back on when it started.

Next afternoon we got into Helena, a division point. Walked round yards through town with a couple of old men and waited in grass for train. Got on end of flat car loaded with railroad rails and alternately lay and stood till morning as it was cold owing to the altitude, about 6,000 feet, and the bad weather.

The next morning at Garrison some others got on the car including two nice guys just out of high school in Butte and out to see some of the country, at present on the way to Seattle. We went together the rest of the way.

From there on to Spokane we rode in a clean, warm empty full of congenial people. Spread out roll and went to bed for some sleep in the afternoon. Talked quite a bit with a colored man (named Corky Watson) from Seattle who bulled an awful lot.

On leaving there was only one empty on the train so it was filled with 26 men, a woman (she, a formidable tourist, climbed in, then hoisted her husband aboard as though he were a suitcase) and a dog. The late arrivals had to sit up against the wall as there was only room for their legs. You had to turn over in unison.

The last day's travel was uneventful.

New Year's, 1944, heading home on leave before taking ship for the South Pacific, bumped off a military plane at Cheyenne by a higher-priority passenger, I went down to the freight yard to seek a ride. A conductor who noticed me hesitating to board a box car from fear of freezing (the cold made such a ride folly to consider, since freezing was not even a risk but a probability), invited me to ride the warm caboose into Idaho. At Hunt, before hitchhiking to Pendleton for a plane ride home, I tried to see Jimmy Sakamoto, a friend interned at the Japanese-American relocation camp.

For almost any kind of travel, reaching the destination was my intended end, and adventure, when it occurred, was an unintended result. This observation includes hitchhiking. The worst cold I ever suffered outside the mountains was waiting beside New England roads in winter. Since college days, my only hitchhiking has been an occasional return to Seattle from elsewhere in the State. I never feared mistreatment by the driver, always rushed for a car slowing down to pick me up. No one ever did me harm, but sometimes the driving has scared me.

Taking off from New York on our first plane ride was an exciting novelty for my Mother, sisters and me. At Chicago we landed in a thunderstorm. Because we knew not what to expect, the hard bump left us undisturbed—until Harriet looked out the window and asked what were the loose bricks doing on the ground. The plane had groundlooped and killed a man when one wing swerved into a building beside the field.

My only other plane mishap occurred in the War. Bringing down an Army transport plane containing thirty soldiers, a sailor and a dog, all sprawled across our baggage, the inexperienced pilot put out the wing flaps and reduced the throttle, making the plane stall and point toward the ground. We tumbled forward in a jumble of duffel bags, sandwiches, pop bottles and banana peels. He pulled out, and we landed. Years later, Harriet, a competent pilot, scared me when she took me over Lake Washington and tilted the small plane into a stall.

Mother taught me to drive a car, letting me sit on her lap to learn to steer. In the summer when I turned fifteen, Edward Ohata and I, with much help from his father, assembled an automobile, mainly from Model T Ford parts. This was interesting and fun. In those days, to start the engine of most planes and many cars—including this composite—one stood in front and pulled hard: down on a propeller arm or up on a crank.

Next year, I got my first driver's license. I do not remember having to take a test for it. Cars never have interested me much, although I like good design and craftsmanship in a physical object, such as a building, a musical instrument, a car or a boat.

Before entering college, after a summer evening at an amusement park, rollerskating with a stranger and driving her home, I started for my home. Anxiety at the prospect of a scolding by my Mother for lateness—and the reason, the naughty act of picking up a girl (first time, an adventure in itself)—spurred me to drive fast. Losing my way over unfamiliar roads took more time, so I drove ever faster until the journey's end when the car went into the brush and came to rest bent around a tree that looked as though it was a mast and the car a boat.

Walking and hitchhiking brought me home late that night. Mother reacted with her customary nerve when she opened the front door and saw my bloody face. First she patched the cuts that next day a doctor would sew shut. Then she reached into my mouth, took hold of my lower front teeth, which were lying on their sides, pointed at my throat. She pried them upright, then pushed them back down to where they belonged—and where, thanks to her, they remained for some years.

No other serious auto accident befell me for forty-nine years, when a collision with a pickup truck on the way to Stevens Pass ended the useful life of my twelve-year-old car but let my daughter Jill and me escape with slight harm.

For a period in my forties, I rode a motorcycle for commuting, errands and taking friends for rides. I had no collisions and sustained no injuries, though took some spills. In satisfying contrast to driving a car, one could feel the surroundings: the rushing air, the unobstructed vision of all one passed and the texture of the road beneath. When the throttle was twisted at the foot of a hill, the machine between your legs and in your hands would surge forward and upward.

For thirteen years (not all consecutive) I rode a bicycle to work and on errands. To me this was not a sport but a useful combination of healthy exercise and convenient transportation. When we greeted, often people would mention the bicycle—as boring as though they had mentioned my toothbrush. Oh to be identified by more dashing features, such as wit, smile, community service or prowess at sport! The rest of the years I commuted by car (mainly), motorcycle, bus and foot.

As a child, I tended to use my left hand, but grownups trained me to use my right instead. Although I have made no effort to shift back to my left hand for difficult skills like writing and throwing, I have made a practice, become habit, of using my left as often as my right for simple tasks such as eating, carrying something, or using a broom, a mop, a rake, a saw, a sledge or an ax.

Until joining the Navy five or six years after starting to shave, I had used a straight razor, imitating Father's practice. Having often cut myself and found it hard to keep the razor sharp, aware that this would be impractical in the Navy life, I bought a safety razor and started to use it on arrival at boot camp. At first my skill was so low that the drill officer, at inspection, doubted my assurance of having shaved. Ever since, I have used only a safety razor and have remained clean shaven, never wearing whiskers as a choice of appearance but only growing them as a consequence of failing to shave during periods of outdoor life spent on Leyte, on expeditions to mountain peaks and when sailing the sea.

After some years of taking cold showers upon rising as a means to improve my character (while taking warm ones in the evening for washing), the effort appearing to have been made without avail, I abandoned the practice.

At five, my tonsils were removed at the Seattle General Hospital, where they kept me for a couple of days. On wakening from the anesthetic, I threw up. (At twenty-seven, when I awoke in this way in a New York hospital after a spinal fusion and again felt nauseated and saw Mother sitting apprehensively beside the bed, remembering the previous experience helped me to resist the impulse to throw up.) The ice cream that my parents brought soothed my sore throat. When asked my preference of a book to be read to me, I replied, "Not *The French Revolution*" (which they had been reading aloud to each other at home). They brought me *Baby Animals*; it had pictures that entertained me.

On about my tenth Christmas my parents gave me a suit of toy armor that I wore sitting up in bed where I was confined with chicken pox. When we got sick, the doctor would come to the house and treat us. Often our throats would be painted with argyrol, mercurochrome or sometimes, worst of all, the dreaded silver nitrate (a caustic germicide, no longer often used).

A two-year disability (eventually cured by a bone fusion operation) from running (along with boxing, the only sport at which my form is good) unexpectedly frustrated me. The simple pleasure of using my body in this way was missed more than the lost utility for athletics, health or catching a bus.

Injuries have been frequent though slight: cutting open the heel of a hand by falling on an ax in the woods; frostbitten fingers from a subzero night out; a cracked rib from plunging my bicycle into the ditch while riding down the White River campground access road, carrying my pack, after an unsuccessful attempt on Rainier; half a dozen broken bones from climbing falls; and a multitude of bruises, cuts and contusions from bicycle spills (and a few from motorcycle spills), skiing falls (eggbeaters or crash-and-burns), and stumbles on mountain climbs. Probably the most extensive single set of these was collected at age sixty-eight on a tumbling slide off a glacier under a sixty-pound pack, bouncing and bumping over the dirty ice knobs like Winnie the Pooh when Christopher Robin dragged him down the stairs. My body has been infested by body lice, bitten by bedbugs, and stung by yellow jackets but never bitten by a snake.

The life of the body, in all aspects, has meant a great deal to me. This trusted companion has served me well. Together we have gone through much. Over the years, I have driven my body hard but rarely have exercised with healthy regularity, often oscillating between excess and sloth. This unevenness has been matched by occasional periods of practicing the eating habits of a boa constrictor. Often I would eat little for long periods when the available food was unappealing or when fatigue took my appetite. At other times, when the food set before me was good and either the importunities of hospitality were hard to resist or eating seemed easier than thinking of things to say, I would shovel in the helpings until at last, heaving myself to my feet, I would feel like the celebrated jumping frog of Calaveras County after it had been stoked with quail shot.

The weather affects my spirits, and its effects may vary according to the condition of my body and mind. When my strength and confidence are low, the cold, wet wind overbears me. When my energy and spirits are high, my body strides through adverse elements, which stimulate and gratify rather than make me recoil.

More than once during my teens Mother offered me a prize if I would not smoke or drink before reaching twenty-one. She did not specify the nature or value of the prize but said it would be substantial. I refused to compete, thinking the issue primarily moral so that to pursue a prize would be ignoble. As it turned out, by twenty-one—and forever after—I drank but did not smoke.

In the spring of freshman year, I tried alcohol by going to a couple of bars and drinking about seventeen glasses of beer. I think. I returned to the room in Lawrance Hall on the Old Campus without feeling much effect and scorned the terrors of drink. My mind was changed by later experiences such as the experiment conducted the next year, this time with a pint of bourbon. Much practice and observation were required before the lesson of excess sank in.

On the carrier *Bogue*, one of the chief torpedomen used to bring to our mess grain alcohol, fuel to propel the torpedoes; mixed with canned grapefruit juice, it was called "torpedo juice." It tasted good, but gave me a headache. Without a taste for drink, I nonetheless have drunk enough, year by year, to risk some harm to health. When I kept company with a woman who withheld her favors from me except when drunk, my efforts to encourage this exception by example may have corroded my innards.

When we were children we knew no one who smoked, except for our grandfather, who smoked a pipe. During my adolescence and early manhood, when most smokers started, cigarettes were seen by many to signify sophisticated maturity. The athletic prowess to which I aspired never was attained, but its quest spared me from capture by the cigarette habit. My smoking peers did not appeal to me as models. Their smoking, combined with their attention to clothes, made them seem af-

fected, perhaps snobbish and not manly. Nor did Hollywood movie stars encourage emulation. Those anti-
septic, shaven, plaster dolls exerted no appeal, sex or
otherwise; and the soigné men left me cold; better were
heroes from history, literature or legend. So although I
have experimentally consumed several substances as
part of education, I never have used tobacco as a practice.

Until recent years, smelling tobacco smoke produced by smokers bothered me not, either as a disagreeable sensation or as unjustified conduct. I did not realize
it might harm a breathing nonsmoker's health and regarded the practice as no more than something mildly
immoral and self-destructive. Seeing others smoke was
similar to seeing them play slot machines for one who
thought such play a probable waste of time and money.

As they do with most people, smells affect me for
better or worse, whether the bracing air from the salt-
water beach below my house or a whiff from a dish left
in my refrigerator too long. This sense affects some
people more. Before mounting her bicycle for school,
one of my daughters would wear her raincoat to breakfast in the kitchen because she so disliked the smell of
bacon on her clothes. The worst for me, exceeding even
some well-filled privies, was the stench thrown off by
soldiers' dead bodies in the hot and humid woods.

When taking part in songs around the campfire
or the living room piano, in my unawareness that the
song "Clementine" was sardonic rather than sad, expressing bathos rather than pathos, it moved me to
tears, thereby amusing some of the grownups.

For a couple of childhood years I was taken to
gentle, effeminate Mr. Hopper, who gave, or rather
offered, me piano lessons. His teaching was unsatisfying

because he did not answer my questions about music (whether he could I do not know) and because he did not require melodies to be practiced along with the finger exercises. After observing neither diligence nor aptitude, Mother gave up. During years seventeen to twenty, I practiced the accordion in a desultory way, never mastering it. In a Pullman car occupied by students returning to college, I started to play a lively schottische. Couples formed and began dancing up and down the aisle. They were frustrated, and I was embarrassed, when I forgot the rest of the piece and had to stop.

In later years the only instrument I have played is a harmonica. Its music never has entertained anyone except some of my children, for whom I played tunes when they were young and perhaps tired of having me read to them. They were invariably entertained when it made the dog howl.

I had been indifferent to classical music, rejecting Mother's occasional recommendation of it, until one evening in sophomore year at college, stopping by a doorway to listen with pleasure to a phonograph playing a Mozart symphony, the Forty-First, I think. In junior year, at an NBC radio studio performance of Beethoven's Second and Fourth Symphonies, conducted by Toscanini, I sat next to Helen Keller. She and the woman beside her conversed through their held hands. (When Mother heard Chaliapin, she could feel his low notes through the soles of her feet.) Among satisfying sounds to me is a deep, strong note from a cello (it is even better than the sound of a sharp plane run smoothly down an even plank). Although I cannot carry a tune, hearing some music has enriched my life.

Contemporary popular music and performers have appealed to me more than those of one or two generations ago, so I have preferred Joan Baez to Bing Crosby, Janis Joplin to Sophie Tucker, Stevie Wonder to Rudy Vallee, Ray Charles to Alec Templeton or Dwight Fiske, Mama Cass to Kate Smith, Tina Turner to Betty Hutton, Johnny Cash to Gene Autry, the Beatles to Guy Lombardo, the Rolling Stones to Paul Whiteman. I never cared for ballroom dancing but after turning fifty enjoyed the free expression of dancing to rock music, its impelling rhythm giving pleasure and release.

Not many lectures, concerts, plays or museums have given me much for which I cared. A number of spectator sports events I have enjoyed, although I prefer to play the games. The most exciting athlete I ever watched was Pancho Gonzales (at the Seattle Tennis Club), followed by Joe Louis. Major league professional sports tend to give more enjoyment on the screen, where one need endure neither the steady high noise level nor the streams of bellowed coaching, comment and self-congratulatory wit emitted by some nearby surly buffoon.

Once on the way from Tokyo to Nikko with daughter Jill, we looked out the train window and saw pine-studded steep hills like the scenes in Japanese prints. Until then, I had thought Japanese art to be highly stylized. The meaning of contemporary art has been an unknown territory for me. This did not begin to frustrate me until Jill became a painter and I wished to understand her work.

Although sometimes pleasure comes from hearing some kinds of noise, and on rare occasions making noise, quiet is a condition I prize. A charm of childhood years was summer days, when what fell on the ear gave relaxation and calm: the stillness broken by an occasional sound of a screen door slammed, a hand lawnmower pushed, bees buzzing, voices faint in the distance. When Dana was returning home at the end of his two years before the mast, his ship, with its yards squared, proceeded through a gentle tropic night with all sails set. An unlettered fellow seaman looked up at the spread and turned to him with the graceful sentence, "How quietly they do their work!" At fifteen, Mozart wrote his sister:

> Above our heads is a violinist, below us another, next door is a singing master who gives lessons, and in the room opposite ours an oboist. This is splendid for composing—it gives you plenty of ideas.

Chacun à son gout.

✦ ✦ ✦

I failed to learn to use vacations properly until middle age was past. Brandeis rightly contended that, "More men have gotten into trouble by the inability to say no, and the failure to take vacations than by more familiar vices." A month's cruise to Scandinavia with my family during college, plus Alaska climbs and a transAtlantic sail, have been my only vacations of more than two weeks in any year, since age sixteen.

As a child I had no work weariness from which to be recreated. In high school and college years, timidity, brooding, doubts and shyness kept me from working hard enough to make a vacation much needed. The War years had enough periods of idleness to make especially assigned recreation periods unnecessary. Intense activity (work, civic affairs, child care, socializing) occupied the first nine post War years (age twenty-six to thirty-five), with little recreation (other than parties) and with consequent impairment of effectiveness. In an unhealthy spiral, I would go on to the point of deep fatigue, then have to devote even longer hours for the same product.

In the next twenty years, vacations were taken, but they were not wholly restful because the time was absorbed with the care of children. After that, most of the time off work was spent in the mountains, skiing and climbing. Though refreshing and soul-restoring, this often left me tired, and the periods were not long enough to allow unwinding. Many climbs were not only short but overdone, cramming a three-day climb into a weekend, transforming what should have been liberating relaxation into grueling toil.

To sail one's boat across the sea, pressing for speed, may be an adventure but it does not relax except insofar as it contrasts with one's accustomed work. I had imagined it to be the perfect way to unwind and rest: Reading challenging and elevating books, devoting sustained reflection to plans for the rest of my life, trailing fingers in the water, like Cleopatra on the Nile. As it turned out, the principal way that this exhausting and monotonous cruise differed from driving non-stop, high speed across the country with schoolmates, taking turns at the wheel and sleeping on the back seat, was that it lasted a month.

Not until late did I learn to play as well as I had learned to work. I had made play an end in itself, as it should be, not making the mistake of treating it as a dosage, a kind of therapy to recreate one for more work. However, play made me feel discomfort—not a delicious sense of naughtiness, but guilt at shirking a job or anxiety at falling behind in the race. Also, instead of simply enjoying play, I often made it a form of achievement. A step forward in learning to live well was taken in my late sixties when, even though a whole weekend had been spent loafing at home, engaged in neither work nor strenuous play, the skies did not fall.

Greenway

6/39

Chapter | 7

TO BE A MAN

Who is there who would not like to be thought
a gentleman? Yet what has that name been built on but
the soldier's choice of honor rather than life?

—HOLMES

When she had me pose at home for a pastel
portrait at age five, Mother read aloud *Horatius at the
Bridge*. One stanza stuck in my mind:

To every man upon this earth
Death cometh soon or late
And how can man die better
Than by facing fearful odds
For the ashes of his fathers
And the temples of his gods.

Father never spoke to me about honor, to my
recollection, but it is hard not to believe that some of my
attachment to that ideal was derived from him, since it
represents so much of that on which the life of the South
is based. For example, the aged Joe Johnston standing
bareheaded in the rain on the New York street outside
the church in which his nemesis, Sherman, lay dead.

In Brookside Park in Los Angeles, Mr. Ohata
broke up a fist fight as it was starting between me and
another boy. A battle of nine-year-olds would have done
little harm. A few weeks later, I had a couple of bouts
with other fourth graders in a school boxing tournament.

Once at the Highlands School, to show off before the older girls and perhaps a teacher, I ran and slid along the floor. The corner of the metal sheathing that edged the linoleum beside the fireplace hearth gashed my right calf. On my bed at home, the doctor stitched it shut, without anesthetic. This was the first of about eight cuts (other than for an operation) that have been sewn shut over the years.

When I threw an icy snowball at another boy outside the Lakeside refectory, it hit him on the cheek, to my surprise (because I rarely hit anything) and alarm (because he was older and big). When he cried, my fear turned to scorn.

Weapons fascinated me as a child—swords, daggers, pistols, guns, clubs. But since then, they have held no interest or appeal. Except for the black shillelagh (about the size of a policeman's flashlight) that Father's father brought back from a visit to Ireland about the turn of the century, no weapon has been kept in my house.

At fourteen and weighing one hundred ten, I convoked a football team composed mainly of Lakeside schoolmates. Without previous practice we played on the Arboretum field against a team composed mainly of Garfield High School boys. We were so overmatched that not until the end of the first quarter—owing to the heavy mist that Saturday morning—did we see the south end goal posts. Half a century later, I played soccer and softball on this field.

Among boys in those days, athletics mattered more than they have for my children's generation. At Kent, our isolation from family, money, work for pay, alcohol, tobacco, girls, cars and commercial entertainment (except for an occasional magazine, radio and 78-

rpm phonograph record), increased the importance to us of sports.

At Kent I played at all the sports, none with success. Football provoked the most effort and provided the most pleasure, satisfaction and disappointment. I longed to make the team and dreamed of becoming a star. The coach once remarked that he did not put me into games because he feared my absent-mindedness might make me run the wrong way. In junior year at college, my last football season, our team won the intramural championship, but although a starter I quit in mid-season because the coach moved me from back to guard.

Anxiety, attention and hope were given to my body's appearance, not for beauty but for resemblance to an athlete's build. Mother's remark that Father's hips had been so slim that only suspenders could hold up his pants discouraged me because my waist above my hips easily could accommodate a belt.

Father had been a successful amateur boxer. For my tenth birthday he gave me a pair of boxing gloves. Later, he was demonstrating a boxing move for me when his strength failed, and he fell back in his bed, bringing to an end our last conversation before he died.

From seventeen to twenty-two, boxing was the most important single object of my attention. I boxed from a wish to do what Father had done, a wish to attain some athletic success and to prove to myself that I was a man. At college the freshman team elected me captain, but my grades remained too low to permit varsity eligibility. I won the Yale title and fought in the amateurs in Western Washington and in New York.

The newspapers referred to fighters as "Polack," "Hebrew," "a lad of color," and "colored flash." My opponents included a fellow named Chester Gasiorowski and a Navy sailor with beetles tattooed on his chest. In Brooklyn, I fought a milkman at an arena called the Ridgewood Grove, after walking far from the subway station, looking for a grove of trees. In training gyms I boxed with some good fighters, including a former world's middleweight champion (Fred Apostoli) and two who had fought for the world heavyweight championship (Harry Mathews, who fought Rocky Marciano, and Lee Ramage, who fought Joe Louis twice).

At a smoker (set of amateur bouts) in a New Haven men's club one evening, we fought on a hardwood floor, within a ring made by a rope stretched between four chairs, a man sitting in each. My opponent and I slipped forward in unison, and his upper teeth took a slice from the bridge of my nose. At the hospital, the doctor, with thought of replanting it, sent me back for the chunk, which my opponent had spit out, thinking that he had bitten off the end of his tongue. But the floor had been swept, and the evening's entertainment had moved on from watching fights to listening to a phonograph record reciting smutty jokes. The resilience of youth made the cavity fill out.

My one professional bout was fought in Danbury under an assumed name, "Al Scott" (my Father's given name), against Stan Steinbeck, with a win by TKO in the third round. Taking part in a professional fight was instructive. The standard of performance did not exceed that of the upper ranks of amateur boxing, but the tone reflected show biz rather than sport.

The slum boys fought hard because their only recognition and fulfillment came from glory in the ring. In this they resembled soldiers of ancient times who did brave deeds for a word of approval from their general, like Caius Crassinius who died for Caesar at Pharsalia. They contrasted with the college boxers who were, on the average, equally good athletes but who tended to regard boxing as diversion for health or pleasure. When you knocked a college boy down he often was slow about getting up, while many of the "dead end" kids would bounce up and knock you down.

My Navy enlistment was undertaken under a program by which Gene Tunney recruited athletes to serve as physical instructors for Navy recruits. It was supposed that athletes might instill a manly ferocity useful to young men at war. The night before my interview with Tunney, he sat at the ringside during a bout I fought at the Washington Athletic Club (where Father had taken me to a smoker a dozen years before) with a fighter from the Georgetown district. When one of my eyes started to swell shut from a blow, the referee considered stopping the fight and awarding it to my opponent as a technical knockout. On my plea to him not to stop it, the referee looked over to the old master, who shook his head; at that, the referee let us proceed. This made me grateful to Tunney, for in the next round I knocked the fellow out.

In my last fight I won the "gold braid championship" of Green Island in the Solomons from a Marine fighter plane pilot at a Seabees' smoker. At the foot of the dark hillside, the canvas in the ring was slick from rain. A voice from the crowd called, "Knock the ensign on his ass!"

Except for those in college and the armed services, everyone in the sport was poor, and almost all the old stock Americans were Black. My social and ethnic singularity drew more attention to my boxing performance than merit justified. A news story read:

". . . Bullitt, scion of . . . decisioned . . . Fort Lewis soldier in the main event." A New York columnist wrote that the sensation of the current Diamond Belt Tournament was "named, s'help me, Stimson Bullitt." Sports Editor Royal Brougham referred to me in the PI as "one of the best amateur boxers in the country." Later, on mentioning the Purple Heart award, he promoted me to "National Intercollegiate champ." Knowing the first to be overstated and the second to be false did not keep these references from pleasing me much. Years later they meant less.

In the Bronx Coliseum, my pattern of starting strong, then wilting, made me lose to a fighter described by the newspaper as "a powerful Negro". In the ring afterward, his handler, a middle-aged Black, told me soberly, in the manner of a Puritan elder toward the village ne'er do-well, "A man can't expect to win fights if he doesn't train." Then Art Robbins from Princeton came to the ringside and joshingly remarked that I must have been doing the nightclub circuit. These remarks hurt because they seemed unfair. Years passed before it sunk in that they were not. After the fight I jumped onto the wrong train, crawling aboard on my stomach; the conductor scolded me for risking having my legs cut off. After a walk through the silent, snowy streets of Port Chester, where the train dropped me, I found a bus that took me to New Haven before dawn. Although this defeat did not make me feel badly at the time, in retrospect it was one of my bitterest disappointments. I have longed to have won.

Six fighters beat me: a Cornell football player, a Yale upperclassman, a Marine private, an Olympic Peninsula logger and Blacks from Aberdeen and Brooklyn.

None outboxed, outpunched or outgamed me. In each
of these fights I won the first round, then faded with
fatigue, and my opponent belted me at will.

Although I practiced often at the gym, I ne-
glected two aspects of training: road work and taking off
weight. This failure to drive my body with the necessary
severity impaired my performance, of course. These
deficiencies owed less to laziness than to my regarding
athletic fitness as a matter of morality rather than physical effort. To me, the requirements of conditioning
were fulfilled by regular exercise and "clean living,"
which meant, on the whole, refraining from experiences
of which Mother would disapprove. Since my heart was
pure, why was my strength not as the strength of ten?
No coach insisted on the right routine, pointing out
that to be a nonsmoking celibate was not enough. But I
was undoubtedly ignorant, maybe stupid, to enter fights
without having trained hard.

Anxious tension that flowed from lack of confidence supplemented my lack of training rigor to impair
my stamina. (By contrast, five and a half decades later on
mountain climbs, my weight was several pounds below
that at which I had fought, and none my age could
outlast me.) Neither the attainment of some competence nor the newspaper attention sufficed to make me
self-assured. For every fight, even the later ones billed
as main events, I had to overcome fear to enter the ring.

The presence of friends and fans, instead of
sustaining me, further reduced my confidence. My assumption was not that they despised me but that, knowing my background and circumstances, they would expect little from a sheltered softy, upholstered by privilege, confronted by an Athlete, a Fighter (scuffing his

feet in the rosin box across the ring). When the bell rang, I would move forward against this (probably anxious) lad, fearing loss likely and perhaps deserved.

In a couple of fights, however, in arenas filled with strangers, assurance came from feeling wholly on my own. The crowd's assumption that both of us in the ring were fighters (else why were we there) tended to free me from the crippling effects of my customary attitude. Likewise, years later, when high in the mountains, on my own resources and finding them adequate, I felt myself a man.

Boxing was more arduous and severe than any other short term use to which my body has been put. As Joyce Carol Oates has observed, one speaks of "playing" football and other rough sports, but no one speaks of "playing" boxing. No bumper sticker proclaims "I'd rather be boxing." Unlike some boxers, players in other body contact sports do not cross themselves just before they start.

However, although amateur boxing calls for nerve, one tends not to be hit hard as often as is supposed by those who have not boxed. Trying to land a hard punch resembles trying to shoot a bird on the wing from a galloping horse, where the bird is shooting back. Professional boxing is more destructive than amateur bouts. Lighter gloves, longer bouts, and the referee allows more harm to be done by allowing a fighter to continue to be hit when he no longer can defend himself.

My ring experience is a valued part of my education and development. However, it provided little pleasure and satisfaction and much frustration and disappointment. The losses were crushing; yet my sense of worthlessness kept me from savoring the cheers and the wins.

My last serious boxing was for a few months at age forty-two. I had become a business executive, everyone seemed to agree with me, and my favor was sought. My personal associations did not seem to furnish that clash with adversity that strengthens character. Reliance on internal challenges for self-improvement being as undependable as exclusive reliance on one's conscience to insure upright conduct, I undertook to spar with professional fighters in the gym, where I received no deference and risked receiving no mercy. Although giving some lumps, I sustained a broken tooth and recurrent black eyes and scattered bruises. This distracting exercise preoccupied me with visions of moves and countermoves in the ring, gloves, ropes, the bright unshadowed light, the referee's portentous index finger and the taste of blood and sweat.

Hardly anyone boxes now; more pleasing sports are at hand. The few who box are poor Blacks, men from countries that offer less opportunity for comfort, and some unbright, low-rated members of the armed forces, where the choices are restricted. Those who seek a personal style that includes a capacity to protect oneself or to injure others with one's body learn an Asian martial art, which demands less austerity and arduous effort and does not so expose one to discomfort, pain and risk of harm.

People have exaggerated (less now than years ago) the degree to which dissipation spoils an athlete's capacity. Some dissipation does little harm to athletic performance. For those athletes who reach the top and who do not dissipate at all, the causal connection between abstention and success is not their austerity but the single-minded intensity of purpose toward athletic preeminence that their austerity reflects.

Mayor Jimmy Walker remarked that he never heard of a girl ruined by a book. This may or may not be true, but a number of good athletes have been "ruined by books" in the sense that the distraction of books kept them from athletic greatness. Dissipation does less to impair athletic performance than does idleness, unwillingness to submit to the discipline of coaching or the self-discipline of training, a strong ambition or preoccupation in some other field, or indifference toward the sport.

Between the ages of fifteen and twenty-two, a few fist fights with other youths enlivened my life. Although the results did me no harm, to enter each encounter took moral effort, depending in degree more on the immediacy of the decision than on the dread that the opponent inspired.

The sight of a grown man in a fist fight offends me. Where braggart clowns use gestures and language as threats and swing for blows they do not mean to land, the scene is contemptible although it may amuse, but it does not offend. A real fight, however, like a hanging, disgusts although it may absorb. Rare is the ideal plot: a decent man put upon who retaliates with triumph. In the common pattern, a bully starts the fight and wins. Typical is the death of the worthy commander at the hands of the base Don Juan. Not only does the undeserving winner inflict injury, fear and pain, but the degradation and brutality humiliate the loser. A severely beaten boxer may be discouraged, disappointed, hurt in all respects, but he is no more humiliated than is a wounded soldier. The movie screen used to make a fist fight trivial by making victory seem easy, just as films used to make war trivial by making it, for the side favored by the audience, seem safe.

At the Grand Coulee Dam construction site, the man at the window dissuaded me from seeking a laborer's job there, telling me to go back to the farm and avoid the accident risks. This led me later to regret the lack of persistence that lost my chance to have had a hand in the largest man-made object of all time, doing romantically virile work on the giant, turbulent river, not yet tamed, and in a setting of cliffs, rock, dust and glaring sun.

When a visitor, hearing of my job on a highway crew, adverted to diverting traffic with a red flag, his failure to recognize my manly work (with ax and cross-cut saw) incensed me. This and other manual labor jobs (as with boxing gyms) enabled me to escape challenging problems of social intercourse. And they made me feel proud.

At some outdoor work I tried from time to time to keep up with the men by taking "snoose" (a Scandinavian colloquialism for snuff). Putting a pinch under one's lower lip was easy enough, but promptly onrushing nausea would keep me from leaving it there. Never could I hold it, much less enjoy it. Another triumph of virtue over vice.

To handle physical pain has not been hard for me. At the San Diego Naval Training Station, the dentist at sick bay undertook to drain an abscessed upper tooth. When the end of his drill broke off, plugging the hole that it had made, he told me to come back Monday morning. On return, after a distressing weekend, my face had swelled until it was about even with the end of my nose. Another dentist promptly yanked the tooth.

The quantity of pain that has afflicted me has probably been about average for men like me (a vague classification). When young, I equated stoicism with much-desired manliness, so tried to bear pain like a Roman or a Mohawk. Sometimes I even would seek tests, as, during college years, having a tooth or two filled without anesthetic. (Looking back, I find this hard to understand.) Since then, a remnant of that attitude—forbearing to escape from pain rather than merely bearing it properly when it cannot be escaped—has been to refrain from more than minimal use of pain-killing drugs when they have been available. The main motives have been health, a rational preference to try to escape even temporary dependence, and an ever-present wish to taste reality.

Although often bothersome, a half century of chronic but intermittent lower back pain has not significantly impaired either the effectiveness of work or the pleasures of play.

As we do with most sore encounters or passages hard to endure, we tend to forget having been hurt. Five times, I made my way out of the Cascades with broken bones, augmented by other damage. This impressed some people but seemed small stuff to me, having taken little moral effort (although hearing that John Stuart, the orthopedist, had referred to me as "one tough cookie" gave me pleasure). It seemed not "agony in stony places," but a necessary chore. The credit and blame others assign us for what we do rarely fit our own judgment of our desserts.

All the sustained pain that has befallen me I've treated with shrugged shoulders and bowed head, as one does the rain. Sharper, briefer pains have required gritted teeth and effort to contain, but among my troubles none has been large.

Of course, this response would be different if the pain were incessant or more intense, such as what my oldest grandchild must have suffered after she had brought a can of gasoline into her motel room, poured it over herself and lit a match. In Camus' *The Fall*, a Paris lawyer who pursued women had one scruple to which he adhered: A friend's wife was sacrosanct. However, he discovered that when the compass needle of his appetite turned to such a woman, somehow her husband ceased to be his friend. Would an inquisitor need to do more than introduce me to his iron maiden, his flames and his rack to make me forget my friends or allies, who should not be betrayed? Jean Moulin, the Resistance leader, could not be made to name his comrades. Tortured until he no longer could speak, he used the pencil and paper given him by the Gestapo to draw a caricature of his tormentors. My conduct probably would fall far short of his exalted fortitude.

To me, pain has been something that ought to be endured without complaint, outcry or altered conduct, but never to be enjoyed or sought. A poet ill-disposed toward me published the lines:

> The unifying principle behind all this is pain
> if it hurts it must be good for you
> everything from getting your teeth knocked
>   out at twenty
> to freezing your balls at 12,000 feet

Sometimes I have felt unworthy of honors or rewards but never that my sins made me deserve to be punished by pain.

I have had much practice putting up with some kinds of discomfort: heat, cold, noise, wet, bugs, filth, stink, bad tastes and places to rest or sleep that were cramped, steeply tilted, or made of sharp rocks. But fate has spared me severe physical scarcity and never made me endure sustained physical hardship, such as hunger. Although many times the stretch between drinks extended until my thoughts became confined to my dry mouth, my thirst never had to be slaked as some peasants in steppe villages who Turgenev wrote were wont "to drink a kind of liquid mud from the ponds."

✧ ✧ ✧

In the War, beyond enlisting, volunteering for sea duty twice and for a landing party once, I did no more than what I was told.

Some of my companions used a double standard to compare the enemy's courage with ours. They claimed that when a Japanese soldier risked or gave his life he was pursuing happiness because he thought he had bought himself a ticket to heaven, while when a Yank went into danger he showed guts. They asserted this, even though American children are taught in Sunday school that they will go to heaven when they die, their passage there insured by worthy conduct such as self-sacrifice, and many of us believed this, yet such belief did not make death less unwelcome. Bertrand Russell told of a man at a dinner party. Asked by Russell what he thought would happen to him when he died, the man replied: "Oh well, I suppose I shall inherit eternal bliss, but I wish you wouldn't talk about such unpleasant subjects."

I asked one of my tent mates, an Intelligence officer, how he questioned prisoners, supposing that a blowtorch was held to their skin, disregarding the laws of war and of humanity in the interest of obtaining needed information from brave men who refused to talk. He said no. Because all had been indoctrinated with the proposition that the Japanese fighting man does not surrender, none had been instructed how to behave as a prisoner: that to disclose military information would hurt his cause. Most were uninhibited by either attitude or conviction from telling all they knew. The interrogators had other problems. In the savage fighting in the Pacific, like that on the Russian-German front, few prisoners were taken, and of them few survived to reach the rear lines. Most who did were members of the lower ranks who, from what they had seen since leaving their father's farm, observed little of use to our side.

An occasional exception appeared. A seaman with a photographic memory resented the Imperial government for not having made him an admiral. In the comfortable tent where he was established on the New Guinea coast, he dictated to a secretary his observations on each day, e.g., "On February 26, 1942, I was in Singapore Harbor. The ships anchored there were _____. The following ships departed for the north _____. . ." There was apprehension that he escape after it was found that he had become expert on how our ships were equipped.

Another exception was a Lieutenant Commander, captain of a destroyer sunk in battle. He had not thought that going down with his ship was a categorical imperative and he willingly took the enemy rope that fished him out of Leyte Gulf. But although a sophisticate he was also a patriot, and to learn much from him would have required a blowtorch. When asked a question, he would reply, unresponsively, in English more graceful than his interrogator's, gliding off into engaging recollections of his term as attaché in Amsterdam and with what pleasure he remembered his American counterpart who had been a Princeton man.

My friend, Art Robbins, was admirable. When he joined the Marines he told his wife that this would be "most interesting," in contrast to so many men who portrayed themselves as martyrs, while behaving as sadists, in describing the hazards ahead. Also, he permitted himself to consider the future and spent his spare time in the South Pacific studying agriculture. Most men facing high risk, knowing the odds that they will miss the chance to enjoy the future, live in the present. To consider the future, other than from the standpoint of a fatalistic onlooker, takes willpower as well as courage where one knows that such effort may go for naught. On the southern tip of Okinawa, on the last day of shooting (bombing went on) in World War II, a sniper's bullet in his belly killed Art.

Brave deeds in the War stirred me. These actions in which men risked or gave their lives out of apparent generosity, loyalty, charity or conviction seemed to come from some elevated dimension of the human spirit rather than from an aberration, an abnormality or an impulse to self-aggrandize.

> I do not know what is true. I do not know the meaning of the universe. But . . . I do not doubt . . . that the faith is true and adorable which leads a soldier to throw away his life in obedience to a blindly accepted duty, in a cause which he little understands, in a plan of campaign of which he has no notion, under tactics of which he does not see the use.
>
> —HOLMES

The soldier's sacrifice made me admire it, without going so far as to share Holmes' passionate regard.

At a scarred and battered clearing in the woods, a soldier told me how the Japanese had run across the field in a bayonet charge with cries of "Banzai!" and the irreverent Yanks responded by climbing out of their holes and counter-charging the Japanese position, shouting "Haba haba!" On the Leyte shore as the files of men tramped into the hills with their guns, the sight reminded me that I was taking much less risk. For some years, I felt a moral regret at not having joined the infantry, those fellows who met reality and the enemy and who did so much to win the War.

To die resisting an enemy used to be a reasonable price for enabling one's posterity to be free from a tyrannical enemy or to survive a predatory one. The weapons of mass destruction now tend to make such a death not noble but futile, a price paid for nothing in that the survivors would be few and unfree. But although soldiers may be obsolescent, they will need courage so long as we must send them forth to fight.

When Mr. Ohata came by the house to say goodbye to Patsy and me (age three and one-half) before he left for Pasadena, a grownup later reported my remark: "I am going to jump on the roof of California and jump down on the house of Pasadena." At the same age, when out with my parents on a walk I would sometimes hide in the shrubbery and say "Peter Roobit's in the busses." Ever since ceasing to identify with Peter Rabbit, I have wanted to be renowned for valor, without transforming such longing into an aspiration, and without abandoning action towards other ends.

Storied heroes always have stirred me: Uncas as a hopeless and gallant survivor; the young soldier in Browning's poem, saying to Napoleon, "Nay, I'm killed, Sire;" Paetus' wife telling him "Paete, non dolet;" Tecumseh, faithful to the followers he had recruited, advancing to his death; Milton's Satan; many of Plutarch's heroes; Radames, erect and unbroken, descending into the vault and finding Aida waiting for him—then their duet, which never fails to move me with melancholy delight, as they sing farewell to each other and to life; Madame Butterfly flinging out her bold hope in triumphant song; James Meredith walking down the Mississippi road; and the opening blast of some bagpipe pieces that seem to say, as the band marches forward, "Here come the men." And movies of soldiers and statesmen facing death: The Seven Samurai, the honorable French and German officers in *Grand Illusion*, Thomas More standing up for his religion and the common law, Lawrence Olivier giving Henry's Saint Crispian's Day speech, and Bergman's returned Crusader contesting with Death at the chess board.

Grand gestures, often with an element of courage, have thrilled me: Alexander as he emptied the helmet onto the desert floor before his army, and later (while handing the letter to his physician), draining his cup; Mucius Scaevola plunging his arm into the brazier; Caesar sending the defector's baggage after him; the six Burghers walking barefoot out the Calais gates, each with a noose about his neck; Olgiati exclaiming while the executioner was breaking his ribs, "Courage, Girolamo! thou wilt long be remembered; death is bitter, but glory is eternal;" Cyrano composing and declaiming witty verse while he whipped a hoodlum gang assassination bent; Andreas Hofer declaring, "A Tyrolean does not buy his life with a lie"; and the Negro slapping the twenty on the Ohio bar and saying, "Bartender, have one with me."

One urge that drove me to justify my favored status, to "rise from the rich," was a lifelong determination to be a man, to make myself immune to a charge of being a languid idler who coasted on his family's assets, connections and renown. An aspect of motive may have been what Sir Kenneth Clark, in *Civilisation*, called heroic, and ascribed to the head of Michaelangelo's <u>David</u>, declaring it "involves a contempt for convenience and a sacrifice of all those pleasures that contribute to what we call civilized life. It is the enemy of happiness. And yet we recognize that to despise material obstacles, and even to defy the blind forces of fate, is man's supreme achievement." I memorized Kipling's *If*, which ends its recital of practices with moral elements by telling the reader that if he could live likewise, "You'll be a man, my son."

During my campaigns for Congress imputations of disloyalty (Communist sympathies) were more serious charges than they might be now, and they angered me, but no more than those who accused me of being a drone with nothing of himself to offer, who sought to float into office on his mother's money and his father's name. For years, the pricking memory of those jibes helped to make me work hard.

My ideal has been one of Plutarch's heroic statesmen or a flower of French knighthood. This thirst for manhood, decorated by daydreams of glory, whence did it come? One small factor may have been a boyhood engrossed by tales of chivalry. The Holy Grail resembled the Heisman Trophy. My devotion to the wild outdoors came directly from tasting and swallowing some of it, before reading about men in the wild outdoors. By contrast, I read of heroic deeds and became enthralled by them and attached to their pursuit long before seeing any examples. For a shy and independent child to turn to books, when books are in reach, is not uncommon. But among all the qualities displayed by people whom one meets in books, why the emphasis on a particular kind of enviable merit? Has an effort to emulate my Father been masked as a quest for manhood? To some, the outlook declared in this chapter proclaims me a pre-Freudian misfit who is a deluded romantic or an adolescent brute.

When first I looked upon the world to see how to behave in it, to be a man seemed easy to understand if not to do. Men, and only men, wore pants, had muscles, spit into spittoons and did not cry. They wore hats, which they would raise to ladies, whose chairs they would push in at table. In ladies' presence, men would refrain from coarse words and without their consent would not smoke. To support their families, six days a week men set forth to work. Women, and only women, wore skirts, had curves, cared for home and children, cried, kept gardens, and tried to civilize men, refining their crudeness and softening their innate roughness. And women needed to be protected by their fathers, husbands and sons.

Manliness appeared to be fortitude, forbearance in the use of power (exercising magnanimity and courtesy), and willingness to lay one's life on the line. It was assumed that men had more such capacity than women. I never doubted that a man has a duty to fulfill a man's role, but when it sunk in that the foregoing qualities—and the concurrent duties to exercise them—were not confined to one sex, the nature of this role, once so clear, became elusive. To regard the distinguishing feature as no more than the capacity to get it up seemed ignoble and inadequate. But what is it? Charles Bukowski lamented:

> it's so easy to be a poet
> and so hard to be
> a man

Aspects of what it is not seemed easier to discern, such as the adolescent he-manism of Ernest Hemingway, the mindless brutality of the American redneck (both white and Black), the vain machismo of a Latin-American major, lurching under the weight of belt, boots, revolver, medals and mustache, and the childish bravado of those who, without a need for hunting or protection, pack a gun to advertise their manhood to others or assert it to themselves.

Since growing up, I thought that women deserved equal economic opportunity, but not until close to fifty did it penetrate that a woman can gain freedom, with consequent justice, by gaining more emotional independence as she becomes defined in greater part by her work and in lesser part by a man—her father, husband or son.

Related to manliness, the meaning of courage is puzzling. Definition is not hard. For utility and effective communication, the term "courage" should be confined to taking risks beyond oneself for some person (e.g., in a burning building), principle (going to the stake for refusing to deny one's religion), or cause (a soldier for his country and explorer for humankind). This includes moral courage, of course, as in standing up for something at the risk of loss of something other than one's body, such as one's reputation, popularity, status or job.

The term "nerve" better fits taking risks for one's personal ends of pleasure, money, popularity and career advancement, by car racing, stunt flying, hang gliding, gambling, duels and so forth. And "fortitude" is withholding your screams and complaints when you hurt. While you can define words as you choose, the significance and moral value of what the term "courage" represents is elusive.

Like nerve and fortitude, to be distinguished from courage is risk, when considered without regard to that for which it is taken. I take risks: life and limb, indignity, embarrassment or financial loss. Often this practice is a means to another end: competition, achievement, others' approval (dares), making a living, getting rich. Another motive is not merely a willingness to undergo risk as a price to be paid for something else but rather enjoyment of the risk for its own sake.

> Or if a path be dangerous known
> The danger's self is lure alone.

Some risks do not attract me. One is gambling for money. The long run odds, dictating a net loss in a commercial game and no gain for the rest, make the expense outweigh the sport. (Betting on oneself in a game of skill is not the same.) Another such unappealing risk is driving fast. In early years, my driving often was dangerous, but from carelessness, absentmindedness or poor judgment, not zest for risk.

A propensity for risk as fun, rather than as a

means, appeals to many males but few females (who seem immune to dares). My only child to share it was Ben.

Although rationality appeals to me, so does heroism, although an ingenious argument is required to show heroism to be rational.

Everyone used to know what heroism meant, just as we knew what manhood was and what was to be expected of a father, a wife, a priest, a sentencing judge, etc. To shoot the works in some great endeavor was not defined as heroism where the aim was a personal goal rather than some cause, interest or person beyond oneself. However, we no longer look at things in such a simple way, divided between "selfish" and "unselfish." All that we do is recognized as done for our own satisfaction. Differences are seen in the distance that the process travels before its impact on oneself—how indirect, how circuitous a journey in space and time for the toppling dominoes to return to us in satisfaction—all the way from dedicating one's life to a sacred abstraction to reaching for a bite of cake. We approve of those whose selfishness is less direct and immediate. Many of us admire them as well, although some prefer Nietzsche's outlook. Although he was intelligent, neither logic nor observation supports Nietzsche's assertion that altruism stems from weakness and that aggressive personal selfishness expresses strength.

The more sophisticated—contemporary, anyway—view leads some people to conclude that the word "heroism," like the word "ghost," stands for a discarded notion. Taking this view, an endeavor may be judged heroic where it is what used to be called "selfless." That is, an action for a cause beyond oneself, albeit in pursuit of personal satisfaction, where one commits a cargo of time, effort, discomfort and the risks of loss: whether failure, pain, ostracism, shame or death.

Today's world has made heroic actions more difficult. News media (for the living) and current biographies (for the dead) tell us high achievers' failures and faults and what prior causes guided their hands. In taking risks for a noble end one may be disheartened by knowing that onlookers refuse to bestow the title of hero. They deny one's deeds heroic significance, regarding them with amused disdain as products of impulses, the background for which the onlookers trace. Although to be recognized as such is not a true hero's primary aim, nonetheless one who stands hesitating whether to step forth on the moral high wire may be dispirited to know that he would be disparaged as a self-destructive showoff, a guilt-expiator or a dupe. One may be further inhibited by looking at himself in the same way that onlookers look at him, thinking of what they surmise to be his motives and their source.

Likewise, bravery is less infrequent in societies that encourage individuals to subscribe to moral principles. Where the surrounding society has inculcated some principles of public or private morality, one is given a basis for exercising courage. This basis is strongest where the courage is emphasized, as by Rome, Japan and France, at periods in their histories. But it is hard to lay on the line your life or your career to defend or assert a principle that is not wholly convincing and accepted as a guide.

Some wise and truthful people who do not display courage do not seem deficient for its lack because they lack beliefs that call for action against strong opposition. However, without courage, whether or not it is currently used, a person lacks merit as a moral leader. Courage must be available to permit one the freedom to change his mind and disagree with those who would oppose him and act on his disagreement. We are surrounded by so many threats to our comforts and peace if we assert definite values that we must face fear if we are to act on independent thought. Even for one who swims with the current, fear is hard to escape.

To oppose or challenge some part of the universe, rather than accepting it all as is, shows that one does not think it already perfect. Where such a challenge defies great powers, as did Prometheus, it shows courage. The challenge shifts from courage to folly only if the odds against success (meaning effective effort, not personal triumph) are hopelessly long.

Other people have beliefs that may clash with powerful elements around them but also believe action of any kind futile. Regardless of their wisdom or honesty, they take no part in moral leadership except to write books about its futility. (Cicero observed how some men, wanting to become glorious for having despised glory, put their names to books in which they disparage the pursuit of fame; and Burckhardt remarked that Dante asserted the emptiness of fame, "although in a manner which betrays that his heart was not free from the longing for it.")

Santayana's intelligence was so deep and broad that he should be called wise in the ordinary meaning of the term. And insofar as he was willing to express himself he appeared to be truthful. However, we cannot tell whether he would have proclaimed his opinion if he had felt it his duty to do so yet knew that this would expose him to harm. The Stoics were right in making wisdom depend on courage. Although Santayana's expressed thoughts may constitute the truth about life and the merits of action, his possible lack of courage may have distorted the wisdom of his thought to direct it to passive conclusions. One would have more confidence in his wisdom if one knew he had the personal freedom provided by courage to reach active conclusions if reason and evidence pointed that way to his mind.

Courage is not to be measured by will power alone, but rather by the net balance between will and fear (between the size of the boat and the size of the waves), as the balance compares with that of other people. If one finds fear in the dustball that he holds, yet overcomes it, is he brave?

And truthfulness does not depend on courage alone because sometimes the pressure toward dishonesty is not fear but passion, cupidity, ambition or some other impulse. Courage does not protect honesty from any temptation except to play it safe. In decisions where a citizen asserts values, these other temptations count, of course, but less so than fear.

The front door of the house that was once my home bore "Virtus et Veritas" engraved on its inner side as a reminder when I went forth. Roman "virtus" was largely civic courage and probity, while "veritas" embraces both truthfulness and the effort of study and approach to the truth, which is about the only way effort can be applied to pursue wisdom. If this formal and visible expression of belief had a hortatory effect on my conduct, it left me unaware of it.

Perhaps a kind of snobbery that Mike Roemer called my patrician morality has caused me to overrate courage. The old maxim that one should hate the sin and love the sinner, so that one should pass judgment only on others' conduct, not on their "selves," is hard to dispute. Nonetheless, over the years, the conduct and character of certain men and women moved me to admire them as brave. But on looking inward on my own experience the matter seems slippery and vague.

In youth, my general outlook was Macbeth's: "I dare do all that may become a man." But, as when I joined the Navy instead of the Infantry, choices of danger more severe than adolescent challenges of fistfights with peers or swinging on a rope above a bluff tempered my boldness and often induced me to shut up instead of put up.

My going after the bleeding soldier on the deck, pure reaction, no decision after choices were weighed, was brave only if bravery simply reflects earlier development as a product of conditioning, so that one resembles Darwin's "heroic little monkey" that braved an enemy to save its keeper.

In 1954, having decided to run again for Congress and after a former U.S. Senator and Congressman had told me he would not seek the nomination, I publicly declared. Later, after he told me he had changed his mind, I did not quit the race. Political good sense for career success called for withdrawal, in light of the long odds that favored him, but to step submissively aside seemed weak. This decision made me feel like one who has enlisted for a war—relief and satisfaction at having chosen the right course, yet not looking forward to the war. If this same question were now to be faced, no sense of role or part to play would press me to repeat the chosen course. However, I do not regret or even disagree with that choice. Its purpose was not to fulfill a moral duty but rather to counter my own past practice of backing down.

The decision to deliver the Viet Nam editorial

(likewise the one on Cambodia), gave me no concern, although the preparation provoked anxiety about the performance. These things needed to be said, and no one had done so. I expected thrown verbal cabbages and lost advertising revenue, but none that would threaten the Company's survival or trouble me. The torrent of congratulations on what was claimed to be my courage (along with a smaller stream of abusive mail calling me yellow) surprised and bemused me. The attacks were no bother because experience in more or less public life had made me take them as part of the game.

The pleasure from the compliments was not great. My self-esteem was too low to accept them fully, and they did not seem apt. Praise for anything is gratifying, and especially for bravery, since I so much would like to be a brave man, but it seemed undeserved because unearned. Some thought it brave because it provoked some who were forceful and strong. But doing what I did took no moral effort because such folk could not do me much harm. In going through the process itself, after the easy decision, the only effort was preparatory labor and the strain of delivery. There were no inner fears to overcome. Having been preparing for this all my life, I felt no more courageous than a baseball player when he, fulfilling his function, fields a hit and throws the ball to first base. Something of the same sort takes place when I go before a hostile crowd. As long as I am prepared on the subject and do not apprehend physical violence, I feel no fear of speaking my piece and responding to challenging remarks.

Taking civic risks has come easily for me, but in some personal relations I have been a coward, by lack of candor about what I felt, holding my tongue in order not to provoke.

Thrice men have robbed me. Once while sitting
on the turf with a red-headed woman as we threw bread
crumbs to the ducks, I felt a sharp prick under my right
ear. A low voice said, "Cool it, man." Standing over us
were three malignant-looking ruffians of mixed Chi-
nese-Filipino extraction. At first tempted to have a go at
the knife-wielder, who was small, I noticed one of the
others, his finger on the trigger of a gun, its hammer
raised. His trembling hand gave me pause. Taking my
wallet, they directed me to walk into Lake Washington,
which I did, wondering if they planned to shoot me
there. When the water reached my knees, I turned
around to ask if this would be far enough. They were
running into the woods.

On the second and third occasions the robbers
bore not only guns but badges as well. A few moments
after setting out for Mount Orizaba from a Mexico City
car rental agency, and while I was driving with the
circumspection that had been employed by civil rights
workers in Mississippi, a police car waved me to a side
street. A big cop with a big revolver climbed into the
car, shut the door and spoke to me at length. He looked
like General Noriega, only meaner. He appeared to be
charging me with a traffic violation. From time to time,
recognizable words would recur: "policia" and "arresto,"
spoken with his wrists crossed. In the dictionary, for the
word "fine" I found "multa." When queried: "Multa?,"
he assented. I wrote: "Multa _____ pesos," and handed
him the pen and paper. He filled the blank with "500,"
so I thought: "Oh, about a dollar, a modest fine, but
here wages and prices are low, so maybe fines are
commensurate." However, he was not finished. He
crossed out "pesos" and substituted "dollars." This
launched me into that ridiculous litany, from time im-

memorial spoken to creditors, tax collectors and robbers by those on whom demand is made for money that they do not have: figuratively pulling empty pockets inside out. After hearing this repeated a few times, he crossed out "500" and substituted "350," then went down to "200." With an air of hopeless resignation, I handed him my wallet. He removed the bills and counted them with a disgusted look. Implored to leave me a little, he did, pocketed the rest and got out.

Relieved to have been caught in a VW bug and not a Mercedes, I replaced money in my wallet from sources elsewhere on my person. Within two blocks, another police car pulled me over, and a similar exaction ensued. When the policeman took the piece of paper (delicacy called for a new piece), he filled in "10,000." On reaching the point in the ritual for me to surrender my wallet, he refused it until he had had me advance the car half a block, beyond the sidewalk bystanders' gaze. Again the look of disgust displayed by a fisherman who has reeled in a minnow, and again a little returned. (The two cops'/robbers' total haul amounted to about $14.) At the end, the swine presented his limp right hand. Prudence overcoming pride, I took it, then drove into the countryside, wondering what predator would fall upon me next. These incidents reinforced my opinion that Mexican justice is to justice as Mexican music is to music.

When the Seattle police told me that a murderous felon in the jail had sought to take out a contract to have me shot when my car left the office garage, this gave me little concern, but nonetheless the next couple of weeks found me looking often at the rear view mirror. And on walking out of the Cascades alone at the head of a logging road, I approached my car apprehensively, but no shadowy figures emerged from the gathering dusk.

Altercations on the street with hostile young Blacks disturbed me about myself. One opened my car door and threatened me with a beating unless I left a restaurant parking lot. In my overcoat and under the steering wheel, I felt like the abusive abolitionist Charles Sumner, with his legs under the desk as Preston Brooks of South Carolina rained blows upon his head. After my polite refusals to go, he did not try to carry out his threat. Then he and his friends, at one table, and I at another, ate our New Year's breakfasts. On a dark street, another attacked me with a few punches and kicks to induce me to surrender my wallet to him; this I refused to do; by and by, he allowed me to mount my bicycle and depart. After each incident the nagging thought obsessed me of failing in a duty to have fought the men despite the substantial risks and slight prospect of gain. All the fighting of different kinds that I have done should have given me enough confidence in my manhood not to feel shame for declining to prove it.

Emerson said, "Always do what you are afraid to do." Like those Roman soldiers who were said to fight the enemy because they feared their officers more, I always have feared to fail to do that which I feared to do. And this was so whether the purpose or end made the question one of nerve rather than courage and whether the fears were moral or physical (boxing matches, some decisions in the War, learning to descend ski race courses and to climb exposed mountain ice and rock). Like the Frenchman who said, "I tremble at the dangers to which my courage is about to expose me," in every case, whichever choice I took—grasping the nettle or taking flight—I yielded simply to the greater fear: what the hazard threatened or self-blame as a coward.

Willi Unsoeld, who lived fully and well until an avalanche smothered him as he descended Cadaver Gap, wrote a few years earlier: "Death is not too high a price to pay for a life fully lived." No, death is too expensive for anything except an act of duty, loyalty or honor to enable others—nation, city, comrades or kin—to survive or to live free. Among the ideals that give worth to our lives, one of the greatest is the willingness to give all you have, that is, all that remains of expected life, especially a prospectively long one, for a cause beyond yourself. Such a sacrifice for your family, your friends, your country or your ship, is to be profoundly admired. I disagree with Horace's maxim *"Dulce et decorum est pro patria mori,"* but do not scorn it. Though it may become one, that bitter draft is not sweet. Of course, that is what makes it to be admired.

My point for balancing choices between life and death falls between those of Willi and of Iphigenia, who told her father that "the worst of lives is better than the proudest death." *Ecclesiastes* may be right in holding that a live dog is better than a dead lion, but to die with honor is better than to live as a dog. And even Iphigenia, when she had thought it over, put patriotic honor first.

Chapter | 8

SOCIAL OUTLOOKS

a stranger and afraid
In a world I never made.

—HOUSMAN

The Highlands, where we lived, had no racial or religious restrictions in its charter, but one could live there only by an approving vote of those already there. Not all members were rich, but since it was formed it has contained more of the richest people in town than any other residential neighborhood. One may doubt that any one else, while living in the Highlands, ever has worked in a factory, ridden freight trains or fought a professional prize fight.

A good place to live for those who made it and built their homes there—energetic, hard-working, successful men, immersed in the world of affairs. For children, its effects were not benign. As time went on, life there became less feudal, artificial, rigid, pretentious and isolated from town. The younger children were subjected to less arid and withering conditions. Among the older ones, however, few amounted to anything. Some became idlers, some drunkards, some dropped out of sight, and half a dozen (a large proportion of the few) did time in mental institutions.

Perhaps in part offsetting the social isolation of the Highlands life was our family's choice to take no part in the social activity of a club—country, tennis, yacht or golf. Such club life insulates many young people from the rest of the community, and thereby narrows their development. Perhaps the absence of a beckoning swimming pool full of playmates made more easy for me the choice to spend summers working at jobs.

During our first dozen years of life, we children were largely cared for and governed by nurses and governesses. They rigidly enforced all kinds of hygiene except mental, of which they were ignorant. In those days before antibiotics, grownups, especially women, addressed anxious care to keeping sanitary our scratches, blisters and cuts. To my Lakeside schoolmates' jibes at having a nurse, I would reply indignantly that she was not that, she was a governess.

Out for a walk one day, meeting Priscilla and me between our homes, our grandfather asked us how we were. When we replied, "Fine!" The nurse reproved us and told us that we were to reply, "Very well, thank you."

A few years ago, Violet Bonham Carter, Prime Minister Asquith's daughter, wrote of upper class British family life in the Victorian and Edwardian eras:

> [C]hildren were...rarely seen and never heard. Parents gave audiences at certain stated times, and for such occasions their children were suitably prepared, washed, brushed up and admonished. Mothers came up to say good night, tender and gleaming visions dressed for dinner, shimmering in diamond necklaces and radiant clothes. But life in the raw from which all intimacey springs often remained unshared.

Although the tone described was more remote than our own childhood experiences, it strikes chords of recognition.

In addition to the family and nurses, others who lived in the house were a cook and a maid; a chauffeur/ handyman lived over the garage.

On growing older, and riding in our grandparents' Rolls Royce, the sight of a friend from the Boy Scout troop standing by the road side would make me turn my head away, hoping he would not recognize me. Considering the Highlands a gilded cage, I envied the boys who lived outside in the "real world," the "wide world," where they were allowed to go to public schools and live what I imagined to be lives of carefree independence like Tom and Huck.

In childhood, the pleasure of Christmas presents often was offset by depression after the morning's excitement, from being pressed to say "thank you," feeling guilty for not having done so soon enough, and feeling the presents undeserved. The Fourth of July was my favorite holiday. We and other families would go to the Highlands Beach for a picnic, with firecrackers during the day and Roman candles and skyrockets after dark.

A couple of winters we children were taken for a while to Palm Springs (then a sleepy village; a substantial proportion of its occupants were Native Americans and tuberculars who hoped the dry air would make them well). Some other winters we spent in Pasadena, where we joined Mother's parents who often wintered there. A couple of times we were taken to the Middick Club where we watched polo games.

When I did farm work one summer on Icicle Creek, most of the neighbors were poor. Some supported themselves by making moonshine. Their diet was limited. One might be invited as a guest for dinner at which the only food offered and eaten was a single type of vegetable, such as beans or peas. A neighbor lad

eft lip, and his speech was hard to understand.
watched his mother twist the wet clothes that she
had been washing. After squeezing out the water, she
threw the twists on the dirty floor.

At the Highlands Chapel sometimes the hymns
would be chosen by request. My favorite was "Jesus,
Tender Shepherd." My parents took me to town a few
times to services at the First Presbyterian Church where
we heard sermons by Mark Mathews, a redoubtable old
fundamentalist with craggy features and long white
hair. In Georgia, he had built his first church with his
own hands. His strong personality, backed by strong
convictions, exerted moral force in Seattle even among
those who did not share his beliefs about public policy
or God.

After a few years of Sunday School, I had a few
more years of Bible class, until fifteen. One member was
Walt Walkinshaw; more than three-score years later he
was my partner and still a friend. At first the class was a
matter of course, and later Mother compelled me. At
age twelve, I joined the Episcopal Church through a
confirmation ceremony.

At Kent, we attended chapel once a day and twice
on Sundays. On Sunday mornings, we wore starched,
detachable collars. The style of services was high church.
Grace was said before and after each meal. Often an
emotional experience that I took to be a religious one
was imparted by the communion service, with its plainsong, stone floors, the windows' colored light and clouds
of incense from the swinging censer.

In college years, I went to church mainly to

please Mother. After one service my letter home said: "Afterwards we went up to the parish house and had a chop suey dinner. I met some nice colored boys." My rate of attendance declined, although in junior year I still served as an acolyte a time or two. After that, I attended religious services of different kinds—Catholic (Polish, French, Australian, American), Congregationalist, Unitarian, Christian Science, Jewish—but my interest was social rather than theological.

By the end of college, although I had acquired negligible education, my faith was gone. Recognizing that much in the world that is important cannot be understood by rational means, but nonetheless unable to believe any proposition unsupported by evidence and reason, I concluded that if there was a God, He was a capricious sadist and certainly not a Christian. In addition to the misery he visits on most of us, he kills us all. Mill's words appeal to me:

> Whatever power such a being may have over me, there is one thing which he shall not do: he shall not compel me to worship him. I will call no being good, who is not what I mean when I apply that epithet to my fellow creatures, and if such a being can sentence me to hell for not so calling him, to hell I will go.

Robert Ingersoll, in language of less precision and more passion, proclaimed a like defiance.

During Navy boot camp, a Protestant chaplain spoke to our unit. He apologized for being a chaplain and explained that he was a good fellow, even though he believed in God. I respected the Catholic chaplains because they did not beg our pardon for their calling.

After the War, until about age thirty-nine, I

attended occasional church services, ushered sometimes, and one season taught a Bible class; but these actions expressed policy (civic responsibility and career ambition) rather than faith.

Although no longer believing in God, I retain a belief—non-rational in part—in moral duty.

One who does not believe in the supernatural nonetheless can evaluate religions on worldly grounds. I would put the Roman Catholic Church above the others. Islam is petrified, oversimplified fundamentalism with excessive emphasis on force. Hinduism, Buddhism and other Eastern mysticisms resort to oblivion as escape from facing a static world of injustice, poverty, filth and heat. Confucianism fails to go beyond respect for authority, moderation, prudence and common sense. The Greek Orthodox Church is anti-intellectual and obscurantist. As Madame de Stael wrote, its ceremonies are "better adapted to captivate the imagination than to regulate the conduct." Judaism is tribalism plus ethics: elevated, encyclopedic, sophisticated and legalistic. Jews who combine piety and intelligence have demolished this proposition when I have advanced it.

Protestant Christianity has little that Catholicism lacks and lacks much of what Catholicism has. The Calvinistic branch has intellect without passion, while the Evangelical branch has passion without intellect. Both lack beauty.

Catholicism appeals to both intellect and emotions, to the conscience and the spirit. It addresses both faith and works. It embodies some of the world's greatest art: all (except for the Parthenon) the twenty best buildings of worship; superior music from plainsong to Verdi's *Requiem*, the *Last Supper*, the Sistine ceiling, the *Pieta* and lots more. It combines the emotional satisfaction of atonement and communion, the reassurance of the sacraments for the principal landmarks in life, the tender warmth of the Nativity, the exaltation of the Crucifixion and Resurrection, a sympathetic woman available to intercede with a stern and powerful father, the blazing glory of the Mass and the brutal glory of the Cross.

In later years, without having made friends with God, I came to recognize merits in the Christian church. Of course, regardless of its truth or merits, its reflection of others' deeply felt beliefs calls for polite treatment. Its rituals and liturgy that link us to our common past (for most of us) invite protection. Its now-tepid passions reduce its harshness toward unbelievers, its encouragement of irrationality and its trading on fear. It still supports certain sensible moral principles and practices and gives consolation to some.

Thoughtful people consider traditional religion as they do constitutional monarchy: an institution useful as a social stabilizer and adhesive but taken seriously only by the ignorant. Yet respect is called for by the gathered thought of searching minds, among them some of the best, struggling for millennia to comprehend who and why we are, what is the nature of evil, why we must die, what should be our purpose before we do, and where in our helplessness can we look for help.

Social justice has concerned me, and social class and its relationship to social justice have interested me. My areas of curiosity have been broad, with concentration on justice-seeking, truth-seeking and the connection between justice, freedom and truth.

In my youth, the question of what kind of people with whom to associate puzzled me. The limitations of those with less education, financial independence and social experience made them appear more candid and direct, with less developed skill in dissembling by speech and action, their faces showing their personalities and moods with less concealment. Among freight train passengers, the life of the soul took forms visible to the eye. Easier for me to approach, to harmonize with, to understand, these people seemed more genuine, more real, and in closer touch with the essentials of life.

On the other hand, those with more advantages and gifts had more skills of expression and conversational give and take and often more candor from independence of situation. Some were better company because their intelligence made them, as Madame de Stael said of Fouché, "occasionally do what conscience would have dictated to others." My choice of companions shifted from the former to the latter as years passed.

Widespread exploration has gratified a long-sustained curiosity about human society and the way its members behave. These observations I have absorbed as a detached participant, avoiding the limitations either of one so immersed that he lacks perspective with which to judge, or of an outsider—whether slumming or pressing one's nose against the window—who does not know how things taste and feel.

Whether for pleasure, curiosity or obligation, I attended social occasions on a wide range: coming-out parties, balls, weddings and funerals in Seattle, New Haven, Boston and Washington, D.C.; dances in farm villages; bohemian intellectual parties where everyone sat on the floor; beer-drinking parties with men where everyone sang, some fought and a few would fall out the houseboat window into the water; tea parties at a minister's house; girls' college teas; diplomatic receptions; taxi dance halls and street fights. A couple of visits to race tracks (outside Melbourne and Renton) and Las Vegas gratified curiosity but left me with no wish to go again.

One weekend I drove down to Seattle from our Chinook Pass work camp and attended a ball at the Sunset Club. During it, the word reached us of the Germans going into Danzig. As some of us stood on the interior balcony, looking over the dancers in their formal clothes, our elegant but carefree scene reminded me of the Duchess of Richmond's ball in Brussels the night before Waterloo. Like the tone portrayed by Thackeray, the news gave a faint chill as a sign of impending calamity for us.

The society of those who rode the freights constituted anarchy with two classes: hobos, who were footloose workers, mainly farm laborers; and bums, mainly older men, who lived by begging (then called "stemming"), scavenging and occasional petty theft. The absence of any law enforcement, letting the rule of claw and fang prevail, showed me that a police force must be exceedingly bad to be worse than none—a limited case in which Hobbes is right. The hobo jungles matched their metaphor, and prudence kept me out of them. To let me live this long, my frequent lack of prudence has been offset by support from others, and by quick reflexes and luck.

During college, because the coach did not coach, although he was a nice old man, I trained much of the time at the New Haven professional boxers' gymnasium. It had a single shower head, no lockers and no working toilet. For the four years, the only other college boy there was one who had a few professional fights before a severe experience in a Brooklyn ring convinced him to concentrate on his studies at the Divinity School.

At the Elm City Gym, talk about gangsters could be heard. Sometimes three or four would come in to inspect and review fighters whom they "owned," one of whom had (briefly) fought Joe Louis. Vain and insecure, they stood around to be seen. Their appearance was as uniform as that of those preoccupied with conforming dress in other walks of life: double-breasted, chalk-stripe suit, white silk shirt buttoned at the neck without a tie, pointed-toed polished shoes, broad-brimmed hat set square on the head, manicured nails, barbered head and pasty, cruel face.

Freshman year in college, after a few dates with a girl from Naugatuck named Janie Lewandowski, my letter home to Mother said I "liked her fine even though she is a Pole." One night we went down to a performance of *Götterdammerung* at the Met, with Melchior and Flagstad.

On a Melbourne trolley car, an Australian sergeant asked me if I was a chaplain. People previously had thought me Jewish, Lithuanian and Polish, and Vivian Mason in Harlem once asked me if I was white, but that was the only time someone thought me a man of the cloth.

From age twenty to age thirty-five I had a number of Nisei friends and acquaintances and in later years knew a number of Japanese in business and professional relationships. Among those of Chinese extraction, I have known only a handful.

Once in my teens I asked Mother what was a Jew, having had no experience or even awareness of what that word might mean. She replied that this was a person

who did not believe in Jesus' divinity. At college I came
to know Jews for the first time. Although few of their
personalities seemed attractive, our gentile schoolmates'
cruel rudeness toward them shocked me. I went through
fraternity rushing but declined to join a fraternity primarily from disagreement with the policy that excluded
Jews. Sophomore year I roomed with Andy Landay, a
Jew whom I had known only slightly but for whom I had
felt pity because the other boys teased and snubbed him.
Voluble, contentious, dogmatic, he was physically small
and weak. By belief he was a Stalinist and by affiliation
a member of the Young Communist League (a rare bird
on the Yale campus). He subscribed to the *Daily Worker*,
which I sometimes read, and I subscribed to *The New
York Times*, which often I did not read. Throughout his
life after college he has been an observing and believing
Catholic. And we remained friends.

Books read in childhood provoked indignation
at injustice that had been done the Indians. It did not
seem wrong for the Western Hemisphere to have been
settled by people from across the sea who landed on the
East Coast, as the Indians' forebears had come down the
West Coast, but it seemed the settlers should have
treated them better in some ways. I also idealized them
but later ceased to do so, on discovering that merits and
their lack were widely distributed among humankind
and on seeing some of these people's descendants, who
inspired more pity than admiration (contrasting with
the Izmir Turks I saw in 1966, who evinced their descent from a warrior race).

I have known only three Native Americans. Two
were non-reservation Klamaths of mixed blood: Lyle
Williams, a logger with whom I sometimes boxed, and
Charlie Scott, with whom I skied, who had the distinc-

tion of being both a cowboy and an Indian. The third, Felix Capoeman, a biker, son of a Hupa and a Quinault, was released from the penitentiary when I got his conviction reversed.

At nineteen, both my acquaintanceship with Blacks and concern with racial injustice began (except for my earlier indignation at the Native Americans' ruin). My previous concern for social justice had related to other kinds, mainly economic. The first Black I came to know—we met on the train to New York—was Oliver Harrington, a graduate student in the Art School. We seemed to share more values than I did with anyone else known during college. Many of the Blacks whom I met were professional prize fighters or aspirants training at the Elm City Gym. Some were kids at the Dixwell Avenue Community House, where I coached boxing and later served on the Board and attended programs— lectures, concerts, sports (e.g., a Black basketball team of medical corpsmen from West Point). I began reading novels and other books about Blacks and went to hear talks by or about Blacks: Walter White of the NAACP; the president of the Rosenwald Fund; a professor from the South; a Trotskyite named James.

One night I wandered around Harlem, struck by the big crowds on the streets at late hours and the all-Black scene, including cab drivers and cops. A diary entry after a visit to the Savoy Ballroom:

It cost 75 cents to get in. Two bands (Benny Carter's and another) spelled each other. Had never heard such dynamic music. Danced cautiously and unsuccessfully with a girl named Wilhelmina Ramsey, who was a nurse with callused hands and who belonged to a "rug cuttahs' club." Talked with one of the huge, unobtrusive guards who stood around in dinner coats. They should not be called bouncers because there seemed to be no demand from anyone to be bounced. They were omnipotent. He said he had been a sparring partner of Joe Louis. He remarked with pride that the ballroom was very "civilized." When I checked out my hat and economics book I had only 30 cents, so I put in a penny and a tax token unobtrusively, but the girl was caustic about it and offered to give them back. So I took back the tax token.

Once I called a telephone number listed under the name of Bullitt in Chicago. The voice of the woman who answered identified her as a Black. I told her I was a lawyer named Bullitt and asked her if her husband was a Bullitt. She said yes. When she realized my curiosity about where her husband's ancestors came from, and that she was not about to hear joyful news of an inheritance proclaimed but that a touchy subject was being approached, her tone shifted from cordial to frosty, and I learned no more.

It is curious why Blacks have done better than Native Americans although they were treated worse. The Blacks' social, that is, tribal, organization was wholly disintegrated. Not only does no tribal identity remain among Blacks, but American Blacks have lost knowledge of their ancestors' tribes.

On the other hand, although the Native Americans' tribal organizations were battered, with some tribes extirpated and others disbanded, many remain as corporate entities, and most Native Americans know their tribal ancestry. Some—through their tribe—have inherited substantial property: farmland, stands of timber, mineral and fishing rights, land with residential and recreational value and Native corporations that own other assets. Some tribes have been granted legal rights to business preferences over non-Indians, such as for cigarettes, gambling and fireworks. Many still live on the lands where their forebears roamed. Those who belong to richer tribes have become a *rentier* class.

In contrast with Native Americans, Blacks inherited nothing by reason of ancestral tribal connection. Black men were called "bucks," not "braves." No image of a Black man has been put on our nickel and our one-cent piece. Americans do not disclose with pride that they have a Black ancestor as they do of an Indian, nor do they name children after admired Blacks, as the parents of William Tecumseh Sherman did of an Indian. Orations have not hailed the noble Black man. Poets have not written in honor of Black leaders, as Whitman did of Osceola and Longfellow of the imagined Hiawatha. No Black names were given to cities, counties or states. No sports teams were named the Washington Blackskins or the Dartmouth, Cleveland or Stanford Blacks. No fraternal order of Blackmen was formed. No popular song was called "Negro Love Call." No one speaks African counterparts of leaving the war path for a powwow to make medicine, smoke a peace pipe and bury the tomahawk.

Yet despite all this, Native Americans have remained alien to the rest of American society, and most are apathetic, without ambition, health or hope, while among all national societies without a Black majority, in ours Blacks now take the largest part in significant responsibilities and roles. And among identifiable groups, perhaps none but the Puritans has exceeded Blacks' contributions to American culture in the field of personal style.

✧ ✧ ✧

Saturday afternoons in the base theater at Navy boot camp, sailors would give musical performances—singing, dancing, playing an instrument—in a kind of amateur hour. Some from the Appalachians, Ozarks or the rural deep South would sing what we would call folk songs but to them were the only songs they knew. The shower puzzled these poor country boys, a flushing toilet alarmed them, and a radio they had not heard. When one of these fellows shouted out "Buffalo Gals Won't You Come Out Tonight" or wailed a more poignant song, he thrilled me as though a time machine had transported me backward.

When boot camp ended, a mate and I drove into the Virginia hills to a dance at Chatham Hall, the prep school then attended by my sister Harriet. We saw the shaven lawns, the stately trees, red brick, white pillars and gracious entrance hall with polished floor and curved staircase down which came sweet girls in lovely dresses. The scene contrasted with Norfolk's grim and grimy squalor (a principal place of recreation for us enlisted men, the Thirtieth Division Club, was known as "Gonorrhea Race Track"). Coming from the frantic immediacy of a wartime port, filled with crowds of strangers hastening to prepare for war or to sail to it, we found this a haven, part of the certain American past. That night in a village hotel where we shared a bed, the other fellow (from western North Carolina) remarked that until he had joined the Navy six weeks before he never had slept alone in a bed.

My first duty assignment was nine months at the San Diego Naval Training Station, helping to train new recruits. In this work I was unsure of myself, unsuccessful and dissatisfied. I got on adequately with most of the chiefs my age, who had come from college, but poorly with most of the older, career Navy chiefs. Of one companion, my journal noted at the time that he did not greet you with "Whadda yah say, boy."

Most of the recruits were teenagers. Many made mistakes on their first sentry watches, not from complexity of the task, but from excitement at the duty to shout at approaching figures in the dark. One, in a faltering voice, chirped, "Halt! Who am I?" Another had been instructed to run and warn the officer within if the Captain should come. Sure enough, along came the Old Man out for an evening stroll. "Halt!" ordered the boot, then turned and raced for the barracks. "Young man," asked the Skipper, "Are you going to leave me standing at attention here all night?" The sentry wheeled and shouted back, "Oh, excuse me, sir; PARADE REST!"

Illiterates would arrive, having been passed by over-zealous recruiting officers wishing to meet their quotas. Inability to read their name on the watch list brought some to tears. Feeling disgraced, they took it hard when they were sent home.

Among the better recruits to take their training at that Station were second generation Mexican-Americans from New Mexico and Arizona. Most were enthusiastic about the Navy life and eager to make good. Only if they spoke Spanish among themselves were they resented.

On the carrier Bogue, all my colleagues and bunkmates were older than I, came from lower class backgrounds, had made the Navy their career and had risen to the rating of chief petty officer. In youth, some had fallen afoul of the law and had enlisted as an alternative to prison.

During a midnight General Quarters, a sailor who shared my battle station told me the only time he had seen a whore blush: When he had walked into a Honolulu whorehouse where he saw a girl from his Texas hamlet, who reportedly had been attending college. When asked if he had blushed, he grinned.

Christmas Eve in Colon, where my ship was docked, I wandered through the town in the afternoon and stopped to watch some boys fly a kite in a vacant lot. A Black man started a conversation, and we went to a bar for a drink. When he asked me if I would like to meet some girls, I said, "Sure," so he took me to the ground floor room of Virginia Dillon, with whom I spent the afternoon and early evening, drinking beer and chatting, she on her bed (occasionally scratching herself in an indelicate way) and I in a chair. This middle-aged Black whore had lost her physical appeal but she had some intelligence and considerable character and spirit and she did not despise herself. When I rose to go, leaving some money for the beer and her time, she asked, "Don't you want a piece of tail, a nice clean piece?" Fear of offending her made me feel uncomfortable and apologetic; she graciously accepted my stumbling explanation of just not in the mood.

Once when my ship was in Norfolk, I picked up a teenage groupie, one of the multitude of females who swarmed in from the southern hinterland to be "where the boys are." Dinner was spent reciting to her verses of Omar Khayam, aiming to convince her that sensate pleasure for the moment was The Right Way. Alarmed, she fled. With other girls, a few years later, playing phonograph records of *Carmina Burana*, Ravel's *Bolero* and the *Rites of Spring* also failed.

Orders took me to Midshipman School on the

Columbia University campus in New York, living in John Jay Hall. The regular Navy chiefs had resented me as a college boy and for not having come up the hard way in the Service as they had; most of the athletes in the Tunney program did not warm up to me nor I to them, to whom I was a bookish sort and not a regular guy. By contrast, my classmates here, fresh from college (most from Princeton or Fordham) thought well of me as an old salt who had Been To Sea.

On a weekend liberty, Oliver Harrington introduced me to Yvonne Gregory, a Black reporter for a radical tabloid owned by the Rev. Adam Clayton Powell, later Congressman. Together we went to *Pagliacci* and *Cavalleria Rusticana* at the Met, the Waldorf Ballroom and to a nightclub where Duke Ellington's orchestra was playing. A friend of her father's, the Duke sat down at our table. He looked so jaded that in later years he surprised me at having lasted so long. One evening, during dinner with Yvonne at the Theresa Hotel in Harlem, I went onto Lennox Avenue seeking cigarettes for her. A passerby, seeing my uniform, introduced me to Ray Robinson, in Army uniform. We chatted briefly in the street. He had the trim build and buoyant gait of the great fighter that he was, and his smile was luminous.

One Saturday night, we returned to her apartment. When she asked me in, visions of sugarplums danced through my head. As we lounged on her bed, she delivered a diatribe at how white men take Black women for granted. In dismay, regarding this as a personal rejection, I plodded out. On our next date, she made a derisive remark at the sight of my hand extended to shake hers at the door. In later years, the memory of having been such a slow learner gave me regret.

I met Edith Davidson in the lobby at the Met, while Yvonne was in the washroom. With Edith I enjoyed going to the Village Vanguard nightclub where we heard Leadbelly and Richard Dyer-Bennet, who were good folk singers. By ancestry and upbringing, Edith was a Jew and by conviction a Communist and an atheist, and she knew me to be an agnostic, yet when I went down to the sea again she gave me a St. Christopher medal. This gesture's irony was amusing, its motive touching.

After attending Symphony concerts (Koussevitzsky conducting) on Navy liberties in Boston, I would pick up ticket stubs from the floor for classmates to show as protective proof that they had not spent the evening in those ways regarded, in the School command's perverse reasoning, as not justifying a liberty pass, although expected of sailors in port.

At times in the Pacific my lot was to censor mail. Aboard a troop ship, almost all used the simile "like sardines" to describe how they were packed; in writing to pals, many mentioned that when they had said goodbye their mothers had taken it hard. One wrote that he had had his first taste of salt water, in the shower, and that he hoped he never would have to taste it anyplace else.

Some wrote home to small towns where the name of the town was sufficient address to reach their correspondent and (seeking to evade the censor) put the place from which they wrote as the street name—such as Bougainville St., Moresby St., etc.—on the envelope.

A few of the epigrams:

I won't write much because I don't want the
censors to know where I'm going.

I guess they keep you here until you go wild;
   then they turn you loose on the Japs.
Today I shoveled dirt again but not in a hole.
I'm in New Caledonia; evidently the Japs found
   out where it is, so the censors don't care
   anymore.
I'm afraid my hair will turn red; all the natives
   their hair is turned red.
There's nothing on this island except military
   organizations and a leper colony. I hope the
   censor doesn't mind this, do you sir?
Didn't go to church today because there isn't any
   around, so read a chapter in the Bible and one
   in the Bluejacket's Manual.
Mother has a heart as big as the moon and as soft
   as cotton.
(Christmas time): We had a White Christmas
   here alright—the cook bleached the beans.
The mosquitoes wear a red cross and give that old
   hard-luck story about wanting donations for
   the blood bank.
They tell me if you're good you die early; I'm not
   taking any chances.
I don't see how you could have gained so much
   weight since I left. Is anything wrong? Be sure
   to let me know.
I wash all my clothes except for the shoulder of my
   skivvy shirt where the lipstick is.
I'll never forget those last few days we spent
   together in San Francisco. They were just like
   a honeymoon except that we weren't married
   and you didn't cook.
Why in hell don't I hear from you more often? I'm
   going to exchange you for one of these darkies

if you don't get on the ball.

I wish you were with me here on the sand under
the palm trees and stars listening to the surf.
You know what I'd do to you? Yes, damn it,
nothing.

You're a pretty good woman, just mean as hell.

But even though you do go out with other guys,
Dear, you don't have to have a party (know
what I mean). It isn't the principle of the thing
I care about, it's the danger of diseases.

When I get back I'll roam across your body like a
wolf through the forest.

So be good, and don't you even think of doing
what I did.

Take a good look at the four walls. When I get
home you'll only see the ceiling.

If you get married before I get back be sure it's a
little guy so it'll be easier for me to beat the
hell out of him.

(the concluding sentence of a Commander): Dar-
ling sugar plum I am fine—movies here every
night—I love you with all my heart.

(The remark of a patronizing censor concerning
the efforts of an illiterate Lothario): "This
guy's a regular Casadona."

The best thing I can say about this place
(Gamadodo) is that officers and men alike
wade through the mud.

I can see the caboose of my train of thought
coming around the corner.

I'm really not afraid of dying; the only thing I fear
is that I'll never get home.

The Australian Army reflected the social equality of the national society. I heard a private introduce an officer to another saying, "I suppose you know this old bastard."

An Australian major told me of the actor, Errol Flynn, with whom he had grown up. He said Flynn had been expelled from boarding school at fourteen for seducing the chambermaids. He would borrow money, default and then use his charm to escape drastic action from creditors. Once as a young man he went to a town that was to hold a swimming race, declared that he would win it and offered to bet on himself. One and all, reacting with loyalty to the local champion and provoked by his arrogance, took him up. Flynn won big. After he had won fame and fortune in Hollywood, some men wrote him asking him to repay £150 that they had lent him long before. He responded by sending them his autographed photograph.

When some of us visited an Italian POW camp in the wooded hills back of Melbourne, we entered a hut and looked at the prisoners, and then the prisoners came outside and looked at us. At lunch one of them came in with his clarinet and played selections from Italian opera and American pop.

Our Navy provided for one's material needs in return for following a few easy rules of conduct. This gave security, tending to offset apprehensions about combat risks. Many of us also felt free in large respects, a common attribute of security. Not until after fifty did I feel as flush with money as I did on liberty in the Navy, with no financial responsibilities for others, modest spending opportunities, modest wants, and enough in pocket to gratify the wants. My condition resembled that of Gibbon, who wrote: "I am indeed rich, since my income is superior to my expense, and my expense is equal to my wishes."

Although for many the Navy's inflexible procedure contributed to a sense of security, it frustrated others, especially where the inflexibility perpetuated some stupid act. A harmless illustration was the rate insignia for electrician's mate. When the rate was established, the order was sent to the designer for a "globe," presumably meaning a light bulb. Misunderstanding this, the designer drew a figure of the earth marked with lines of the equator and tropical boundaries looking like the lacing on a baseball. Before the mistake was discovered, this had passed the desks necessary to become official; it was not corrected.

The Navy's rules and its members' attitudes both expressed views of sex that now would be regarded as ultramontane. Use of whores by enlisted men was tolerated and expected. Homosexuality evoked horror. A young recruit in San Diego was accused of masturbating in the shower (his defense: "just washing it fast").

Personnel decisions annoyed me, where made by men who were neither wise nor right and, more importantly, made without a hearing. A request to allow the other side to be heard would be rejected as insubordinate. To be charged with some misdeed, then after you had been acquitted, to be told, "You are forgiven," was hard to take.

To me, the two worst injustices were the treatment of Blacks (the Services were wholly segregated until the final couple of months of the War) and what has been called the "Franklin Field complex." This was an Army vs. Navy refusal to cooperate: "You run your war, and we'll run ours." This vice, infecting some officers in the middle range of rank (insignia from oak leaf to eagle), sometimes resulted in our side's units butchering each other from failure to exchange recognition signals or operational plans.

In the Navy, one saw little social discrimination against members of minority or other ill-favored groups:—Jews, Catholics, sons of immigrants, people from the wrong side of the tracks. Men were not segregated by background (except the Blacks, against whom prejudice was harsh). Background differences were invisible or obscured. No one could be measured by his parents, his neighborhood, his home, his checkbook, his clothes or his car. People tended to measure one another by conduct and personality rather than by a conception of the alien, and perhaps competing, group with which another was identified. The most common bigotry was aimed at those far enough off not to be harmed. For example, some men hated the British so much that they told me they would prefer that we were at war with England than with Germany.

While off duty, one almost always wore his uniform. He was proud of it, and the civilians held him dear for it. When I walked through Harlem restaurants and nightclubs in 1943, people at tables would pluck my sleeve and wish me well. Later, when I visited the Norfolk Virginia *Pilot* and in mild tones asked the editors if they perhaps had mislaid a letter I had written to it, defending the American Japanese, they apologized and published it. We were popular and accepted.

✧ ✧ ✧

Compared to other non-farm children of my

generation, I saw few movies as a child—and perhaps have overcompensated since age thirty. Until about eleven, I never had seen a movie in a theater. We children had seen rented movies (primitive cartoons) and ones taken by our Mother, screened by her (and sometimes the chauffeur) in the living room or in the Norcliffe ballroom. One day at home she casually asked me to choose between something since forgotten, or attend a movie at a theater. Immediately and eagerly, I chose the latter. It was a Western in which Gary Cooper disputed, then shot, a man who was cheating him in a card game. A year or two later, when we three children were taken to *Moby Dick*, the scene upset me when the sailors cauterized the stump of Ahab's leg on the Pequod's deck. As the redhot whaling tool was pressed against him, John Barrymore convulsively bit into and spat out an apple that he had been given to divert or comfort him. This reminded me of grandfather Stimson as he was dying. The Lakeside music teacher took a group of us boys to town to see the movie *Hell's Angels*. The flyers' brave and dramatic deeds impressed me, as did the German Zeppelin crew who stepped through the hatch to lighten the ship so it could escape.

In New York, when I was fourteen, Mother took me to my first musical comedy. It thrilled me, although I was tired and dozed a little, and my romantic idealism was disappointed when the hero applied a bandage to the heroine's knee, showing the audience part of her leg. During the next seven years, several plays and musical comedies in New York and New Haven were big events for me. Cole Porter's *Anything Goes* was exciting then, and forty-three years later, a Yale Dramat production of it, attended with daughter, Margaret, a freshman, gave me equal delight.

Failure to realize the narrow range of audience interest kept me from understanding why the lyrics of popular music were confined to courtship rather than also reflecting other human interests, as the old songbooks did: friendship, farewell, patriotism, worship and work.

Mother instructed me—and I questioned her rigorously to make sure I had grasped the doctrine— that until betrothed a nice woman was never kissed. The logical corollary—that a woman who lets you kiss her without a promise of marriage was not nice—led to heartless treatment of women who had done no wrong. Ignorance had not ceased to veil my eyes eleven years after leaving home. During part of our recreational time at the close of the War, my fellow Navy officers and I enjoyed the company of young ladies from Melbourne's polite society: at balls, concerts and so forth. On the return voyage I was surprised to discover that my colleagues' well-bred girl friends had taken them to bed.

For a while I adopted an attitude of *weltschmerz:* one quarter pose and the rest discovery of a few disappointing features of the human predicament. In late-night conversations, an effort might be made to impress my listener by reciting the whole of Byron's *Stanza for Music* (written at age twenty-seven) that starts with the lines:

> There's not a joy the world can give like that
>   it takes away,
> When the glow of early thought declines in
>   feeling's dull decay

On the islands in the South Pacific during the War, many men resented women's visits, which disturbed and frustrated rather than soothed or satisfied. A woman's presence denied the men the slack deportment permitted in all-male company. While one or two got the pleasure of her company, the rest, in lonely envy, had to mind their manners and seethe.

Men were ill-humored with one another, tired and uncomfortable, tempers worn from putting up with much they did not like. Because military discipline denied them the indulgence of losing their tempers, the tone was peevish rather than explosive. Expecting never to see one another again, men knew they could get away with discourtesy. Violence or name calling was forbidden, but petty nastiness was permitted. In contrast to the Frontier and the Old South, where verbal restraint was common because (among other reasons) men went armed, one's hands were tied, but one's tongue was free to be rude.

Once at a long table occupied by men eating their meal in silence, I remarked, apropos of nothing, "After the War, won't hostesses have a problem getting their ex-servicemen guests to resume the art of dinner table conversation? We'll have forgotten." After a few moments more silence, a lieutenant commander burst out that as far as he was concerned, he wanted to see the War won and he spent his meal thinking about his work and to hell with the hostesses and social chatter; and he thought there was entirely too much complacency at home, etc. Then he apologized and talked awhile more about himself to make up for apologizing and then stopped, and silence resumed. At another meal I tried this, and a couple of men looked up and smiled and said, "Yeah, that's the way it is, all right, isn't it," and returned to their food.

During college years, I danced at private dances

and at public places. The bands were big: Paul Whiteman, Glenn Miller and others. Large parties during college, whether the function was dancing, drinking or both, I usually disliked, although kept attending because girls were there. Those fleeting attempts at conversation in the turbulence made me nervously frustrated. It was hard to keep from hopping up and down, as though the floor were hot.

During my time in politics, a personal news article about the scene at an evening political reception mentioned me as seen wandering about "like a lost child." While the scorn annoyed me, it nonetheless accurately described my behavior at big parties throughout my adult life.

Since prep school days, at parties I would find myself sinking into a bitter, isolated and hostile mood, envying others' easy fluency of speech, comparing myself with them as to achievement and personal worth, feeling an impulse to hurry away to some quiet place of work to try to get ahead, to exceed those people in some way, and then return to merit their respect without the need for aggressive assertion on my part. Not until old age did it dawn on me that the conversations were trivial, and likewise the parties, yet that nonetheless these occasions could be enjoyed.

At social gatherings in Spokane or Tacoma drab scenes and unimpressive people have made me wonder if this is how we in Seattle look to New Yorkers; and if so, if the New Yorkers' view of us is correct. Then apprehensions of mediocrity are dispelled by hearing educated Easterners place Seattle in Oregon and by attending New York parties.

Attitudes in Seattle have become less provincial. No longer does one hear strong reactions to a British accent: Some people used to detest it as snobbery, while others doted on it as displaying a cultural superiority that they aspired to share.

In my years of growing up, association among the young had sweetness, charm, closeness and safe contact with less risk than now from passions that then might do one harm. But the risked harms (pregnancy, ostracism, shame, lowered value on the marriage market) were greater then, and the price of avoiding them was insipid experience, while shallow relationships are the price paid now. For most, sex back then was furtive, risky, squalid and, above all, infrequent.

Some of the passive young rebels of this generation have undertaken to interpret life through the supernatural rather than to exert the intellectual effort required to understand the natural world. For this, rejecting doctrines of Western religious institutions as representing established society and as connected to the past, they chose as vehicles non-Western mystical faiths.

Rebellious youth of the '60s thought that by denouncing the past, which binds us all, they could escape it. The French Revolutionary leaders and the '60s youth both repudiated the past and both failed. The former sought to reorganize society on a basis of reason and first principles, while the latter hoped for a society open to expression of impulse. They may live out their years ignorant of the past and what it means, an ignorance owing to lack of education, a timid refusal to look on harsh facts that they dislike, and the ease with which a modern urbanite can live oblivious of the past. Their experience contrasts with that of an earlier day when society's slow continuity kept it before one's eyes. Just as the burning of the library at Alexandria denied it a later impact, the '60s youth, by disregarding the past, may succeed in escaping that aspect of its control over us that comes from the transmission of knowledge.

The counterculture movement appeared commendable for favoring spontaneity and opposing materialism, both needed to offset excesses the other way. It made some deplorable mistakes: Pretending that incompetence is a virtue; using adherence to a life of unfettered impulse as an excuse for lack of self-discipline and acquired skills; in some cases, in order to be Byron's "thing of impulse and a child of song," taking advantage of other people (e.g., stealing to avoid being a money-grubber); the hypocrisy, or at least inconsistency, of decrying pollution and chemical additives, yet living in dirty homes and consuming and distributing unhealthy drugs; and the notion that not only is experience the only worthwhile thing in life (this can be argued) but that only *passive* experience counts. One should not become a hippie before reaching old age.

I used to think that conspicuous early success was a misfortune because it tended to impair personality. One watches the pathetic middle and old age of the high school or college athletic star who suffered arrested development, frozen in that championship season, the rest of his life a letdown, looking backward while going through the routines of an obscure drudge. But I no longer deplore celebrated success in youth. Risks of a warped outlook remain, but life assures so many defeats and disappointments that if a chance comes your way for some recognition or triumph, even though superficial and brief if measured on a grand scale, go for it. The gain outweighs the risk you will be spoiled. The pleasure is great, the good memories can be cherished, and such a chance may not come again.

Nor any longer do I think it unfair to others or corrupting to your own character to take advantage of every asset that comes your way, whether by inheritance or other forms of luck: finding money in the street, using the musical talent that your grandmother had, accepting an offered favor from an influential uncle. For other reasons, I do not regret having chosen Yale, but would not now have rejected Princeton because my Father's good name there would smooth my path. The leading men of the Kennedy clan do not deserve blame for failing to reject the support given them by those who exaggerated these men's merits and idolized them in a cult that made a myth.

A child who discovers his family stretching out behind him, long-established in the upper reaches of the national society, may react by taking the high road or the low. He may be challenged, taking a path that must be climbed, or he may be soothed, riding the momentum of his heritage. Gibbon wrote of a Germanic tribe that moved into northern Italy and made out well, until the tribesmen's "valor became so eroded by prosperity that their cups were heavier than their swords."

You do wrong, of course, to treat those assets that come to you as gifts as a means to escape the challenge essential to develop your potential and then to exercise it. But on the whole, life inflicts so many tough breaks that you need to take every helpful outstretched hand. Hubert Humphrey used to say that in Minneapolis he was blamed when it rained, so he felt it not unfair to claim credit when the sun shone. One who refuses opportunity not offered to others resembles a jockey who, knowing his mount is fast, carries more weight than the rules require. Let society do such equalizing as it deems fit.

To help themselves rise in the world, some ambitious young men cut ethical corners. Many intend to greet the onset of success by adopting more scrupulous ethics as a luxury that at last they could afford. Some do, but others fail to break their habit, after repeated postponements of reform. The differences come from the comparative balance between ambition and scruple, not from the place on the ladder where one starts, because even one born high may be consumed by ambition to rise.

In the early years of law practice, my obscurity kept clients from identifying me with anything but my profession. Later, many people came to identify me with my money, and this hindered my practice, acquainting me with the frustration felt by a woman with a tempting body who cannot divert men's attention to her mind. Some people refrained from retaining me because they supposed me uninterested in their modest prospective fee, while others supposed that since their failure to pay would not make me miss any meals, I would not mind working for them without charge, and a few resented the prospect of their own sacrifice to pay some one who did not need to make a sacrifice for such help for himself. Still others who came dashed my hopes by revealing that they wanted not professional service but an investment or a loan.

In later years, my partners' awareness of my wealth deterred me from urging on them measures for the firm that I thought either fulfilled our professional or civic duties, at risk of income loss, or for long run firm income at the cost of short run expense. I feared they would reject my proposals on their unspoken belief that my financial security would make me indifferent to their money problems. Perhaps I judged them unfairly to have assumed they might brush me off for not invariably voting my purse above all.

Criticism about money from contradictory directions has left me exasperated and amused. Some have disparaged me for insufficient effort to gather money and keep it. Yet once while we sought to settle mutual accounts, a former associate shouted at me, "To you, money is king!" Some have charged me with being a socialist, advocating that money should be taken from its rightful owners and given to the government to be distributed in wasteful equality among the undeserving idle, while others have called me an economic royalist, who grinds the faces of the poor.

Although money has not occupied much thought or been among those topics that have kept me awake at night, reflection on it always has left me perplexed. If a man chases it, he is money mad; if he keeps it, he is a capitalist; if he spends it, he is a playboy; if he does not try to get it, he is a ne'er-do-well; if he gives it away, he's an exhibitionist; if he gets it without working for it, he's a parasite; and if he accumulates it after a lifetime of hard work, he is a fool who never got anything out of life. How does one keep money in its proper place, between obsession and neglect? How does one subordinate it to higher things, yet get it and keep it, so it can provide independence, influence and time for pursuit of those higher things?

Proudhon's claim that "Property is theft" (How can there be theft without property?), may be admired for its succinct expression, but not much more. Riches and power corrupt less than poverty and impotence.

Those who regard the rich as wicked, yet consider crime the consequence of poverty, seem to believe that one's parents' failure to accumulate money gives one moral superiority over those who work for motives other than the lash of want. Their logic resembles that of those who regard themselves, because their ancestors came past the Statue of Liberty, as morally superior to those whose ancestors erected it. Of course, the converse attitude applies with equal force.

Those who regard me as a dollar sign, failing to recognize other worthwhile things done by me, have to be considered both ignorant and excessively idolatrous of dollars, whether they react with awe, envy, resentment or contempt. One morning as I lurched on crutches into a crowded elevator, a state Senator, later a member of the Supreme Court, looked at my cast and remarked: "What'd you do, Stimmy, drop your money on your foot?"

Those who despise *noblesse oblige*, both in moral conception and in practice, would do well to shift their misplaced fervor to improving those institutional arrangements that now provide insufficient protection for the less fortunate, thus leaving *noblesse oblige* by individuals to fill a need.

Except for books and pieces of furniture, my sisters and I received no worldly goods from Father. Throughout Mother's life we received material gifts from her. She treated us generously and, on the whole, impartially. After we had ceased to write letters to Santa Claus, we never asked her for anything. We were grateful to her for all that she provided us. We knew she owed us nothing and we felt responsible for supporting ourselves. Those adults lack my respect who believe their parents have a moral duty to provide for them, who rather than work, prefer to grumble or beg.

✧ ✧ ✧

After Mother had been in business for almost twenty years, she changed the name of the family corporation to the Bullitt Company, thinking to please us children. I disliked this, wishing not to have our name used "in trade." Because she had put so much of herself into this company and taken out so much satisfaction, she felt identified with it and was upset by my extinguishing this name in a merger a score of years later. My attitude expressed mingled pride and snobbery about our family name.

During the decade at King, I remained a member of my law firm, from attachment to the profession that was my ancestors' and is my own, pleasure in the processes of law practice (although I had little time to spend on them beyond handling an occasional appeal), enjoyment of my partners and a hedge against risks that lay ahead.

When I told my old friend Georgia-Mae Gallivan of how my older son Scott was a humanitarian radical who lived poor and followed his convictions, giving money to panhandlers whose clothes were less tattered than his, she recalled that fifty years before, I had behaved likewise. Except for the shabby clothes, neither my friend John Robinson nor I remember that.

On wet, cold nights in childhood and for a few years after, I would feel a tender pity for the toys left outside in the sandbox. A Japanese saying goes: "Kind is he who visits the cherry tree after the blossoms are fallen." I have given more friendly attention to those who seemed to need it more: among beggars, to the repulsive; on an election night visit to campaign headquarters, to a loser, as a winner has plenty of well-wishers and would be rejoicing even without them. The only remembered election night visit to a winner was when Hugh Mitchell beat me (badly) in the Democratic primary for Congress. As I walked through the merry-making crowd of his supporters, to deliver him a congratulatory note, wishing him success in the general election, a jeer from my ex-wife, reclining on a table, was the only voice I heard.

While I admire the New England tradition and am charmed by scenes of its countryside and small towns, I feel less identified with it than with Virginia and Kentucky, although my background is equally divided between the two regions. With my friend Shelby Scates, I exchange anecdotes from the Southern experience with an easy understanding that cannot be matched with some one from New England about his region. Perhaps in part this owes to New England having changed more than the South had done by the time Shelby grew up in Obion County, Tennessee.

G. K. Chesterton wrote that the Catholic Church, with its nineteen centuries and its expectation of plenty more, was one thing that saved a man from the degrading servitude of being a child of his own time. Without my belonging to that institution, my own isolation, acceptance of tradition, familial examples and sense of historical continuity have given me some independence from the conventions of the day. Of course, they have not kept me from the condition of being, like all the rest of us, "a child of my own time."

Some attitudes show me to be an anachronism, born two hundred years too late; in others, such as toward race and sex, my children's contemporary. On a warm spring evening in a college courtyard, children of alumni were dancing to a slow piece, while the pounding beat drove through the loins of all in earshot. One of my middle-aged classmates on the sidelines made me feel out of touch with my own generation when he turned to me and said, "Kind of sensual, isn't it?"

Non-conformity has been a large factor in my conduct, while a sense of anachronism has been slight. Like most of us, I have found that submission to conformity is not so hard when compelled, just as discomfort is easier to bear when shared. From an armed service at war I had expected harsh discipline and arduous work but found at boot camp that the main demand was to conform. Even arising at an uncivilized hour to jump around in unison in the chill winter dark is not hard to endure when you know it is temporary and is shared by all the other occupants of your big bedroom.

By not becoming closely connected with a set of people from any one homogeneous group, I never belonged to a "crowd," among whose members one might hear the remark about a big party that "Everyone was there." (Aside from law groups, I belong to no organization except the Massachusetts Historical Society and the American Alpine Club.) On the whole, my social experience has been broad. About the only kinds of people I have not known have been undertakers, chiropractors, models, beggars and whores. Knowing people over a wide range of society gave me the advantage of a large pool from which to find my friends, and thus attachments of deep and precise congeniality came to bless me. However, the lack of comforting immersion in a warm and supportive group, and without much to turn to at home, was isolating.

Without full knowledge of either my background

or my inner life, some people think I have sought to break away from my background. Despite struggles to pursue ideals, to achieve ambitions, to win contests and to survive, my partial departure from the milieu of my birth was not done for that purpose. Although one's past cannot be escaped, effort may lift a person above his or her parents' station or enable approach to other ends. For a Pullman porter's son to become a U. S. Army colonel he must work hard to overtake those who acquired more of the necessary skills and knowledge in childhood. But to forsake companions for whose company you do not care takes no iron resolve. To adopt a style of life that you prefer to that in which you were placed by birth and that may be followed by the children of your parents' friends is easy if your taste impels you that way. And, of course, one should not forget that whether one struggles to hold one's patrimony, to climb a social ladder or to seek an ideal, or whether one merely strolls across the social street, all depends on what one's background—social and biological—has provided and decreed.

Although lacking confidence in both social relations and personal capacity, I never have felt social insecurity. This owed not to a sense of power from membership in a strong family and the American upper class, but a deeper feeling, that of being at home in the whole society, as though it were air in which I moved and breathed.

To belong to a well-favored family brought me obvious advantages and some inconveniences but it never gave me shame. Although I never felt guilt for my property or privilege, or for that of my parents, I have felt a continuing burden of duty to justify those unearned conditions that had been received as gifts. Along with this has been a sense of like duty to maintain the standard of contributions to the society that my parents and grandparents had made.

1928

as ghost news reporter on Yale Hope Mission 5/41

Chapter | 9

TRYING TO GROW UP

Oh as I was young and easy in the mercy of
his means,
    Time held me green and dying
  Though I sang in my chains like the sea.

                         —THOMAS

Sometimes on summer days, when maybe eleven
or twelve, I would lie on the woodpile beside the garage,
watch the clouds passing overhead and reflect about
life's meaning. Passing thought was devoted to questions that probably had simple answers, such as why
screech owls do not screech and the Three Musketeers
did not shoot. More time was spent on the fundamental
questions; because perhaps unanswerable, they all are
old.

One must sympathize with those who appear to
have missed such unhurried, meditative experience.
Periods of sustained, isolated reflection, where one
seeks to discover how one fits into the universe, are
useful, perhaps essential, to the integrated development
of some people. This is better than looking wholly
inward as though one *were* the universe or wholly out-
ward, unaware of a separate identity. Time should be
spent looking for ways to make the parts connect.

Spiritual enlightenment I have neither found
nor sought. However, starting in adolescence and for
years thereafter, I pondered right and wrong and the
question "Why be good?" "What is the Almighty, that
we should serve him? and what profit should we have, if
we pray unto him?" —Job.

My attitude, which was more a reaction than either a conviction—because not held with certainty—or a belief—because not thought through—caused me to see difficulty as a measure of moral merit. How could an act have moral worth if it did not come hard? This contrasted with Edith Wharton's Lily Bart, who "craved and really felt herself entitled to . . . a situation in which the noblest attitude should also be the easiest."

Doing good came hard—always has in some respects—but rejecting the crowd's approval as a guide to conduct was easy. When young, not yet having recognized that the crowd is capricious, its judgment often impaired by passion, ignorance and muddled thought, I simply was indifferent to it. I early concurred with Saint Augustine's disparagement of the fashionable and arrogant youth who were "ashamed not to be shameless." My peers' approval—a popular incentive today—likewise had little pull, although it counted for more than that of the crowd. It seemed craven to adjust one's conduct to either group any more than one must in order to get along.

The question whether we need illusions caused puzzlement. For institutions and deities to be used for our benefit seemed useful and just. Yet to make our relationship to them work, it seemed we must pretend the opposite, calling for self-deception, which seems wrong.

Despite these uncertainties, it nonetheless has revolted me to hear people advised to forbear from harming others in order to avoid feelings of anxiety and guilt. It is morally repulsive to be exhorted to do good deeds "because it will make you feel good" or to hear an expression of grief treated, not as an inescapable reaction to pain, but as a means of comfort. ("Go on and cry, it will do you good.") Likewise, to be exhorted to

"Worship God in church because it will make you feel better" turns one's relationship to the universe into a therapy. It makes trivial the questions of mortality, destiny, duty and right and wrong. However, does the attitude of those who speak this way differ much from that of our forebears who advocated good works or true faith as a ticket to an everlasting happy afterlife?

And should our beliefs about the ultimate and infinite be passionate? For a religious believer, even a Laodicean, merely to "like" God is hard to comprehend. Yet passion creates dangers of both error and injustice when it concerns an absolute not subject to tempering by reason.

Another perplexity that lasted for many years and never was resolved was where should two balances be struck. The emotional question was how to gain enough confidence to be effective and enjoy life, yet not come to feel, or reveal, a sense of such exaggerated worth that one offends others and becomes blind to opportunities of learning from them. The philosophic question concerns how to realize that you, as a member of a species, are not the center of the universe and not morally entitled to have your own way in all things, yet to escape seeing your place to be so small and brief that the indifference of the cosmos overcomes you with despair. The former question was largely one of self-mastery, while the latter was half intellectual and half common sense.

In my early years, it seemed that youth was the time to discover self and fix a course and that the rest of life should be spent propelling oneself along the course. This resembles a French critic's definition of a great life: a thought conceived in youth and realized in later years.

To put this another way, one should grow up as a member of the "twice-born" (e.g., Hamlet or Tonio Kröger), "living in the question," in Rilke's phrase, wondering, doubting and seeking fundamental truth about how to live. Then after developing a design for one's conduct, a set of aims and standards, one may do well to transform oneself into a member of the "once-born" (e.g., Billy Budd or Tonio's friend Hans Hansen), settle on some ends, for better or worse, and pursue them. Speculation should become an extracurricular activity confined to the fireside, since life is too short not to be mainly lived rather than thought about. In other words, youth should be spent studying form sheets, then you place your bets and stake your life on them. Later years have left me not so sure.

After the world of affairs came to preoccupy me, these speculations were largely set aside as insoluble although of course, as with most people, my life continued a never-ending process of trying to reconcile what you want with what you ought.

One notion grew to become a fixed conviction: that you should strive to fulfill your own potential. You should try to put out all your energies in pursuit of your ends so that you go to the junkyard with no gas left in your tank.

Much time in the war years was wasted. Like an illness, this was regretted as a misfortune rather than a mistake. But the five years following the War, during my age span twenty-six to thirty-one, contained lost time that seemed my fault: trivial errands, making deliveries, civic meetings at which nothing happened, business undertakings that neither gained nor seemed to educate, waiting in office ante-rooms for appointments, spending time with people whom I neither helped nor enjoyed, pursuing projects that came to nothing and sitting in restaurants and bars listening to empty conversations and shallow music. Other time was wasted submitting to vacuous monologues when I could think of no polite way to make the speaker stop boasting, trying to amuse or selling something that I did not want (insurance, a business deal, a political measure, a public policy or a charitable cause).

In addition to the slow learning process, this wasted time reflects, in part, restrictions on efficient time-use that those with influence or authority impose on a young person who lacks it. One must stand and wait until Mr. Success has finished his phone calls, interviews and lunch. (Most people never climb out of this situation, but their life-long limitation owes to circumstances outside them.) In later years I have envied those able young folk who operate more efficiently than I did, doing significant work from the start in professional or executive functions, leaving errands and other routine work to the less trained.

A life can be made more productive and more satisfying by living most of it belonging to one community, after first seeing other parts of the world as part of one's education. To live in one place offers benefits that outweigh the cost (unless you appear to be a better person than others in time will discover you to be; a criminal who does not look like one may find he does better to keep moving). One comes to know places, routes, people, opportunities and other sources of one's needs for information, assistance, credit, affection, approval, comforts. Effectiveness and satisfaction can be gained from being trusted, sought, respected, needed and heeded. One's reputation gives one the benefit of doubts.

And a sense of security is gained from sustained association with a related set of places and people. To be recognized by strangers has meant little to me, but recognizing known and friendly faces gives me pleasure and sometimes a sense of being connected to the surroundings. Passing familiar scenes and faces in the community amounts to thumbing random pages of your autobiography. Nabokov wrote, "One is always at home in one's past."

On the minus side fall the importunities from, and obligations toward, friends and relatives from a tangle of long-accumulated ties: weddings, funerals, name givings, baptisms, brisses, bar mitzvahs, graduations, retirements, testimonial dinners, hospital visits, letters of condolence, letters of recommendation for college or employment, requests for money, and so forth. Of course, it works both ways. If you stay in one place, people attend your ceremonial occasions and care for you when you fall sick. If you choose to forgo the attachments and the blessings that flow from them, these opportunities can be escaped.

If asked to address members of a graduating class, I would advise them to limit the scope of their pursuits (not the same as a low level of aspiration or a narrow focus of interest). Although the lesson should be given because useful for a better life, it is difficult to teach and to learn because it is new, caused by our expanded range of choice.

One's productiveness is threatened not only by fulfilling, or at least responding to, a multitude of loyalties and obligations but also by the glittering distractions to which we are now exposed. Fascinating periodicals divert us from good books. Like shoppers at a mall or guests in a restaurant with a long bill of fare, each of us is surrounded by inviting activities. These conditions call for narrowing one's practices, if not one's tastes, enough to keep one's career from resembling the course of a bee in a flower garden. One's education should be broad, and one should resist the tendency to excessive specialization in work and in training for work. But in play, hobbies and other interests that are coming to compose such a large part of life outside of principal employment, one's course may earn more satisfaction if one can keep from perpetually tasting everything on the list.

To narrow one's aim all the way down to pursuit of no more than some single end may be justified only if this offers enough personal rewards to outweigh both the sacrifice of human ties and, by betting all on one square, increasing the risk of losing all.

✧ ✧ ✧

At about age eight, in a Palm Springs pool, I tried to ride on Mother's back as she had let me do a couple of years before. She sank under my weight, and we began to drown. The poolside loungers did not respond to her screamed "Help!," but a passer-by threw off his coat, jumped in and pulled us out. Although this scared me, it induced no reflection on death.

I have observed people in severe pain, others dying, and a few men smashed into dusty meat. I have watched men in danger, some responding firmly, others (like a companion beside whom I sprawled under a truck during a dive bombing) drooling and quaking in fright.

I have seen men under enough stress to make them lose their respectable human qualities and turn temporarily into animals, whimpering, snarling, grunting, twitching and groveling—performances that disgust and shock but offer a lesson of human nature and of society: That although demanding challenge is essential to personal development, we should organize our society to limit that excessive stress that degrades or breaks even the strongest among us.

As for lacks, I never have had a brother; killed or maimed anyone; been beaten up, although I gave a beating once; been knocked unconscious; had a tailor make a suit; had sex with a man; had a manicure; used a deodorant; attended a dog race; jumped with a parachute or committed what most people would regard as a crime.

Institutional injustice to me has been slight. In the Navy were a few instances. On the whole, my fellow lawyers have treated me well. Having received little injustice, I have had the combined benefit and burden of having no one to blame but myself.

As have we all, I have been subjected to personal unfairness in action and in attitude—that is, unjust treatment and snobbery: a little direct snobbery in the Navy and in college, and some inverted snobbery (more in politics than in law, business or elsewhere). But, as I have mentioned to my children, inverse snobbery from below is easier to take than snobbery from above.

As our formal rules have been reformed, so have our practices in the names with which we are tagged. Even people of some refinement used nicknames of a kind that gave annoyance, discomfort and pain: Fatty, Skinny, Stinky, Slats, Balmy, Snowball, Butterball (Father was a pallbearer at his funeral) and some not fit to print. A Seattle lumberman, "Flatwheel" McCormick, was a cripple with a limp.

Until I grew up, most people called me "Stimmy" (what some of her friends called Mother when she was young) and since then "Stim." Those who now call me "Stimmy" either knew me when, use it (often behind my back) as a pejorative, pretend a familiarity they lack, or know no better, as perhaps was the case with Father when he called Governor Roosevelt "Frank." Christened "Charles Stimson" after my Mother's father, I dropped the "Charles" as perhaps pretentious as an initial and unnecessary to avoid confusion with others. When one of my little children got up from the family dinner table to answer the telephone he was heard to ask, "Stim who?"

From age eleven to twenty-eight I was immersed in a society that ranged from mainly male to all male. My friend David Riesman recalls that, because he was shy with females when he was young, a boys' school and men's college enabled him to flourish. But a sound measure may be applied to excess. Although Mother's decision to send me off to prep school rested, in part, on the sensible aim to remove me from the one-sided environment of what had become, with Father's death, an all-female household (mother, sisters and servants), it put me in a condition even more one-sided the other way because it embraced the whole of its members' days.

Of those formative years in male society, four were spent in the Navy and thirteen in school and on summer jobs. Most of the living was in dormitories, barracks or bunkhouses or aboard ship. My only contact with females was at college, with girls who were not fellow students; in the Navy, when on liberty or leave;

and at home until age fifteen, during parts of vacations until twenty-two and for law school.

Amounting to most of "seventeen years in a locker room," this deficient experience limited my comprehension and probably warped my outlook. It may have contributed to my hunger for manhood, although in the past century many men in England and the U.S. had similar experience, yet a substantial proportion of them do not seem to have been much concerned with manhood.

Other than a few months with my Mother, and a few more with a wife, I never have lived with a woman except in conjunction with others (Father, sisters or my children) as part of our household.

Although at different times having experienced most of the sensations connected with being in love, I doubt that I have learned as much about love with women as many men have learned. My parents and children tapped deeper and stronger feelings than anyone else; to give my child a happy smile made me happy. Except for those in impersonal working relationships, the only women with whom I have gotten on well in any close, long association have been my sisters and daughters.

Good fortune has let me suffer few blows of fate. Close to me have been a few deaths, no bankruptcies, crime convictions, crippled children or extended painful diseases. The major lacks have been intellectual and emotional. All in all, the weight of "those numberless afflictions," in Jefferson's words, "which render it doubtful whether heaven has given life to us in mercy or in wrath" that have fallen to my lot has not been hard to bear. What has made me suffer have been conditions, not events. Whatever the cause of my gloom, it rarely could be attributed to an event. Fate did not club me down.

In the summer when I was about eight, grandfather came upon Skooky and me when we were starting to make a "clubhouse" of some scraps of boards, boxes, and so forth, in the bushes. He said we should have a real house. Then he had concrete foundations laid and a child-size house built on them just north of the vegetable garden. Grown-ups (parents, grandparents, nurses and workmen) gathered there and made a to-do about the construction. Father remarked that he was a laborer and grandfather the foreman. Mother had a cornerstone laid in the cement and put some funnies (comic strips) in it. A hammer was handed to me from time to time, and I was directed where to pound, and also directed to shift the hammer to my right hand from my left. Mother took movies. Near the end of the process after the crowd had ceased to gather, Skooky and I nailed most of the shingles on the roof and stained them; this we enjoyed. The house remained and was still there when I left for the War. We never had played in it much.

One fall evening at age thirteen, I walked up the road to my cousins' house for the night. I was on bad terms with the nurse/governess and did not seek her permission but just shouted out in the hall where I was going. She apparently did not hear. While lying in bed awake with cousin David, I heard a radio in another part of the house broadcasting a speech by FDR, who had come to town in his campaign. He was declaring his regret for the loss of my Father. Soon a servant came at

Mother's direction to have me routed from bed and brought back.

Among schoolmates at the City Ice Arena, one repeatedly teased another (a frequent butt whom I too had teased) by pulling off his cap and throwing it up among the seats. I asked him to stop. When he did it again I skated over to him by the boards and punched him once in the stomach, knocking his wind out. That evening, on my telling Mother of this episode, she asked, "Did you hit Roger below the belt?" Until my age passed thirty, she often disappointed me by expecting from me the least or the worst. When in her presence, I tended to retaliate by fulfilling what she expected. It did not seem possible to win her approval until my middle age.

Although perhaps excessively self-preoccupied (it is hard to know the length of one's own McLandress Dimension), for most of my life my opinion of myself has been low. Mother gave me to believe that to think well of oneself was wrong. She condemned conceit as a serious fault and readily discerned it in a modest boast. She detested Cellini. Because she tended to confuse egoism with egotism—the conditions, not the words— she regarded my self-centeredness as arrogance and concluded that the best remedy was to take me down a few pegs. In fact, this treatment intensified the self-centeredness because the condition was partly caused by lack of assurance.

During teen years, perhaps in response to my discouragement at not doing well enough, Mother, reacting to my awe at some other boys' impressive abilities, told me repeatedly that what counts is "what you are, not what you do." She was putting character above forms of worldly success. With this I would agree, then and now. But then—though without arguing with her—I thought her mistaken because "what you are," your character, tends to be determined and reflected by what you do.

When I was seventeen, she remarked that I never had wanted anything very much. Although I was not sure whether her criticism was sound, my awareness of it encouraged me in later years to pursue goals.

One summer evening between college and the Navy, my discouragement and discontent with my menial job (in the Smith Tower basement) were met by her reminder to me not to expect the sort of job available to boys with a college degree. The flint point from that one stuck in my hide, furnishing impetus for developing my long-sustained purpose to achieve education and success.

Over the years, her diatribes, delivered with cold, controlled force, repeatedly left me crushed. In response to her upbringing, my ambition rose and confidence dropped.

Only late in my life did awareness come that she had not felt as critical as I had supposed. In her old age these things were brushed aside, with never a retrospective comment, and we got on well.

In college I disparaged grades, in law school disregarded them, and ever since, have exaggerated their importance. Awareness of never having graduated from anything but high school has weighed on my mind, generating a mixture of attitudes toward degree holders, including envy, a sense of being unqualified and a determination to become educated. Others' academic credentials have overly impressed me. My partners' Rhodes Scholarships, law review editorships, summas and Coifs have awed me and added to my pride in these colleagues. The friendly attention of college professors has flattered me.

Then one afternoon, my daughter Dorothy brought me a package. It contained a diploma, Juris Doctor, conferred forty years after the last class that the University of Washington Law School had allowed me to attend. She had called the School's attention to the matter, and it had taken its action as "a correction of administrative error." After all this time, the new status left me with a confused reaction, but unblurred was my profound pleasure at the love her act expressed.

As a young lawyer, the sense of belonging to a profession and being respectably employed was satisfying. Before a boxing bout, nervous and fearful, I would envy the other fighter who would walk down the aisle to the ring apparently confident, enjoying the crowd's attention, and looking forward to the performance that he felt ready to handle, or so I thought. Going to the office made me feel the way I wish to have felt before a fight: Looking forward to hearing that work bell ring.

However, the disappointments of maturity renewed the self-doubts of youth. How I have longed to be able to stride into a crowded room like Escamillo, declaiming with joyful confidence! My sense has been the opposite of Alberti's and Cellini's happy self-esteem.

Feeling insecure and of little worth put me in awe of Mike Roemer's effective personality. In contrast to my solid social position and extended family, he had no family backing, even from his father, and had fled from another hemisphere where his country's government and many of his fellow citizens were exterminating all his kind.

Although applause pleases me, as it does most

people, I tend to find it hard to accept and shut it out of my ears, so that I am only dimly aware of it.

Not until late in life did I learn to accept compliments in the right way. Spared the mistake of believing them to be true, which would infect me with conceit, I failed to take them as one should, with skepticism and pleasure, but shut them out the way I do applause, considering that those who praised me did so from motives of either charity or to gain their way with me.

At forty, receiving some notes of compliment on a talk (introducing Chester Bowles) gave me pleasure but made me feel a retarded child who had taken forty years to learn to speak. My speeches became good ones about the time they became infrequent. After competence had been achieved, the process shifted to easy pleasure from painful effort. As to appearing before a microphone, a camera or a crowd, I used to long for the spotlight, yet fear it. Experience and acquired confidence now relieve me from either longing or fear.

People seem to have become less susceptible to being moved by spoken words than they were a century ago. Those with aptitude for their use no longer develop eloquence because such gifts do not promise results. My Father's closing arguments would make some jury members cry. He could not do this today.

Likewise, although circumstance directs us as much as ever, we seem less bound by symbols. When sworn to the truth, Christians used to be impelled to testify more truthfully if they had a hand on the Bible. Once in court in Louisville, before my Father's father tried a commercial dispute between two Orthodox Jews, his client advised him to require the opposing party to put on his hat before he was sworn as a witness; then, during trial, he plucked grandfather's sleeve and withdrew the suggestion. "Why?" "Because then he might have me put on my hat."

The local daily papers have covered my activities in different roles: boxer, at war in the Navy, civic activist, socialite, politician, lawyer, author, broadcaster, mountaineer, real estate developer, litigant, robbery victim, bereaved parent. I never have sought publicity (except in politics), often enjoyed it and in other instances disliked it. My feelings toward public recognition or even notice have been mixed—like T. E. Lawrence, hungering for it, yet taking flight from it.

Although my family, past and present, gives me pride, it is hard not to show annoyance with those people who do not measure you by what you are doing with your life but who acclaim you for your pedigree as though you were a colt whose parents had run fast. After growing up, I disliked being introduced as someone's son rather than as someone who might have something to contribute more than honorable connections.

When I took examinations to support an application for a scholarship at Yale, my Mother concealed from me the fact that our family's resources made me ineligible for a scholarship. She feared that knowing we were rich might make me purse proud.

With deep pride in my parents, I sought to earn my Mother's approval and to live up to my vision of my Father. Because I knew little of him, I could imagine much.

In childhood, my sisters and I saw few other children and not many grownups. Our principal associates, and consequent mentors, were our parents' servants. They spoke well of our parents when they spoke to us of them. Hearing this raised still further our view of our parents' moral merit, and extended in our minds the gulf between our moral station and our parents' lofty plane. (Cf. Winston's nanny, the loving Mrs. Everest, who encouraged him to idealize his distant parents.)

For a long time the sense of falling short of my parents' levels of character and achievement discouraged me. Their heredity and environment had been no better than mine. As a hybrid, produced by the confluence of family streams from New England and the South, I might have been expected to surpass them. After *Who's Who in America* had listed my parents, both grandfathers, Father's three brothers, my ex-wife and a few cousins, my own listing gave me less satisfaction than relief at not having failed to reach a level that seemed uniform for my kin. Eventually, on my realizing that I had overestimated my parents' height and that in part an equivalence had been attained, that source of discouragement faded out.

✧ ✧ ✧

The privileges, applause and special attentions of high station, although they had appeal, were not the magnets that drew me on. Rather, "the land breeze that sped my bark" was an honored name, laurel wreaths, medals for valor and escape from risk of shame.

Regardless of one's achievement level, one has no right to hold up his head if he confines himself to the shelter of a protected class. To achieve excellence, to succeed and to be a man it was necessary to seek out competition, which my life's circumstances did not thrust upon me. Mother sent me east, wanting me out of the provincial and protective home and hometown surroundings, against my conviction that the effete east would enervate and corrupt. She was right. At home one could coast on one's background and connections, while elsewhere, among strangers, one could not.

Yet while in those distant parts I was better treated in some ways than I was treated at home before I had made a mark. In Seattle, some people scorned me as having advantages without having demonstrated or even asserted any merit. Away, I escaped that adverse presumption. Those eleven years far from home were useful. On return home I sought competition, and to forego peace and *ex parte* matters has not been hard.

Some people's ambition is ignited by the thought of doing well at a vocation that appeals to them. Others, whether or not a particular kind of work attracts them, are stirred by putting one foot on any ladder's bottom rung. In my case, wishing to succeed, having come to know that others were more gifted, I found a slowly grown resolve not to let others outwork me.

After the second defeat for Congress, plunging back into law practice at age thirty-five, weary and without bounce, I put out all that could be squeezed. In desperation rather than enthusiasm, I pressed to make up for lost time and to scramble harder to succeed at something. Unlike the reaction of Dr. Johnson, who knew he had genius and felt guilty when a stretch of indolence buried it, fear of idleness compelled me to stay on some race track.

At a picnic or a barbecue, poking at the fire, enduring screams and chatter, and morosely sipping bourbon from a paper cup, I jump with joy when a game of softball or volleyball starts. The sight of figures below me, toiling upward on a climb, never fails to spur me to step up the pace. Because to aim lower seems the coward's or idler's course, I have sought to "run with the swift": ski-racing with Gabl, climbing with Bertulis, boxing with inner-city Black professionals, practicing law with good lawyers, tackling long-sustained business challenges.

Although my behavior toward other people has been shy and unaggressive to the point of timidity, it has been competitive. On the whole, the competition has not been compulsive, but has been a pleasure; the chance to win seems worth the risk of loss. In fact, sometimes the outcome has not mattered, but simply joy in the process. More than once a climber with whom I had exchanged pleasantries when we came upon each other has asked me in polite puzzlement, "Are you engaged in some kind of race?" Most of the time in the mountains this fast pace was an enthusiastic exercise. Feeling able to go anywhere and surmount any obstacle in sight contrasted with the frequent sense of mousehood on returning to town.

An aspect of competition has been self challenge, of which in turn an aspect is tests of nerve or fortitude. The moral effort to enter the ring closely resembled that required to lead a climb above an abyss on rock that pushed me to the limits of my strength and skill. On Snow Creek Wall, on a route called "Outer Space," after which I named my sailboat, I took a forty-foot fall and (only) broke my foot. Next summer I tried five more times; on the first four losing my nerve and turning back, making it on the fifth.

✧ ✧ ✧

In all activities—work, play, errands, travel—impatience has afflicted me more than boredom. During the Navy years, in those frequent periods when nothing of us was either required or allowed, the wasted time was frustrating. After my sloop had taken refuge in Casablanca, a Third World Oakland, my comrades' reluctance to proceed with the voyage drove me wild. Later, the monotony of thirty unchanging days and nights on the empty ocean did not bore me because demands were made for my attention and effort, and we were crossing the Atlantic. Not until a few days before her death in her ninety-eighth year, as all her human equipment was disintegrating at once, and she had made her farewells, did Mother tell me, "I'm bored with life." Although I'll not live to her age, my senses, powers and choices would have to have ebbed as far as hers before no aspect of life would longer interest me.

✧ ✧ ✧

Unaware that my personality made an impact, I never asserted it much, either for good or ill. Eventual awareness came so late that the long-sustained forbearance to use it had become a habit hard to break. Perhaps akin to the sense of invisibility as to my dress, this unawareness may have owed to a wish to be invisible, from a notion that to be visible was to be conspicuous, which in turn was to show off.

Since emergence from an adolescence during which I rarely dared speak to others, my manner of address has tended to be humble and soft-spoken. One motive was a form of timidity, a fear to confront and be scolded. Another was fear that aggressiveness might be taken as bombast, that apparent assurance might be considered conceit. This habitual hesitation to assert has hindered me in those aspects of leadership that call for such behavior at a stressful moment, whether leading a business organization, a Naval unit or a boat.

A third cause of not speaking out with force when it was called for has been a stiff-backed unwillingness to use personality or noise to get my way, a willingness to fail if reason and authority did not suffice. In fast-moving conversation, my slowness at thinking what to say next augmented my hesitance. Others reacted, not with the approval to which I felt this humility entitled me, but with indifference or condescension. Not until several decades had passed and a reputation had become attached to me, conferring authority of certain kinds, did my words come to be heeded.

It seemed to me unnecessary and improper to try to influence people by expressions of personal force, such as to shout, pound on the table or display the trappings of authority. For example, when she saw me beset by debt, with income small, my then-wife decided that my heavy spending on a campaign had entitled her to an equivalence, rather than a call for frugality. Concerned that my resources could not sustain this outflow if it continued much longer, I remonstrated over the telephone with a credit supervisor of the most expensive women's clothing store (I. Magnin), asking that it stop granting my wife credit for purchases charged to me. Speaking in a snippy tone, the supervisor refused. I submitted, while had I gone to the store and made a loud complaint to the manager, he might have granted relief.

At King Broadcasting my modest personal style led to consequences that gave me regret. This mistake was failure to heed Machiavelli's admonition (in his 2nd Book of *Discourses*) that humility toward an adversary, especially one who is a subordinate, tends to be futile. Seeking to reassure insecure vice presidents or to propitiate their vanity, I took a small, windowless office and would visit them instead of summoning them. They took advantage of this. One device, which stemmed perhaps no more from presumption than from obtuseness, was used when the corporate officer sat down for the ostensible purpose of our conferring to seek a decision. Not examining the aspects of the matter before us, he would deliver a sales pitch for what he wanted. At the end of the time allotted for the conference he would finish his monologue, stand up and lay before me a piece of paper to sign.

Another executive would keep me waiting. While I sat before his big desk, blinking into the sun that shone past his head, he would take phone calls. Had my behavior been less self-effacing and more like that of Louis XIV, he might have earned thanks and promotion instead of being treated with ever-increasing remoteness.

Executives who were Mother's former colleagues would come to her imposing office and seek her concurrence with their opposition to my policies. Her consent, more often implied than expressed, encouraged them to brush me off. Sometimes a secretary would come into a room where I was meeting with executives and say, "Mr. Bullitt, your mother wants you on the phone." The secretary would be told the call would be returned as soon as the conference was finished. She would leave and pop back a moment later with the message, "Your mother says you are to come to the phone now." I would rise and go out. My passive submission to all this, and allowing it to continue, impaired both my effectiveness and enthusiasm during the decade in that job.

Eventually it sunk in that my forbearing to exert personal force was a mistake. Many people would rather submit to the impact of one's personality than expose themselves to a penalty that one may have the power to inflict: fire, demote, desert, divorce, quit, strike, sue, withhold credit, report to superior officer or have arrested.

Others have heard few complaints from me, but, until late in life, much pity was poured on me by myself. I have made few demands on others but sometimes have been disappointed by the lack of attention or help that might have been received by asking for it.

One step further removed from rational argument than an *ad hominem* argument is a harsh confrontation. In all areas of living, these encounters, calling on me to demand, accuse, apologize or admit, with my fear to face an angry countenance, have baffled and defeated me. Their prospect has made me shrink from them, sometimes by evasion. Unable to think of an effective response, averse to being upbraided, I hesitate to provoke by blunt words.

Evading confrontation has gotten me into trouble. Half a dozen times, when I took some action that would disappoint others—for example, dissolving a business connection or cutting off a flow of money for a retainer or a sinecure—action that was my right and not unfair, I did not tell those affected but allowed them to discover what had been done. Instead of merely disappointing, it caused a deep offense.

In sullen silence, I have endured many tirades, more of them by women, and have resented them without end. When treated like a Catiline, my absence of response would exacerbate the tone, and my passivity would encourage duration and repetition by reassuring my castigator that reprisal was not risked. I feared and resented those diatribes, delivered in sarcastic or derisive tones from one who joins cleverness and malice to interpret one's merits as contemptible pretensions, one's motives as weak or base and one's achievement as unearned. Such a person would claim that St. Francis, to gratify his ego, sought the title of the world's humblest man or that Justice Holmes, in making the United States the residuary beneficiary of his will, displayed not lofty idealism toward the Union for which he had been employed for his most important work and for which he was wounded three times, but rather an old man with neither imagination nor friends.

Even when facing one who would not scold me, I often would withhold words that might offend. Fearing to provoke a subordinate by criticizing his performance, I would glower at him, giving him the uneasy sense that he had displeased me, but leaving him in the dark as to how or when.

Mother once explained to me, when a child, that from love of me she often did things for me that made her suffer. When asked for an example, she mentioned that she had had a headache on a recent afternoon when she had accompanied me on a walk where I had shown off to her with pleasure, jumping from one boulder to another (in Tahquitz Canyon, over the ridge from Tahquitz Rock where I climbed technical routes sixty years later). This opened a vista for me. Until grown I continued to feel occasional remorse to think of her generous actions, performed for my benefit, that caused her discomfort or pain. However, often during my youth when Mother made me unhappy I would try to punish her by dropping into a dark sulk and spurning offered pleasures to demonstrate how she should feel sorry for the way she had made me feel. Deplorably, in adult years I sometimes resorted to this device with other people, a course always foolish and often unfair.

Never having learned to exercise controlled anger, I have stifled it, regarding such a confrontation as no more or less than an invitation to enter a street fight, which should be abjured except in extreme cases of principle—honor or the protection of others. It is a no-win proposition: A loser goes to the hospital or morgue; a winner may go to jail. Rather than confront an angry face and exchange harsh words, I withdraw in silence, turning away or backing down. Self deception appears to be the cause of my confusing such a verbal confrontation with a lethal fight.

In a reaction common to many, my resentment has been provoked less by injuries than by slights: slurs on my honor, domestic humiliations, or charges of disloyalty to my country. Perhaps the next most upsetting kind of experience has been annoyance at myself for staying silent and allowing something to be done against my wishes or principles when my speaking out could have offset it.

During the decade in the broadcasting business (and occasionally for a few years after that, as some people thought me still in charge of King, just as during that period some continued to think it headed by Mother), criticisms came at me for the Company's actions, mostly relating to TV programs: content, schedule and preemption. Commercial broadcasting, in part a public trust, calls for courteous attention to complaints, even though they are peevish, tedious or even rude. My one exception was made for an insult sent by a sneak: anonymous phone calls (one cannot respond to anonymous mail), almost all of which would invade my home at night.

In time, these voices impelled me to develop a routine response. When a caller's first words would show a hostile purpose I would ask the caller's name. If he or she refused to be identified and proceeded toward a verbal blow, I would cut in with a monologue as offensive as in my power to make: loud, abusive, obscene; would mention the despicable creature's craven anonymity and declare gratitude to be allowed to impart these opinions of him. The malediction would continue until exasperation made the swine hang up, never having been allowed a pause in which to interrupt with a retort. Afterward, it seemed prudent to leave the phone off the hook. These unaccustomed outbursts would so alarm daughter Dorothy (later a formidable personality at will) that she would run and hide under her bed. However, they gave me pleasure. To speak thus to a stranger by phone was much easier than using harsh words to someone's face.

Words that might advance or protect my interests in a social situation come to me never or too late. On my way down the corridor toward Mother's office to greet her on my return from the War, a friend of hers, Mrs. White, came past and said, "I don't want to miss this." She turned back and followed me through the door to watch the deeply felt embrace. But for my slowness to think of a courteous but firm word to turn away this obtuse intruder, this episode would not have left me at a boil.

I never learned to respond to disparaging words with a mordant thrust. Oh to have made comebacks like Guizot's response to the opposition charge that his foreign policy was subservient to England: "You may raise the pile of calumny as high as you will; vous n'arriverez jamais à la hauteur de mon dedain!" My initial assumption that the other person was right would further extend the time lag in laboriously trying to formulate some response. Others have made fools of themselves in my presence, but never with my help. I used to envy those who could make fools of opponents until observing that the momentary pleasure of the trenchant blow is outweighed by incurring long-sustained resentment that impairs one's career advance. The lack of such a defensive weapon has deprived me of comfort and relief but spared me the enduring enmity of those who might have been embittered by a scourging wit.

Forms of rebuke change with the times. In the 1920s others called me "naughty," in the 1930s "bad," then a few decades of "wicked," and of late "sick"—all in response to my having incurred disapproval or given offense, and leading me to wonder what I will be next.

After Dr. Wanamaker had painted my sore throat with silver nitrate and had left, I cried and told Mother that he was "god-damned son of a bitch." Swearing in Mother's presence was treated by Father as a severe moral breach for which I earned a whipping with a hairbrush as I lay on my bed with the covers pulled back. Then for a few months I was forbidden to read fiction or the comics page of the newspaper. How this (for me) serious event at age eleven may have affected any moral quality of my later conduct is not clear.

As years passed my explosive temper was subdued—not mellowed but submerged—and my emotional expression constricted. During my youth Mother would react with a smile to anything said by me that showed strong feeling (provided it was not rude). She probably felt affection, but to me it meant disdain. This made me try to contain my emotion. In my twenties, friends urged me to expand and relax, calling me stiffly formal, rigidly polite and cautiously reserved. On the other hand, Mother charged me with the opposite: rashness, failure to curb my temper and often, by an offensive manner, showing no thought of consequences. Regrettably, I believed her and thereafter tried even harder to contain. I would refrain from disclosing a defeat, a wound or a win for fear the listener would repeat the remark in scorn for it as a weakness or a boast.

Sustained containment became a habitual inhibiting cork at work, play and home—discreet, watching step, withholding anger and keeping my mouth shut. Drink, tears, growls, shouts, angry outbursts and so forth, none of the common methods would suffice to solve the problem. As to each, either I could not comprehend how to use it, scorned its use, lacked the willpower to use it, or found it did not work. For me, emotional release is limited to indirect means: laughter, the creative process (writing and giving an occasional speech) and moments of success ("Oh Black boy, where is the slave ship now!").

I cried aloud no more than about ten times in the half century between the deaths of my Father and my son and always alone except for a time or two in the presence of my older son, Scott. (Beyond my power to withhold, tears come less infrequently, sometimes not from pain or grief but from other feelings, such as pity, pride or joy. They would have poured had I been among the listeners on V-E Day when the Boston Symphony played that German's Ninth.) A tight-lipped stance, nursing grudges against others, resenting myself, all made a corrosive inner life that festered and stewed.

✧ ✧ ✧

Impartiality, which in John Stuart Mill and others has stirred my admiration, is easy for me, giving me security, providing a kind of certainty that some people obtain from religious belief. In fact, I cannot be otherwise than impartial. Usually this has been an asset in law practice, although sometimes a client has felt that my recognition of what could be said for the other side showed a lack of the fierce partisanship that reassures many clients and the absence of which some take to show one to be disloyal or slack.

Sometimes I have looked at a current situation in light of such far distant conditions that action to alter events now would not make enough difference to warrant effort. For me, this passive response has been a sign less of maturity than escape: Lethargy and cowardice leading to an admission of defeat, which might be seen as much a cause for old men's skeptical objectivity as is wisdom. However, this has not bothered me because, after looking at all sides, I usually do make a choice.

The aspect of litigation that appeals to me, other than competition, is the chance to enjoy the pleasure of argument. Of course, one argues in many of the mansions of the great house that our profession constitutes, but litigation offers more opportunities.

An opponent's use of an *ad hominem* argument offends me, as it does most of us. Part of this comes from affront at the suggestion that one's background or interests bias one's position, and part owes to scorn of those who fail to meet the issue. He who claims that objective judgment or disinterested action lies beyond his opponent's reach exposes himself to similar doubts. Such argument is the last resort of a debater whose case is weak and who is willing to stoop. An appealing feature of law practice is the comparative absence of that kind of fire aimed at counsel. (Witnesses sometimes are such targets, but what is opposed is their credibility or knowledge, not their reasoning.) The customs and attitudes of the game played teach most lawyers that such an approach is counterproductive.

I enjoy broad reflections on as much of the world as I can comprehend. For example, the impact on intellectual and emotional history, respectively, of the zero and the Cross. And modern physicists' observation that a human stands in size about equidistant between an atom and a star—giving more concreteness and drama to Pascal's placing the zone of human life and comprehension between the infinitely large and the infinitely small.

Clear thinking appeals to me. Other kinds may have worth only in groping toward a hypothesis or as verbal music. At a social gathering one may be disappointed to find many guests' minds either empty or closed. With those—like Rousseau and Marshall McLuhan—whose thinking is muddled, even though from time to time providing valuable insights, my patience runs thin.

Along with the intellectual merit of clear thinking go the moral merit of truthfulness and the emotional asset of realistic thought. Although I have always been susceptible to romantic and idealistic pulls, my thinking has shunned conceptualism, preferring to look behind the phrases to what they meant. Rationalism appeals to me, while pragmatism, as an approach to truth, not to choices of action, seems repulsive.

Idealism guides my social purpose and morals—private and public—while my notions of the meaning of life and the process of reaching conclusions are those of a rational skeptic.

Now that we know that most events have natural causes, and often know the causal chain behind them for a long way, we have largely lost our belief that God acts to punish or reward or to express a whim. Yet, curiously, this knowledge has not reduced irrational beliefs about the causes of events: astrology, channeling, psychic forecasting, crystals, tarot cards, lotteries. Likewise, despite awareness of the far-reaching law of causality, acceptance of the evolution theory and the archeological discoveries that show multiple sources for the Bible's tales, one may wonder at the continued attachment by many to some branch of the Christian church.

Once I refereed a grudge fight, as a crowd of amused sailors stood around an outdoor boxing ring. The purpose was to "decide" the combatants' dispute over the comparative merits of a Chevrolet and a Ford. The men did each other little harm, despite their zeal, and the performance enabled me – with relief – to declare the bout a draw. Although the measure taken was as repugnant as it was ridiculous, it seemed no less likely to reach a sound conclusion than other irrational methods such as prayer, impulse or picking petals from a flower.

Sophistication about truthfulness means lack of self-deception; that is, one knows it when one lies. E. M. Forster remarked that the Oriental's demon is suspicion, while the Westerner's is hypocrisy. One is an assumption of others' dishonesty, the other itself a form of dishonesty. Lawyers are not notably afflicted by either demon. (If self-deception reduces moral guilt,

then lawyers—who tend to be aware of issues of truth—
may be commensurably more wicked.) As for myself,
nothing is to be sought as more desirable than to keep
one's promises and to tell the truth in knowledge that
one will be made to suffer for one's act. I have always
considered honesty a paramount virtue and have practiced it in all areas of conduct, with the lamentable
exception of some dealings with some women (none
relations), with suspicion and resentment, regarding
the other as an intruder on my privacy or as an enemy of
sorts.

Unawareness of one's premises not only causes
unsound thinking but also, by self-deception, is often
ignoble as well as unwise. I never have resolved, or even
explained, the contradictions between my resort to day-
dreams, more to imagine achievements that I had not
performed than blessings not received, with my constant wish to face reality, to know the whole truth, the
bad news as well as the good. I have felt that not to look
at the thermometer resembles accepting a blindfold
before they shoot you.

For many years I resented Mother's failure to
tell us children that Father was dying, so we could tell
him goodbye and pay attention rather than disregard
him as a convalescent. Then she told me that he wanted
not to know. If we children had been told, we would
have run to his bedside in tears. For my Father, I
stretched to sympathize and excuse, but this put on his
balance sheet a small minus item—diminished when I
learned, at sixty-three, that he did know he soon would
die, but not how soon.

Cynicism has seemed to afflict some of those
who have comfort without power and others who have

suffered a naive disenchantment, provoking a shift of outlook from thinking all is good to thinking all is bad. Cynicism never has infected my outlook (partially excepting some aspects of relations between men and women—a feeling rather than a reasoned opinion).

By age twenty-one my views on policies for the pursuit of racial justice were both advanced and sound. This contrasted with my backwardness in grasping some other features of life, obvious to others but surprising to me. David Stimson's remark that a dog likes you because you feed it disappointed me because its evident truth made me abandon my previously held notion that a dog loves you for yourself. Later, a woman friend's mention that she was fond of her father shocked me. I had thought of parents as like the vault of heaven, towards whom duty called for an attitude of reverent affection that implies no emotional choice. Perhaps this dim sightedness came from a childhood immersed in literary romantic adventure, leading me to resemble Milton in the sense that Dryden observed he "saw nature through the spectacles of books."

The lives and living conditions of many of my ancestors have become known to me. My memory of my own early years has been supplemented and corrected by ample records. Introspection has been a common pastime for me. I have consulted psychiatrists. Yet despite all these, and a reflective nature, my self-understanding has remained small. My observations of who and what I am are fairly sound, but they have not been accompanied by comprehension of why. Some people are deeply disappointed at others' failure to understand them. Among my disappointments, my failure to understand myself has not made the list, much less taken high rank.

✧ ✧ ✧

From the onset of adolescence to the end of war service I lived in a slough of despond from feelings of moral and intellectual mediocrity. Thereafter, although some success had brought some self-esteem, the emphasis of discouragement shifted, in part, from lack of achievement and moral worth to loneliness and frustration from my personal life. Some of the loneliest people I have ever known were hired hands on Western farms. My circumstances differ from theirs. I live in a community inhabited by kin to whom I feel indissolubly bound, work with colleagues who are friends, and have a multitude of friendly acquaintances whose cheerful greeting when we pass on the street remind me of human ties. But I live and think as a loner. Nabokov wrote, "Loneliness as a situation can be corrected, but as a state of mind is an incurable illness." I always have thought that mine was the former but feared it might be the latter. Not long before he died, a New York writer named David Boroff became a friendly acquaintance. We hit it off well together. When he said he thought me probably unappreciated in Seattle and therefore lonely, I took his remark as half compliment (which gave me pleasure) and half snobbery toward the provinces (which I did not share), and reflected that I probably would be lonely in New York even if acclaimed there.

Among all my days and nights, the loneliest were endured in marriage. With more than average emotional self-sufficiency, I can get along alone, but the cumulative effect of long-sustained isolation left me in a loneliness that was not intense but was numb. Without escaping from this affliction, I retreated for recurrent sustained periods into sullen gloom, corrosive remorse and the craven vice of daydreams.

As the product of our genes and our experience, we have no good reason to eat our hearts for most of what we have done or been, but nonetheless, early and late, what has put me down has not been misfortune but feeling of merit lacked; dissatisfaction with self and not with the world. I never have doubted the worth of my pursuits, only my performance. For a long time even memories of wicked impulses long past would give me shame, despite my failure to have yielded to them. Without pessimism about either life's meaning or the nature or future of humankind, I never have felt we are engaged in decline or fall, or that we deserve consignment to outer darkness or that the individual cannot affect society or that life is futile. My stars suited me, but myself did not.

Most of us so abhor death that one's life must be exceedingly miserable or hopeless to make us prefer death. Nonetheless, suicide preoccupied me for about seven years, starting at age forty-three. My motive was neither escape from endless pain nor a substitute for killing another person whom I wished to hurt; nor for shame at defeat, like Brutus or dishonor like Ajax; nor to avoid being killed by a despised enemy, like Saul; nor out of loyalty and grief, like Saul's armor bearer; nor in obedience to a moral code, like the Japanese officers who jumped off the Okinawa cliff; nor to escape the indignity of being executed by others, like Socrates, Paetus and Seneca; nor from pride, like the captured Granius Petro, when offered pardon, who, saying that Caesar's soldiers were accustomed to give mercy, not to accept it, fell upon his sword.

Rather, it was black despair. On return to town

from "an errand into the wilderness," the quick shift from fearing death to wishing for it would amuse me by its irony. Dragged along by a sense of duty, I despised myself for the cowardice of brooding over suicide without committing it. Awareness of the weakness increased the dejection, as did shame at the appalling irresponsibility of considering abandonment of six children under twenty. My conduct contrasted me with Saint Martin, of whom it was said that he neither feared to die nor refused to live.

By and by, the inner debate, to go on living or not, dwindled to an end, but the self-destructive impulse may have continued as an underground stream, revealed by the practices of riding a motorcycle and making solo climbs.

For a few years before turning sixty, an intermediate stage prevailed: no longer an angry or hopeless longing to destroy myself but an indifference to living. I felt over the hill, not needed, either professionally or personally. At the time of our Liberty Ridge climb, I had been planning to climb Mt. McKinley in a few weeks, solo and by a new route (toe of West Buttress). Success would be worth much and to come home after turning back short of the summit would mean only one more failed effort. Yet the risk of not returning carried slight weight because I did not care; I proceeded with preparations and conditioning efforts. Yet when the bitter cup was offered me, sitting in the snow, it was unwelcome. Then after survival the reckless plan was dropped. (In part, this plan rested on lack of imagination. Standing at the foot of this difficult route, I would have thought better of it and turned back. Follies committed by me on climbs have been few.) This shift of attitude made me feel a hypocrite and coward in dealings between my own divided selves. But I did not despise myself for this, only laughed.

My steam pressure continued low, my engine stoked with stoicism (a poor fuel) in which I took a secret pride. Animal vitality, duty, habit and the satisfaction of sometimes-productive work impelled me through daily routines without the spur of joy or hope.

Disheartened by my present and future plight, I declined to take commonly used measures to escape this dejection—drinking, cheer-up pills, seeking friends, listening to music and so forth—regarding their use as an evasion of the facts and cowardly self-manipulation. (Two mood-altering drugs, alcohol and coffee, I have taken for pleasure but not for cheer.) Yielding to this condition was irrational and weak. Nor did I address this gloom and haul myself out of it by correcting my behavior and the look on my face. Long ago I accepted the truth of Ella Wheeler Wilcox's verse: "Laugh, and the world laughs with you; Weep, and you weep alone," but failed to follow it in practice. I did not weep but did brood alone.

The Liberty Ridge episode and its aftermath taught me two lessons, notable because they endured. First, I was touched by expressions of concern and relief by relatives, friends and acquaintances, in letters, phone calls and stops on the street. Discovering their affection was gratifying because I had thought myself unseen.

The other lesson was to relish the pleasures of each day, delighting in this process that had come to seem so precious. It made me so savor life that not even turning sixty a month later could sink me into deep gloom.

1919

1921

1921

1927

ca. 1941

Chapter | 10

GROWING OLDER

> Though much is taken, much abides: and though
> We are not now that strength which in old days
> Moved earth and heaven; that which we are, we are;
> One equal temper of heroic hearts,
> Made weak by time and fate, but strong in will
> To strive, to seek, to find, and not to yield.
>
> —TENNYSON

To many people the past surpasses the present because they survived it. They see in it the security of certainty, without the present apprehension of what is about to happen. When they look back on past times and conditions in their lives, supposing that then they were happy, they merely reflect their wish to be transported to that place and state even though at the time they never much enjoyed or appreciated them. They consider to be the "good old days" either their childhood or some earlier period of history that they find enhanced by the charming glow of long ago. Most of those who long for the past have forgotten what it was like when they were young, or are ignorant of history or have just sustained a run of bad luck. Although much of my life I would repeat, for a chance to do it better, only small parts would I enjoy reliving for the way they felt. And those from earlier eras whose lives I have envied for their pleasures, comforts and satisfactions—as distinguished from achievements and virtues—are exceedingly few.

Old people's memories captivate me when they

connect one to the past. Ivan Best (né Lovich) told me of when, in his home town of Odessa, he had stood in line all night to buy a ticket to a new play about to open. It was *The Cherry Orchard*.

When Justice Holmes was a child, John Quincy Adams, who lived nearby, lit his fire each morning with flint and steel. In the 1920s, a page of Greek reminded Holmes of The Seven Days, when they marched at night, fought by day, were parched with thirst and, like Ulysses, longed to see that evening sun go down. The news of the Great Coal Strike in England reminded him of when he had walked to a lecture by John Stuart Mill on the predicted exhaustion of Britain's coal supply. Later, Holmes wrote to Francis Biddle's son, born after me:

> My grandmother died when I was fighting in the battle before Richmond in 1862. I remember her well and she remembered moving out of Boston when the British troops came in at the beginning of the Revolution. Later in London I talked with a man who had been a school mate of Lord Byron and a friend of Charles Lamb. This will mean nothing to you now, but if you remember it someday it will carry you back a good way.

As a child, Mother used to see Princess Angeline selling baskets on the sidewalk at Third and Yesler. Angeline is buried in Lakeview Cemetery, near the graves of Mother's maternal grandparents and other kin. When Angeline's father, Chief Seattle, was a child, his father, Chief Kitsap, took him in a canoe off Suquamish to circle Captain Vancouver's ship, bearing the Old World's first visitors to these parts.

My Aunt D's grandparents, Charles and Mary Terry, were married in Chief Seattle's presence on Puget Sound in a canoe supplied by the Chief. Charles, who had landed at Alki Point in 1851, crossed Elliott Bay and laid out the town-to-be. Years later, the settlement having become Seattle, he invited some of his fellow citizens to a ball. John Redmond, after whom the Town of Redmond was named, entered Terry's office with an invitation in one hand and a pistol in the other and threatened to shoot Terry. He desisted only on being assured that "Esqu." after his name did not mean "and squaw."

On visits to Louisville, I stayed at Oxmoor, built by my great-great-grandfather in 1785. Sleeping in the original portion of the house, in the small room where my grandfather and great-grandfather had been born, did not make me feel either burdened or uplifted but gave a satisfying sense of continuity with the past.

Although the stories that revive a bygone day are enchanting, those old folk whose company pleases me most are mainly absorbed by the present and future, rather than with musing and reminiscing. When Joshua Green, at his home, my grandparents' former home on First Hill, mentioned that he remembered reading in the papers the news of Custer's massacre, he frustrated me by disregarding my question about the public reaction at that time and turning the conversation to the current fall duckshooting. His forward attention probably was one reason why he then had reached 101.

At my college class's twenty-fifth reunion, the range of apparent age had extended far from that of college days. Some looked like old men, and others as they had looked on Commencement Day. Their faces and general appearance showed a like range as reflecting the comparative progress of their lives. Some showed a distinguished splendor; others evidently had fallen on stony ground. (Such gatherings, of course, are not attended by those who have sustained the worst defeats.) Among the crowd of classmates, my old shyness, insecurity and self-measurement in comparison to the others swept back over me in a wave.

Although these men's paths and personalities had diverged, the self-selection process for those who came accentuated the uniformity of the dominant pattern: upper-middle class WASPs living in the suburbs of a large city, each with a wife, children, a respectable job and a country club membership. On visits to Yale decades after attending it, the most striking change seen is the expanded range of background among the students.

At the fiftieth reunion, the spread in apparent age seemed no greater than it had at the twenty-five-year mark. Probably those who had aged faster than average had died or reached a condition that otherwise did not permit them to come. I went fearing depression at seeing all those old men, and aware I was one of them. Tedium was also feared: To endure medical reports ("Let me tell you about my bypass"), grandchild snapshots, detailed recitals of how each hole was played on each course, and—as Castiglione remarked of old folk in his day—sour growls about how the country was going to pot, smothered by government and rotted by youth dissolute from drugs and sex. But the event was happy. When a number of classmates met me with warmth and respect, their response surprised, pleased and touched me. Perhaps a dozen mentioned a memory of having been battered by me in a boxing ring. The thought of punching these seventy-two-year-olds bemused me.

Genial recollections and anecdotes were exchanged. At dinner, a man who had lived in the same entry at Timothy Dwight inquired: "There's a personal question I hope you wouldn't mind being asked." "No, no." "In the bathroom, I noticed you shaving with a straight razor and have wondered why, and if you still do." My explanation that mentioned Navy enlistment evoked his reminiscence of how he too had joined the Navy, and had made it his career. He recalled going out to Saigon (as Vice Admiral) in command of the U. S. Naval forces there and reporting to the aged Ambassador Ellsworth Bunker, who, after the courtesy cup of tea, had told him, "Now, do not forget, son, that I graduated from Yale two years before you were born." The latter reunion helped me to reconcile myself to mortality and to resign myself to my lot by seeing others in the same fix.

After passing fifty, I became more aware of advancing age and what it means: accumulated defeats, follies, missed opportunities; dreams and hopes replaced by memories and regrets; the shutoff of options—for achievement, for pleasure, for paying debts of duty; the setting sun, approaching darkness. One day I was surprised to discover that my life had lasted so long I was not only older than the President but older than the Pope. Far from home, one can count on no kindly light to lead one on. As his long day wanes, a man may wistfully admire Tennyson's Ulysses but he rarely can emulate him. In Eliot's words:

> The cold friction of expiring sense
> Without enchantment, offering no promise
> But bitter tastelessness of shadow fruit
> As body and soul begin to fall asunder.

When you first compete in any field, you are disappointed when others exceed or defeat you. By and by, you learn the limits of your capacity and realize you never will calculate like John von Neuman or pitch 90 mph strikes. You are discouraged no longer by having your betters outdo you but only by failing to put out the best you think you have in yourself.

When your performance falls short of what it did in days of yore, you feel not discouragement but rather frustration and regret at your diminished capacity. Lagging far below your younger pals, kicking steps up a long snow pitch, as you gasp you wonder if this means you are not yet back in full health from a bug that has kept you in bed, or does it mean your age has caught up with you, a state from which you will not be restored? The lines from *Beowulf* exhort an aging warrior to charge against adversity:

> Harder should be the spirit, the heart all the
>   bolder,
> Courage the greater, as strength grows less.

But this rhetorical whip applied to one's withered flanks does not bring on a gallop.

On attaining middle age, some people are reassured by comparing their perhaps prosaic lives with lamentable destinies of many who were their peers during youth and who have fallen by the wayside: dead, in an institution, a bar fly, on the bum (whether in a doorway or on an afterdeck), or dropped out of sight. At fifty, to be self-supporting, without more, makes one a winner compared to many with whom one started the race. For others of us, however, survival without disgrace does not suffice to set at ease.

Through most of your life, to learn of a peer's death gives sadness, if not for the loss of one for whom you cared, at least as a reminder of your mortality. But when you are old, as you achieve less and less, the probable sadness at the news of a peer's death is accompanied by a sense of success at merely surviving those your age whom you have known for long. Confining to the living your comparisons of others with yourself effortlessly raises your ratings as the class diminishes. To take petty satisfaction from becoming the last sere and yellow leaf on the tree, a form of inheritance, luck alone, reflects one's narrowed scope.

The following lines express an aging man's wistful awareness of that to which he no longer can aspire.

To the Rising Sun

I

Greetings, Rising Sun, how good
    To have you in our sky!
Providing light, the means of sight,
    You rescue me from dark.
The landscape, blank and black before
    You came, you decorate
With shape and color, then adorn
    It with yourself. Almost
Since first from dim-seen hills you sent
    Up streaks to end the night,
Your level, blazing rays throughout
    In spirit, body, mind,
Have penetrated me. Unlike
    The roasting noonday sun,
Its own caloric sending, you've
    Ignited flame in me,
Inert until you struck your swift,

Involuntary match.
Infusing all my blood with fire,
    Your diathermic flash
Now kindles every factor of
    My nature (numb and scarred)
With ardent, melting, tender zeal.
    Your animating beams
Awaken me from apathy,
    Refresh and liberate;
They stir me both to spurn despair
    And to defy my fate.

II

You start exalted music, chime
    And peal, to mesh the gears
And grease the wheels, your melody
    And rhythm bringing me
By integrating harmony
    In touch with human kind.
Your dazzling brilliance, perfect form,
    Enchanting, gorgeous bloom,
Your symmetry, simplicity,
    Your upward-mounting flight,
And, counting most of all, your own
    Sweet singularity,
Dispose me to prefer to live,
    And furnish fortitude
For persevering in the fray.
    To help a seeker stay
In merit's quest, you offer far
    More than the stars or star;
They merely represent a prize
    Which you both symbolize
And splendidly incarnate; they

Suggest an aim, require
Disciples to be self-propelled,
    While you, Bright Sun, inspire!
No matter where your ground, your place,
    For me is always found
At center of my universe
    As though you were my god.

III

Hail, Heavenly Rose, may your
    Felicity match mine,
By you bestowed. With gratitude
    Your suppliant salutes
You for creation of the dawn
    And for yourself, applauds
Your soaring rise with eager cheers
    Beseeching, yearning eyes.
Despite you're wanted, needed, craved
    And understood, we both
Yet know, nor can for long forget,
    That grinding, rolling time,
In regulating which you take
    The main celestial part,
Will move you on, returning me
    To dark and to decline;
Then you'll ascend beyond from new
    Horizons, there to shine
On other heads, transcending mine,
    Your image, warmth and light.
But although all good things must end
    Such as this day's delight,
Their finiteness does not deny
    Their worth. Climb on, Dear Sun

Into your sky; pray radiate
Your glory, gifts impart,
Rewards receive, and tolerate
An all-adoring heart.

Cicero acclaimed old age as liberating from the bonds of passion. Is such deliverance a prize? Yeats wrote, "The only business of the head in this world is to bow a ceaseless obeisance to the heart," and "Reason is, and ought only to be," as Hume observed, "the slave of the passions." Sitting at the fireside, all passion spent, and reason having lost its master to serve, what purpose has one left? Most people still held in thrall by "the bonds of passion" do not welcome the prospect of release. To subside into a posture of repose may express not relief but regret.

Byron overstated the delights of youth:

The days of our youth are the days of our glory;
And the myrtle and ivy of sweet two-and-twenty
Are worth all your laurels, though ever so
    plenty.

The music of "Bright College Years" appeals to me but not the line "Those happy, golden bygone days!" Yet, Rabbi Ben Ezra likewise overrated the satisfactions of old age. Few may hope to resemble Cornaro in his mid-eighties, living not only an active and productive life but one that was happy as well. With health, life at any age can be gratifying. Yet should you welcome a farewell to all the pleasures of the senses but scratching where you itch?

As you slide into decrepitude, your friends may not be life's only remaining pleasure, but they steadily become an ever larger proportion of what you most enjoy. Ongoing experience keeps reminding you that those long odds against putting out a sample of your best are much reduced by having good friends: comforted by their kindness and emulating their merits—except where those merits are so exalted that instead of inspiring emulation they daunt. Probably the best part is the pleasure of their company. Friends make accepting mortality no easier but they improve your life while it lasts.

Of all audiences on earth with whom you may converse, your friends of many years are the easiest. All your shared experience makes reaching each other's mind less difficult than with any one else. You only risk boring them by things they have heard from you before. And they are easy because, although their critical faculties may be impressive to the point of intimidation, their affection lets them tolerate from you fuzzy logic, fractured syntax, non-sequiturs, unfunny jokes and lapses of memory and taste.

Grown wary of having your words and revealed feelings used against you, you may give others less of yourself, leaving that lonely space between. Yet among your long-time friends you may acquire such a deep understanding that, with little emotional disclosure, you may reach each other more fully than can those who are discovering the world with excited surprise.

When young we assume that forever we will be alive and vital, if not young, like those lads and lasses chasing each other around Keats' Grecian urn. In later years, however, our creaking internal machinery and knowing we are seen as paltry things remind us that although our lives may not be nasty or brutish, they are damned short.

When old, we learn little more than what that brutal taskmaster, experience, grinds into us. Our horizons of understanding may broaden, but our expectations for ourselves contract and subside. Likewise, our open mindedness is increased by release from ambition and by humility from defeats, although it is diminished by habit, skepticism, hardening of the brain, and indifference toward arguments heard so many times before.

Except on concrete matters within their experience, most old folks' thinking, having become commonplace, calls on them to use effort to state their frozen views in new and graceful ways. To avoid the boredom of thinking and saying the same things after years of repetition, one may stick to the particular so as to let the subject matter supply the originality that has left one's mind. Only the truly venerable old can get away with general conclusions into which particulars of experience have been distilled.

You may disappoint some younger folk who mistakenly expect that one who has survived for long must have wisdom to impart, having observed the world, addressed its problems and mysteries, pondered them and come to understand them. When you have reached an advanced age, you find you reach few conclusions with any certainty. Long ago you will have decided that the meaning of life resembles the inside of a hot dog. You do not know what it is, and realize that that is just as well. Likewise, although the quality of justice dispensed by a given society, legal system or court may differ from that of another, you have concluded that life over all is no more or less just than a flipped coin.

You tolerate human frailty because you have come to know that we are sinners all. You lose patience with those who interfere with you or distract you, yet you gain patience to endure frustration or pain from inanimate things, despite momentary anger at some trespassing bug. Your disposition is not sweetened, but the taste of life becomes ever more sweet.

In memory, as hills and valleys level out when seen from distant height, the spread contracts between the best and worst of one's experiences long past.

Because your capacity to forecast your future does not improve enough to make a difference, unexpected conditions and events confront you as often as they did when you were young. But they startle you less. Having learned that life is full of surprises, you have come to expect the unexpected.

Although the quantity of unforeseen experience washing over you does not abate, you less often encounter conditions and events of a kind that you have not met before. Particulars are new, but the types are not. This familiarity softens their impact. Your spirits are not pushed up or down as far as they were when you had nothing with which to compare the new experience that affected your life.

Looking back on the methods and practices that you have tried, you see a string of stumbles and failures but find a residue that has worked well—a recipe, contract language, a travel route. You put them to repeated effective use.

You may become cautious from acquired prudence but after many timorous years you are not easily made to flinch or hide. Facing risk of harm or defeat comes easier at the two ends of your life: In youth, when you are unused to failure and have not yet realized that you are mortal; and at the far end, with a short life expectancy and small chance to fulfill ambition, you have less to lose. You even may acquire a serene courage, like Attalus, the Second Century martyr, sent to be devoured by beasts before the crowd, who strode into the Lugdunum arena "with confidence derived from the memory of his life."

The risks to you of accidental death do not increase. The advice "Don't press your luck," means not that your past run of good luck may impair your prospects for more. It merely warns you not to conclude that your having survived past risks gives you some charm exempting you from future risks. The odds of accident are kept constant by the blindness of the dice.

But although the chances remain unchanged, the penalty declines. Like other aging perishable goods, your life's price tag is marked down. In advanced years, the cost to you of losing your life declines as your life expectancy and responsibilities both shrink. However, this reduced concern may be offset in part by your long-grown attachment to your life, attachment that may have helped you to survive for so long.

If you retain vitality you can transmit to younger people rich diversity of your experience, giving them pleasure and glimpses of abundance. Much "autumnal felicity" one truly can enjoy. In Longfellow's words on the opportunities of age,

> And as the evening twilight fades away,
> The sky is filled with stars, invisible by day.

However, after you have been seeing "the young in one another's arms, birds in the trees," and then a young person tells you that "You must have lived an interesting life," it is hard not to retort that you are not done yet. Those who assume that having "drunk life to the lees," you must be satisfied, make you feel as though they are asking you, "What, you want three meals to-day? Why, you had three only yesterday."

In your body's use, the balance tilts from joy to effort, sometimes grim. Exertion takes no more units of energy but, as though you start out tired, takes more will. To stay fit takes more effort. You lack the buoy-ance of yore seen in young dogs and horses as they jump and run for fun. When you cross a surface both slippery and hard, you feel less like a soccer ball and more like a china cup.

When your body is new, you sense it as a total organism as you cross the earth which you so lightly tread. After you have left your youth behind, you be-come aware of your organs and members, each with its awkwardness, numbness, stiffness, murmurs, ache or twinge. You feel like a well-used car, full of rattles and undependable parts. Conrad wrote:

> I remember my youth and the feeling that will never come back any more—the feeling that I could last forever, outlast the sea, the earth, and all men; the deceitful feeling that lures us on to joys, to perils, to love, to vain effort—to death; the triumphant convic-tion of strength, the heat of life in the handful of dust, the glow in the heart that with every year grows dim.

About the time I ceased to feel worthless as a person, my fading body started to give increasingly frequent reminders of its temporary nature and of my terminal illness: life. Yet sometimes even now, high in the moun-tains with everything going well, that sense returns of my body as a smooth-working instrument, its parts for-gotten, its whole giving joy.

I have not planned, or even considered, retirement. People's inquiries—yet or when—make me bristle, dismayed by their implication that my willingness or capacity to work has gone. Lawyers are not compelled to retire. They are allowed to dwindle. To me, the prospect of retirement repels or appalls. It repels if you must retire because your impaired equipment relegates you to wheelchair, ear trumpet and the company of others in like plight, varied only by an occasional doctor or nurse. It appalls if you abdicate while still able to work— leaving action that is challenging, socially useful and sometimes fun, for an endless round of fishing, drinking, gardening, travel and so forth, long ago summed up: "If all the year were playing holidays, to sport would be as tedious as to work."

To keep my gears meshed in significant action remains my aim.

> Death closes all: but something ere the end,
> Some work of noble note may yet be done,
> Not unbecoming men that strove with Gods.

Cicero wrote of an Athenian in his eighties, whose sons concluded that dad was losing his marbles and neglecting his affairs. They petitioned the court to appoint a guardian to look after the old man's property. He defended himself successfully in this proceeding by reading aloud to the jury from the manuscript on which he was working: *Oedipus at Colonus.*

As middle age reminded me of my declining powers, old age brought awareness that you cannot make your death an exalted occasion as grand opera makes *de rigueur.* A corpse may be given a funeral of

majestic pageantry, like that of de Lattre de Tassigny,
but you cannot die in stately dignity. As the curtain
comes down, instead of singing gloriously, you fade.
You cannot rage against the dying of the light, you must
go gentle. You may grumble to yourself but you do not
burn or rave at close of day. You may agree with Joyce:

> Better pass boldly into that other world, in the
> full glory of some passion, than fade and wither dis-
> mally with age.

Yet if the former has not been your fate, you may find
that some degree of the latter you are not unwilling to
accept.

I have wished to die outdoors in the rain. Sword
in hand, fallen amid a ring of slain foes, wounded every
place upon my body but my back. Propped on an elbow,
I would harangue family and friends with elevated philosophic thoughts, like Buddha, Bayard or Julian the
Apostate, parting with an embrace to each. At the last,
lapsing into murmured Latin aphorisms before the silence. Of course, the final scene may be played in a
hospital bed, doped up, slipping back and forth between
stupor and woozy awareness, maybe babbling of green
fields, as officious hospital staff come and go and my
depressed and anxious children wait out the event.

I would like, but do not expect, to conduct the
affairs related to my dying like Guillaume le Marèchal,
Earl of Pembroke, with active, precise control: He
assigned his titles, divided and distributed his worldly
goods, made farewells to family and friends (his best
friends came in wearing his finest robes), accepted
mourners' grief, directed the terms of his funeral and
burial, committed his soul to God, then died.

Brief exposures to danger in the War taught me

that previous meditation on death does not affect one's behavior in sudden events that bring or threaten death; only habits and conditioned responses count. Devoting thought to the subject may affect one's conduct somehow (the term "useful" is useless here) where the event is a process rather than a moment, so that the final moment can be anticipated, and one can choose how to meet it. But when death comes at you without warning, or where desperate action absorbs you, what goes on within you does not matter. Our reactions do not permit reflection and are unaffected by prior reflection. Melville wrote:

> There is no faith, and no stoicism, and no philosophy, that a mortal man can possibly evoke, which will stand the final test in a real impassioned onset of Life and Passion upon him. Faith and philosophy are air, but events are brass.

If aware that one is dying, having known much solitude may make facing this prospect less difficult.

> 'Tis solitude should teach us how to die;
> It hath no flatterers;
>
> —BYRON

But not much.

Nor is past experience. At social occasions, a remark to you that your experience must have made you familiar with death, implying that you and death have made friends, seems rubbish. As Epicurus wrote, we never even meet death. Like passing in a revolving door, it arrives as we depart. To "face death" means to face its immediate prospect.

The final scene is not significant. Montaigne wrote:

> In everything else there may be sham. . . .But in the last scene, between death and ourselves, there is no more pretending; we must talk plain French, we must show what there is that is good and clean at the bottom of the pot. . . .That is why all the other actions of our life must be tried and tested by this last act. It is the master day, the day that is the judge of all the others.

One may question this wise man's opinion that one's philosophy and courage are measured best by how one comports oneself "in the last scene." (Like the Stoics, he may have made too much of death.) Elsewhere he too observed otherwise, contradicting himself as he often did. A closer measure may be taken from the way one seeks amusement. As Samuel Johnson put it, "No man is a hypocrite in his pleasures."

When our forebears attended to the subject, they gave the manner of dying more importance than is justified for us. Then one lived in death's ever-present shadow, one died in the presence of those who might measure and remember him, and the pain that so often accompanied one's final hours made willed composure desired and difficult. Far less often than now did one die long after losing lucid thought, without having confronted oncoming death. One was likely to believe one was about to embark on a new life—for better or worse—and therefore needed to give oneself a proper sendoff.

One's death may be noble or base, but its quality does not measure one's life. In the words of Job: "One dieth in his full strength, being wholly at ease and quiet....And another dieth in the bitterness of his soul, and never eateth with pleasure." To live is harder than to die, and even the noblest philosopher cannot make his living dying. Roger Downey wrote that "Death makes a great curtain but a lousy story line." Since your experience of life is all that counts, the way you bear yourself when you face this final transaction matters only as to how it fits your own standards of behavior for yourself or how you think it will affect others, if you care. On the whole, most of us have such little choice in the matter. As he lay dying in the spring sunshine from his garden, Mirabeau asked his friend for a shave, saying, "When one has come to that, all one can do is be perfumed, crowned with flowers, enveloped in music and wait comfortably for the sleep from which one will never awake."

To sacrifice one's life for others may help to justify one's life and may ennoble one's death, while to die during undignified or disreputable conduct—on a toilet or a whore—may embarrass or disappoint some survivors. But although the manner of your departure may become you more or less than all that went before, it makes a negligible difference to the sum of worth by which your life may be measured. What you may be doing at the moment when you lose concern with all else should matter little to those who care much for you; and to you it matters not at all.

Although many people care about their prospective deportment at death, few prefer their death to come while they are absorbed in their favorite pleasure. Some comment on a mountaineering death that the victim was "doing what he loved," as though this means of execution fulfilled him and thereby made death somehow less a dirty trick. Nonsense! For him whose life has been snuffed out did the mountaineering that gave him such delight include being killed? Was he fulfilled by shivering lost, huddled on a wet log? By stumbling numb, by spinning in accelerating somersaults, by gasping for breath as his lungs gurgled, by hurtling toward rocks? Or at the dark bottom of a crevasse, wedged in an icy cleft? If a sudden fire barbecues a man, are his friends made to think the loss less harsh by recalling that he was taken in a nightclub, living it up? When Jon Goldmark's son Chuck and Chuck's wife and little sons were beaten to death, were those who mourned them consoled by knowing they had met their end together by their hearth on Christmas Eve?

Approving death for its having directly followed pleasure is as senseless as expressing relief that death has brought peace to a tormented soul. Many whose souls have been tormented feel gratitude that relief came to them from the passage of time rather than from death.

In old age, you do not come to fear death. What strikes fear in any one is risk of harm, and for you imminent death is not risk but certainty. Although you do not fear it, you hate it, as a prisoner hates the executioner who awaits him. To one whose life expectancy is seven years or less, testing HIV positive would give little shock.

In her ninety-eighth year, Mother still could be upset and, at that, by matters beyond herself, such as her children's behavior and her grandchildren's misfortunes. What a remarkable engagement with the world around her! At that age, many people would be congealed in resignation from which on occasion they might be aroused to no more than the outlook of a convict on death row, absorbed by his fate, wits fixed on his own plight.

✧ ✧ ✧

If your health has not forsaken you, the main drawback to old age is knowing that your time will soon run out. Gibbon observed: "The abbreviation of time and the failure of hope will always tinge with a browner shade the evening of life."

You make fewer and shorter plans. Longfellow greeted his Harvard classmates at their 50th reunion with the gladiators' declamation: "Morituri te salutamus." The remaining moments, ever more dear as their supply grows scarce, we hear ticked off by a clock or taxi meter, counterparts of the hourglass that medieval art depicted in Death's grasp. You oscillate between reminding yourself to slow down in order to extend your life and enjoy it (relax, have a good time) and to speed up to make the most of the time you have left (hurry, work to be done, pleasure to be sought).

Most of us fail at some undertakings into which we have invested time, effort and hope: a garden, a new business, a friendship, an elaborate party, an invention that costs more than the labor it saves. When young, we often find we can accept such failure, knowing we can try again—and again. Our loss is offset in part by the lesson learned, an asset on which to build. But when we have grown old, failure offers no residual value. You must win results, your investment is a total waste unless its payoff is direct and prompt. You do not seek training as an accountant or start to learn to play golf.

No form of self-improvement effort works. If someone suggests that hardship, exhaustion, deprivation and risk will build your character, you recall the courtesy visit paid by FDR to just-retired Justice Holmes, ninety-two. When the President-elect was wheeled in he found the judge in a rocking chair, reading Plato in

Greek. He asked him why. With an ironic smile, Holmes replied, "To improve my mind, Mr. President." Do not tell an old man to improve himself by becoming even more ascetic than his state and condition already impose on him.

Your ambition and hope of gain decline because the fruits of those pursuits—achievements—please only as honors or awards, not through later fruits that they in turn will bear. Cicero questioned what can be more absurd in the traveler than to increase his baggage as he nears his journey's end. Thomas More wrote that to be covetous when old resembles a thief who steals on his way to the noose.

In the frontier West, the phrase that a man had "cashed in his chips" meant he had died. That term might be applied as well to the efforts of one with a short life expectancy yet whose personality has not yet dimmed to a smoking ember. One seeks to turn his chips to cash—and spend it, reaping forthwith all that he has sown. Like life in wartime, one turns to pleasures of today. As Sassoon wrote, of soldiers in war, you "draw no dividend from time's tomorrows." Yet the knowledge sinks in that to pass each day as though he were a sailor on shore leave about to head out on a North Sea convoy will further shorten that life expectancy, the shortness of which was what impelled him thus to act.

One comes to measure out one's indulgences of all available kinds to fit the time that appears to remain. One paces oneself. On Liberty Ridge, while our supplies grew lower as the expected time for consumption extended, each day we diminished the ration from what we had consumed the day before. As a converse counterpart, when one's time ahead grows shorter, the portions are increased.

A popular fallacy among the young about the old

is the notion that long range consequences become the motivating guide for one for whom awareness of distant consequences has been acquired through long experience. In old age, your mind and body have equipped you to develop careful plans and then patiently tend them until they ripen for harvest. Yet your heart exhorts you to take pleasure from each moment; to follow the adage to live each day as though it were your last, because you know perhaps it is.

Omar's admonition to "Take the cash and let the credit go" has been thought to strike its most responsive chord in hot-blooded and impatient youth. But a young man or woman, possessed of self-discipline and either ambition or prudence, is more likely to defer gratifying impulses and to pursue long-range ends than is a gaffer to whom the choice is not between pleasure now and pleasure late but between now and never. You may take a long view in exercise of judgment about matters beyond yourself but not as to the conduct of your own life. To enjoy each day becomes ever more compelling, for "At my back I always hear, Time's winged chariot hurrying near." Unwilling to play a waiting game, you see no gain from deferring pleasures that you thereby put beyond your reach.

The morality of your behavior comes to depend more on habit than conviction. Pursuing elevated goals— by definition distant—encourages morally principled action. But when you no longer have a future for which to plan, a concern for posterity, often not compelling, remains your only motive to put off indulging impulse.

Although life is too short either to squander or to hoard, many of us devote our span to each course. By the time one learns to strike a fruitful balance between these wild swings, one has the capacity to hoard but the inclination to spend.

Rilke wrote that the spirit of Paris "is the desire to live in haste, in pursuit; it is the impatience to possess all of life right away, right here. Paris is full of this desire; that is why it is so close to death."

On my turning sixty-five, family and friends gathered on the terrace of my house to make merry and console me. After some had stood up and reminisced about experience with me, in a sort of oral *festschrift*, my response remarked the final steps on the way to life's gallows and what these guests meant to me:

These stories—fanciful, apocryphal, though most pleasing to hear—strike no chords of recognition. However, the sight of your faces evokes what those who mistakenly think they are drowning reportedly see pass before their eyes.

The shortness of life has been given plenty of attention: from poets, philosophers, theologians, . . . actuaries. But overlooked is how small is that portion during which you can make the most and best of what you have in you or around you. That is, how short is your "good time," a phrase used by convicts and family counselors. And that short stretch is further shrunk for those of us who are slow learners or who have trouble avoiding excess and achieving balance. This narrowed span of felicitous living gives one's human connections more import.

A long period of pursuing aspirations is followed by fulfillment too late, a rewarding harvest too short. After at last acquiring the knowledge or skill essential to doing something you want to do, you find your power to do it slipping away. Just about the time you get the hang of skiing fast, you begin to falter and wobble down the hill when you shoot the works.

This applies to the mind as well as the body. Hardly has your personality been ripened to the age of reason when your reason starts to stumble and blur. When your maturing process broadens your perspective, so that you extend your range of vision to distant horizons and recognize the significance of the long run, just about then you have to admit that as far as you're concerned, the short run is all that counts. You may freely think in terms of centuries, as though you were the Catholic Church, but for your own conduct you know that to take out low-rate magazine subscriptions is reckless presumption.

When people greet you by name on the street, and although their faces are familiar you cannot recall their names, you first react: To be known by the unknown, that shows one has become a Leading Figure. Then you realize it shows you have become a frequent forgetter.

Before some people have stopped identifying you as Dorothy's son, others start coming to know you as Dorothy's father.

After a lifetime aspiring to receive deference, when it comes you spit it out. For years you may yearn to be addressed as "Sir." The title connotes in your mind the Knights of the Round Table, or valiant gentlemen, generally played by Laurence Olivier. But when one day you are so addressed, the term turns to ashes in your ears. Not a recognition of honored rank, as you'd hoped, it's an embittering affront, a euphemism, veiled with insulting thinness: "Sir" means "fossil."

On so many a weary evening journey home, you heave yourself out of your seat and offer it to the infirm or the weak. Yet when one day *you* are offered a place to sit down—by one who thinks your age is to be dated by carbon 14—you are plunged into despair, provoking an impulse to get off at the next stop and throw yourself beneath the bus.

When you are young, you may read Justice Holmes's remark that, "Life is an end in itself, and the only question as to whether it is worth living is whether you have enough of it." And you may think, "That's frivolous, philosophically shallow, perhaps irreverent toward life, and of course it leaves out a lot. There must be exalted absolutes to guide our steps on some elevated course." Then a few misspent decades later you may conclude, well, maybe shallow, maybe deep, Holmes probably had it right. And you regret having failed to pay more attention to getting enough of "it," whatever your preferred form of "it" may be.

As one learns parenthood at the expense of one's children, so one learns how to live at one's own expense. A stock figure of comedy is the boob who spends a life of self-denying toil, deferring pleasures, and when the long-awaited time for self-indulgence comes, the only means that still remain within his reach to gratify such appetites as have not left him is to sip broth and sniff salt air on an ocean cruise as he wanly plucks the lap robe in the deck chair, while enduring his companion's querulous grumbles.

But although people laugh at that fellow, they despise one who does the opposite, who from adolescence on seeks not to develop and contribute but careens along as though he were a rock star after a concert, or, with less expensive tastes, as though it always were Saturday night in Forks.

The perplexities and frustrations that beset a

slow learner who also has trouble seeking that elusive golden mean give special importance to one's human relations, whether for better or for worse. With some of you, I've shared miserable times—discomfort, defeat, grief or other misfortune. And with each of you I've shared some mighty good times—good enough to make the prospect of more seem appealing—an extended run of living, longer than a miserly providence tends to be willing to allow. I'm a better man for having known you. Without you, my life would amount to little, would be ineffectual and stale. Over the years, you have given me so much kindness and encouragement and good company.

As far as life's pleasures may be derived from human association, you have blessed me with much of the best. Consolation in the bad times and pleasure in the good ones, the honor and privilege of some connection with each of you, make me look forward to lots more.

Whereupon I drained my glass.

In youth, resisting temptation preoccupied me. In the middle years, adherence to a moral code concerned me. Late in life, my moral assurance rose, and I began to relax. After many years of looking forward with anxiety and backward with remorse I stopped caring so much either way. When I reached the final quarter of my life and started looking a short way forward and a long way back, my condition brightened, shifting from hopelessness to melancholy. It was further lifted by assurance derived from experience of what I have done

and been. The roller coaster of my spirits did not flatten
but it has ceased to plunge into deep troughs. Following
a more rational pursuit of emotional ends, I try to resist
insensibly sliding even further into the life of an eccentric recluse.

Although without self-devotion I would not have
survived so many vicissitudes, much of the time for most
of my life I have been propelled by a gleam of hope as a
carrot and by fear of shame as a stick. But in my seventh
decade I largely mastered—or grew out of—this craven
defeatism, came to think well of myself, ceased to take
myself and life so seriously and came to look at most
personal decisions less as heavy principle than as matters of taste. My practices having crystallized into habits, good and bad, my principles largely were forgotten.
Eventually a growing contentment with self enabled me
to enjoy that passionate hunger for life that had been
felt all along, so that I came to enjoy many things.

Despite continued loneliness, reduced powers
and narrowed prospects, my frame of mind became not
cynical or despondent but lighthearted and less earnest,
yearning and sober. It echoed the appealing Viennese
saying that life is "hopeless but not serious." To some
this may seem pleasure-seeking selfishness, but nonetheless it warmed my relations with others rather than
cooling them. At ease, I reach out to enjoy human
contacts as I had not done when more fearful of others,
more uncertain what to say, hesitant to speak and anx-
iously pursuing a morality that was grim and strict.
These later years have been the best.

Sisters

Chapter | *11*

A LINK IN THE CHAIN

A. Posterity

Love descends.

—SCOTT BULLITT

From each of us, in a fan that doubles at each tier, our ancestors extend backward toward the start of the biological reproductive process. Depending on my offspring, an expanding set may descend from me. Some day this would make an ancestor: not of me, of course, but of some information connected to my name, plus the genes and experience passed along by me. For someone nine generations ahead, 512 other members of my generation (255 men and 256 women) will share my part.

We start the process of becoming an ancestor with great presumption because when we add a child to the world we are playing God, even though thinking, perhaps, that we are only playing. If allowed to live for a couple of centuries, few would fail to be surprised at what they had wrought.

We know many of the causes for a given person reaching a station in life far below or above that of one of his or her grandparents. But we know little about the reasons for the patterns of rise or fall. Why is fluctuation so great? I never have known a family in which a couple and all their grandchildren achieved much.

John Marshall's father, Thomas Marshall (my great-great-great-grandfather), rose well above both his background and his surrounding society. In turn, John rose well above his father, then was followed by children whose lives were unimpressive. One often sees this pattern: an eminent father, a preeminent son and no significant grandchild.

Xanthippus	Pericles
Hamilcar	Hannibal
Aemilius Paulus	Scipio the Younger
Nicholas Bacon	Francis Bacon
Henry VIII	Elizabeth I
William II	William of Orange
James Mill	John Stuart Mill
O. W. Holmes	O. W. Holmes, Jr.
Alexander Melville Bell	Alexander Graham Bell
Randolph Churchill	Winston Churchill
Arthur MacArthur	Douglas MacArthur
Motilal Nehru	Jawaharlal Nehru

These are suggested to illustrate the pattern, not to define the words "eminent" or "preeminent." Must not many sons of prominent men have wondered to themselves when young: "Is my father a Philip so that I may become an Alexander, or was my grandfather the Philip so that I will be nothing?" (Fewer older men, when successful, perhaps have wondered: "Am I an Alexander, so my children will count for naught?")

What causes this pattern? Admiration, envy, ambition or fear of shame may inspire the able son of a notable man to surpass his father. And his father's success may assist him upward. Yet a great man's children suffer from neglect by a father who puts all his efforts into his work, and his stature may discourage them rather than inspire them to excel.

Lacking both a father's career to emulate and children to be measured, the great Popes did not follow this pattern. At first glance it seems surprising that so few kings seem to have fitted it. If your father had been a king or a general (roles so often combined in the past) the inherited station and opportunity for training far superior to what most other people used to receive gave a head start toward greatness. However, although many of the great kings and captains (e.g., Charlemagne) who had prominent fathers seem to fall outside the pattern because they had prominent children, the children were nonentities in everything but inherited title, so these lines do fit.

On the other hand, those who possess notable creative gifts are not found to follow a path of steps upward to the brink, but instead go "shirt sleeves to shirt sleeves in three generations." Thus:

While visiting the Western Isles, Johnson wrote: "[W]hat genius could be expected in a poet by inheritance?" And Boileau told Racine's son, who aspired to write:

> It is not that I consider it impossible for you to become capable some day of writing good [verse], but I mistrust what is without precedent, and never, since the world was world, has there been seen a great poet son of a great poet.

✧ ✧ ✧

With all the uncertainties of the historic record, we nonetheless can comprehend our past 2,500 years. But for the future, our expectations for more than a couple of decades become wild fancies; our hopes and fears extend little more than a generation. And except for astronomical regularities, one cannot even contemplate the next two and a half millennia, much less "the never-ending flight of future days."

During my formative years, ignorant of my ancestors' nature and experience beyond a couple of generations, my outlook on the world was unaffected by knowledge of them. Likewise, many of these ancestors probably knew less about their more distant forebears than I have been able to discover, so they, too, may have been unaffected by such knowledge. In later life, learning about these ancestors has helped me better to understand what and where I came from. And perhaps even during my early years these people's experiences and values reached me by means of which I was unaware.

The Romans were admirable in their wish, and sometimes their effort, to seek noble achievements that would honor the memory of glorious ancestors and be remembered with approval by their posterity. But my conduct, and feelings about conduct, have been no more affected by thoughts of descendants beyond my children than they have by thoughts of ancestors behind my parents and grandparents. I have sought to make my own record strengthen and adorn that of my ancestors, not for posterity but to avoid letting down the team.

Wondering sometimes how some of my ancestors might have been pleased by compliments given to their memory after they were dead has reminded me to tell people the good things I think and feel about them rather than to postpone these words until standing at their graves.

This need does not deny the social value of honoring achievements of the dead. Such a practice toward the past tends to encourage behavior in the interest of the future. It is well for people to be re-minded that posterity sometimes expresses gratitude to the memory of its benefactors.

Because one deserves no credit for one's ances-tors' merits and achievements, the pride taken in them must be inner and private. Each generation must earn its own distinction. When treated with scorn by a patri-cian for his plebeian origin, an able and rising ancient Roman responded: "Your family ends with you; mine starts with me."

How can a child be taught to live up to standards set by those who went before him without acquiring at the same time the notion that he can rest on the past, that his ancestors' achievements have become his own, for which he should be respected and rewarded? My great-great-grandfather, Alexander Scott Bullitt, who migrated from Virginia to Kentucky from which his great-grandson and namesake had migrated to Seattle one hundred and thirty-five years later, wrote a family history for his children. He introduced it with the words: "Of gentle blood past shed in honor's cause each parent sprung." And he concluded with the hope that "the example of your forefathers will have some effect upon your conduct through life. I entertain a hope that when you reflect upon the characters of your forefa-thers, when you reflect that they have all been men of sense, courage and enterprise, you will blush at the thought of being less respectable than they have been."

Burckhardt wrote of Dante's belief that: "[N]oble origin , . . . is but a mantle from which time is ever cutting something away, unless we ourselves add daily fresh worth to it."

> A people which takes no pride in the noble achievements of remote ancestors will never achieve anything worthy to be remembered with pride by remote descendants.
>
> —MACAULAY

That for which we are remembered, to which our name longest is attached, often does not reflect the deepest furrow that we have ploughed. As the foremost orator of his day, Cicero perhaps put as significant events in motion by what he spoke as by his essays and letters (and transcribed speeches) by which we remember him. Some people are long remembered because their names are attached to something both durable and visible—something written, painted or built. Some make a mark on their times by writing a tune or slogan that captivates the crowd and moves it to action but that the next generation ignores and then forgets. The action has enduring consequences, but the identity is lost. Some others—soldiers, administrators, prophets—who have caused a major impact, whether preservation or change, may be not remembered unless a record of their acts is written well enough to be preserved and read. So what does it mean or matter to be remembered?

Our only immortality is the ongoing chain of consequences of our acts, which extends forever, or until causality stops. Our identity, by contrast, always terminates. Its duration is one of degree. After death one's name—to whatever it may be attached—resembles a fading trademark.

Rarely has posterity occupied my thoughts. As W. S. Gilbert said (incorrectly for himself), "Posterity shall know as little of me as I shall know of posterity." On going to work each day, I never have thought like Tycho Brahe, who said that he spent his life counting the stars so that posterity would have fewer to count. My children have been intensely and deeply important to me but with a sense of immediacy that does not go beyond their own life expectancies. To me they have been my family, to be loved and brought up to be free when launched, and maybe good.

Although I value constructive family tradition, I have not considered my descendants as perpetuation of self or an escape from mortality. DeTocqueville wrote:

> What is called family pride is often founded upon an illusion of self-love. A man wishes to perpetuate and immortalize himself, as it were, in his great-grandchildren.

However, the sight of a distinguished family line come to an end has saddened me, and knowledge that the Bullitt name in these parts ends with my children makes me wistful. So does the awareness that our family's century-long pattern of contribution to this community soon may end.

During exposure to the risks undergone in the Second World War, I cannot remember giving thought to improving or protecting the lives of my descendants (I apprehended having none). Considerations went backward to honoring and justifying my forebears and forward to the future life of my national society, but not to those who some day would bear my genes.

In contrast to those more distant in the chain, my parents and children have strongly affected my efforts to lead a constructive and upright life: Wishing for approval of both; wishing not to disgrace either; seeking to maintain the standards set by parents and grandparents to avoid embarrassing myself by falling short; and seeking to set an example for my children both for their early development and for my eventual reputation with which they will have to live when I am gone.

"Although all good things must end," the best of them being life itself, some pleasures do not end as soon as we may fear. My unexamined assumption had been that when my children grew up and left home, my delight with them would cease because our association would be slight, our only contact an occasional envelope containing snapshots of their children and an annual holiday reunion marred by the coldness of those treating the occasion as to be endured and by the acrimony of those who found it unendurable. To my surprise, the pleasures went on. Some disappointments were more than offset by relief from previous contention, exasperation and worry. Warm and felicitous association continued, with much affectionate mutual attention, exchange of problems and advice, shared experiences, anecdotes, laughter, confidences in easy trust and some shoptalk.

The possible duration of such tender parental relations was shown to me after having skinned a knee in a tumble playing baseball (two blocks from the front yard where my last fist fight had been fought, almost half a century before). My Mother, ninety-two, took me upstairs to her bathroom, climbed on top of the toilet to reach the fixings from the medicine cabinet on its high shelf, then bandaged my knee, remarking that this recalled old times.

How much effect will we have on who and what

come after us? In the past, the whole society's impact on succeeding generations was small. The principal means by which parents could affect their descendants' lives (beyond genes and upbringing) was to build or gather for them. This also, of course, would affect the whole environment in a small way. Care was put into social machinery for passing on to one's survivors what had been gathered or built: rules to make meaning certain, others to enforce intent, all aimed to carry out the wishes of one who had expressed them but would not be present to carry them out.

Change was slow. Economic scarcity, limiting the number who could afford time away from survival, combined with a cumbersome social structure that limited recognition of merit. This confined to a tiny few those whose potential talent joined the chance to realize it and then to exercise it. A genius in science or art could make a large and permanent change. A dynamic leader might find his city brick and leave it marble. Others, with more humble gifts, would make incremental additions by what they discovered, organized, sustained or built.

Those few who could substantially affect the conditions and events that followed them tended to possess notable gifts and to perpetuate themselves through work rather than through children. Bacon wrote:

> [T]he noblest works and foundations have proceeded from childless men, which have sought to express the images of their minds where those of their bodies have failed: so the care of posterity is most in them that have no posterity.

Emerson wrote of Plato, that "No wife, no children,

had he, and the thinkers of all civilized nations are his posterity."

But now, by contrast, our powers over the earth have risen to where the practices of us all, taken together, may ruin or save those who succeed us. The majority will tends to find expression in legislation and other public policy. Many interests and groups that do not make a majority nonetheless protect themselves by political organization that expresses itself in public policy. But two large and significant groups do not make themselves heard. One is those who combine ignorance and poverty, and the other is the unborn. Despite the fact that, although in some precincts votes have been cast in the names of the dead, no one among the unborn ever votes. We nonetheless may hope that some leaders will persuade enough voters to let the leaders act for posterity's good.

Since our forebears and other predecessors started to settle this country in Massachusetts and Virginia, we have had almost four centuries of rising material conditions. Almost all of every generation expected their children to enjoy a higher material standard of living than they had. And they were right. Now, for the first time in this long span, most people in our country do not expect their children to live in a larger home than theirs; they are not confident that their children's level of material conditions will equal or exceed their own. (An exception is those undereducated Blacks whose children become educated.)

The impact on us of about fourteen generations of improving material experience will not be canceled by our ceasing to hold these expectations any more than the shape given to our lives by a few thousand past years of belief in the supernatural will be obliterated by many people ceasing to share such belief.

Society has made large changes that will affect future lives. Because otherwise reflection on the human future would lack point, let us assume we escape extensive use of the weapons of mass destruction. Although the angle of material betterment appears to have dropped, we reasonably can expect our descendants—perhaps better to say children, because to look further may be too speculative—to live better than our parents lived in three respects. (Comparison is made between children and their grandparents because the three-generation contrast may be more easily visible.) How will they live better? They will suffer less physical pain and enjoy longer life and more fulfilled individual potential.

Many people used to suffer much physical pain. Some was inflicted by others as punishment of servants, children and convicts and as torture to extract confessions or information from prisoners. But most pain came from physical ailments: toothache, headache, earache, backache, childbirth, burns, boils, ulcers, cancer, broken bones, infection and going under the knife. Customs and laws have largely done away with the former, and anesthesia technology and drug chemistry have much diminished the latter. No longer is medicine so disagreeable that to be swallowed takes fortitude ("took their medicine like men"), nor do some dentists distinguish themselves from others by advertising themselves as "painless dentists." Those who now suffer physical pain may indignantly deny this proposition that pain has been much reduced. Such indignation testifies not to the proposition's falsity but to pain's importance. Although reducing pain makes a large social impact, it is hard to see how it may alter one's influence on his or her offspring.

A second respect in which our children probably will live better than our parents did is longer life. When he wrote that less is more, Mies was not referring to life. This extension owes to medical science, public health methods, diet, shelter, clothing and lighter and safer work. Longer life probably will both decrease and increase parents' influence on their posterity.

Our attitudes toward our lives vary with life expectancy. (Historians underrate life expectancy more than any other factor affecting human behavior.) The old prayer, "Now I lay me down to sleep; if I die before I wake . . ." seems remote from the way most of us now think when we turn in. Unlike ancient Egyptian merry makers, we would not put a skull on the banquet table to remind each other to enjoy today.

The prospect of longer lives, tending to assure the chance to perpetuate oneself, may make people feel that perpetuating themselves is less important than people used to feel. Demographers have remarked how a reduced death rate among children reduces parents' need and wish to multiply. Few have noted how an increased span, enabling one to watch his parents and their generation wither and decay, and even see his own children pass the zenith of their bloom, attenuates the link between generations. When most fathers died when their sons were barely old enough to earn their living, the sons may have cared more deeply than do we to perpetuate themselves because they had come to know the precariousness of passing the torch.

In the past, some parents deferred putting an emotional investment in a child because they feared the disappointment of the child's death. Now such an early investment becomes a safer bet. The lesser need to multiply—for survival of the family and society—brings improved odds on achieving satisfying results by parental care. Parental effort may be encouraged by the prospect that it will bear fruit.

The third way our children may live better than our parents is by a better chance to fulfill their individual potential. This comes from an increased diversity of functions coupled with extended opportunity to enter a role that suits one's taste and aptitude. The lives of most members of our society are being improved by the shift in means of personal fulfillment from rising to a higher station in a hierarchy to adjusting and training oneself to fill a role with the special configuration that fits one's particular gifts. Not only is this means becoming available to many rather than, by definition, to only a few, but it tends to provide more personal gratification as well.

Formerly, at least 99 percent of the members of society had no choice of role. For 98 percent, if a man, he was to be a farmer or a farm laborer; if a woman, the wife of a farmer or farm laborer. One was stuck with that even though one's highest aptitude was to be a third baseman, a cellist, an appropriations committee chairman, a dermatologist, an interior designer or an abstract impressionist. For the remaining two percent, one had little choice to vary from the role of one's parent of the same sex.

Now the rich diversity of roles—domestic, civic, economic—comes from a collection of related things: affluence enabling people to go beyond subsistence agriculture and the complex elaboration of both technology and social and economic organizations.

This increased opportunity to occupy a role that allows you to fulfill what you have in you owes to three causes. Supplementing the proliferation of roles have been the changes in our laws and customs that remove bars to entry. These include the abolition of slavery and of primogeniture, extension of literacy and further educational opportunities, and particular rules that forbid barring people from an occupation for reasons unconnected with their qualification for it. The third cause has been the new technology that qualifies a larger proportion of people to perform some of these roles. Perhaps the two most important are machinery replacing the requirement of much muscular strength and other measures enabling the choice whether or not to have a child.

Enlarged prospects of personality fulfillment offer factors that both increase and diminish parents' influence on their posterity. One is reduced transmissibility of parents' own skills and knowledge.

Formerly, parents passed on to their children their vocational skills, and their vocation as well, so a family might acquire its name from its members' occupation: Abbot, Alderman, Archer, Arrowsmith, Baker, Barber, Baxter, Brewster, Butcher, Carpenter, Carter, Dean, Draper, Dyer, Earl, Farmer, Fisher, Fletcher, Fowler, Fuller and so on. But now no longer, just as our mobility and our multitudes no longer let our names refer to where we live, e.g., John of Gaunt. In part, this owes to the rapid changes in our technology and in the conduct of our lives, making no longer venerable the accumulated knowledge of the old. And in part it owes to children's divergence from their parents in roles and functions. For a child to follow a parent's vocation, formerly a matter of destiny, has become such a free choice that by taking it a child tends to compliment the emulated parent. By this divergence, children stand less to profit now by learning what their parents have to teach. Tom Wolfe has written:

> [M]ost people historically, have *not* lived their lives as if thinking, "I have only one life to live." Instead, they have lived as if they are living their ancestors' lives and their offsprings' lives.

Now that a child is less likely to repeat the pattern of his parents' lives, varied by a negligible margin, his parents may see him less a precious replica of themselves. And parents may not try as hard to serve as models when they see that their children emulate them less than children did their parents in the past.

On the other hand, these increased opportunities for individual fulfillment may increase parents' shaping influence in other ways. In the past, many people sensed that their efforts could improve their descendants' lives by leaving them a farm that they had found a swamp or by heaping up riches for them in other ways. Now the opportunities have spread for exercise of talents that have been developed. Insofar as our society follows the model of a wide-open meritocracy, one in which merit is primarily measured by the directed capacity of developed minds, parents' efforts in the early training of their children may give even more of an advantage than passing on wealth used to do.

Ironically, the differentiating effects of this process at an early age, combined with the practice of grouping young people on the level of certain aspects (e.g., not musical or athletic) of their apparent unfulfilled potential, may deny fulfillment for many by stretching the high and stunting the low.

For parental behavior to matter so much in determining what a child becomes depends on the opportunity that the society allows for full development and use of talent, that is, that keeps the doors for all roles open to all. Such parental effectiveness will be limited by the extent of leveling social policies that seek equality of condition or result. Examples are the universal franchise, public schools, the military draft and progressive tax rates on personal income and estate transfers. Achievement of a large degree of this kind of equality is attainable only at a price that diminishes rather than increases social justice. And full equality of this kind would come only at the heavy price stated by Thierry Maulnier of l'Académie Francaise:

> La seule arme absolue contre l'inegalité est la sterilisation des élites. L'incapacité de se reproduire est la seule inegalité qui ne soit assurement pas transmissible et qui rendrait transmissible toutes les autres.

To reduce shock to those high minded people who suffer from the illusion that full equality of condition or result is a sublime goal for public policy, the foregoing remark is left in the language in which it was written, as Gibbon would leave "veiled in the obscurity of a learned language" a naughty or scandalous footnote. Such leveling policies may reduce, but not remove, the strong effect of parents' influence on their children through what they are trained and taught.

Toward those who have gone before us we feel gratitude for the world that they have provided us, a world we enjoy much more than the one that we would have if we had lived long ago. But the debt that goes with that gratitude we can seek to pay only to those who will succeed us. As my Father told Mother, love descends, and so does duty to forbears.

B. *Trial Balance*

> To say less of yourself than is true is stupidity, not modesty. To pay less than you are worth is cowardice and pusillanimity, according to Aristotle. No virtue is helped by falsehood, and truth is never subject to error. To say more of yourself than is true is not always presumption; it too is often stupidity.
>
> —MONTAIGNE

Not long ago, mistaken about the truth of the ideals they pursued, people often sought false goals. Now a common error is failure to recognize what used to be assumed without conscious recognition: That life is hardly worth living without regarding some things as worth dying for and without trying to produce something of your own to offer the world, to leave a ploughed furrow rather than a blank. This, of course, requires pursuit of ideals. Strenuous action for its own sake, or creation in order to "be creative," is ignoble self-manipulation that regards life as a substance to be consumed, and with cautious nibbles at that.

George Orwell wrote that every life, viewed from within, is a series of defeats. Probably this is so, in the sense that few people have achieved anything without having aspired to more. For the racing dogs to run fast, the mechanical rabbit must go faster.

I wanted to achieve and to do good but was sure that gratitude and recognition are undependable standards and also that my efforts should not be measured by how much they had changed the world. Without self-deception, one is almost sure to be disappointed by, at most, slight evidence of slight change in one small sector. Even if some resulting change can be perceived, it may not have done good. Most people who are productive workers and good citizens sustain the society, adding something of value to it by keeping it going, with an incremental contribution such as what an ant adds to its anthill. But having helped to make the world go around cannot be measured in a comparative way.

Wise men have concurred in thinking that human merit should be measured against the practices of the time. In the past, compared to us, the most admired leaders of action, creation or thought faced more difficult conditions under which to achieve what they did, yet the peers with whom they competed and against whom they were measured were fewer in number and had less knowledge and shorter careers. Nor were the enemy hosts as large or as strong. Montaigne wrote:

> We do not note in commendation of a man that he cares for the education of his children, since this is a common action, however just, any more than we note a great tree when all the forest is like it.

—and Gibbon:

> Our estimate of personal merit is relative to the common faculties of mankind. The efforts of genius or virtue, either in active or speculative life, are measured not so much by their real elevation as by the height to which they ascend above the level of their age or country; and the same stature, which in a people of giants would pass unnoticed, must appear conspicuous in a race of pygmies. Leonidas and his three hundred companions devoted their lives at Thermopylae; but the education of the infant, the boy, and the man, had prepared, and almost ensured, this memorable sacrifice; and each Spartan would approve, rather than

admire, an act of duty of which himself and eight thousand of his fellow-citizens were equally capable. The great Pompeii might inscribe on his trophies, that he had defeated in battle two millions of enemies and reduced fifteen hundred cities from the lake of Maeotis to the Red Sea; but the fortune of Rome flew before his eagles; the nations were oppressed by their own fears; and the invincible legions which he commanded had been formed by the habits of conquest and the discipline of ages. In this view, the character of Belisarius may be deservedly placed above the heroes of the ancient republics. His imperfections flowed from the contagion of the times; his virtues were his own.

and Lynn Swann of the Pittsburgh Steelers, after a Super Bowl:

> . . . I think it was Booker T. Washington who said you measure a man's success not by what he has achieved but by the obstacles he has overcome.

When applied to comparative performances, these observations seem beyond argument. Paavo Nurmi must be judged to have been a great runner because he so far excelled in his day, even though second-raters now can beat his times. But when we consider personal merit, it seems to disappear as virtue or wickedness for praise or blame. Gibbon wrote of Belisarius that "his virtues were his own." But, of course, nothing is our own.

Likewise, one should expect more from those who appear better equipped but not be disappointed if they do not perform to expectations. The term "appear" implies a range of error. Since we are what we have been made, no one acts above or below his true capacity. If we fall below our apparent capacity, we merely show that we have been mistakenly measured. A parent's disappointment that a child grew up to have less merit than expected shows that the hopes erred. The divergence of a golfer's score from his handicap shows that on that day his handicap was inaccurate. No one transcends himself or is unworthy of himself; we just have good days and bad.

Earlier passages in this book have reflected that we cannot be but what we are, while others have suggested that some people surpass themselves, displaying some elevated dimension of the spirit. To reconcile these irreconcilable notions of determinism and free will will have to be left to my betters. Some have thought my conduct showed a resolute nature (if they did not think it showed an obstinate one), but I never have felt much command over my destiny. In Raymond Carver's words: "Compulsion and error, just like everybody else."

The best measure of what you have done seems to be how much of your potential you have fulfilled, how far have you made the most of yourself. On this measure, Gene Tunney, Picasso and Artur Rubinstein scored high. Consider how far you have spent your powers, going all out, in a direction that seems to you to be right.

Despite the perplexities of measurement, one can try to judge with realism both one's surroundings and one's own performance. And one may present to others one's self-prepared balance sheet. Montaigne (whose *Essays* I carried ashore in the landing at Red Beach) appeared to think this. The results may be measured, but to measure their causes cannot be done. It is futile to differentiate attributions between achievements, contributions, gifts from without and within, blessings and luck.

Not all people react the same way to the same conduct or apparent personality. For a millennium, Jews despised Gentiles because they farmed and fought, while the latter despised the former because they did not. (Happily, a few years of Israeli history sufficed to dissolve the scorn of both.) Reflecting different ways an observer may interpret features of my personality, some alternate meanings are offered: distinctive/difficult; analytical/cold-blooded; agnostic/godless; ardent for lives of both mind and body/an intellectual, carnal jock; self-sufficient/a perverse loner; rich/privileged; original/eccentric; strong/rigid; zest for life/animal spirit; resolute/obstinate; young at heart/immature; experienced/old; discriminating/an intolerant snob; successful/obsessed with fear of failure; a political and social liberal/fatuous bleeding heart; wilderness lover/tree hugger.

Several causes—my Father, my old-fashioned upbringing and seeing life through books—combined to make me, in part, an alien in the world in which I have been placed. As an alien, I have been an observer. Insofar as I have been a player, it has been with an outlook of abstract idealism, driven by a 19th century sense of duty and role. And much of my action and passion have been engaged in personal pursuits only distantly connected with the surrounding society.

Measured by effort and sacrifice—that is, by what was given—my largest civic contribution was the Navy service. Measured by impact—that is, what others received —it was the Vietnam stand. Some efforts advanced racial justice in the community and region. The direction and tone given the Broadcasting Company had a constructive effect on local media standards. Most of my direct civic contributions have been small: doorbelling, giving blood and money, wrangling in committees, drafting resolutions and making speeches that seldom either gave heart to the persuaded or convinced those in doubt.

Toward my ancestors, my feeling resembles that toward my city and country: I do not love them but I belong to them (like my feeling for British culture, less preference than sense of being a part of it): as part of a tradition from their share in the American Experience and in the pursuit of the American Dream. I am proud of some, although the luster of their deeds adds no credit to mine. I feel deep pride in belonging to that country whose people have directed a long-sustained civic course by a set of exalted ideas, who have sacrificed much for noble dreams; the only nation in which young men ever laid down their lives to liberate members of a race not their own.

Companies pay more for wise strategy than for competent administration because it is a more important executive function and more scarce. However, administration is essential, and it is a function I have not done well either in business or in the other aspects of the world of affairs. The complexity of living keeps me struggling enmeshed, swamped in detail—housekeeping, shuffling papers, looking up telephone numbers, and so forth, the counterpart of the "asphalt road and a thousand lost golf balls." With more skill at ordering my affairs, I would be subjected to fewer of these unsatisfying chores. Keynes wrote of Newton that he was able at conducting affairs and that "it must not be inferred from his introspection, his absentmindedness, his secrecy and his solitude that he lacked aptitude for affairs." Sharing some of these qualities with Newton has not been enough.

In hiring, firing and promotion, my capacity to measure merit and talent was better than most. But in getting people to do what I wanted, whether by giving directions or inducing others to follow my lead, my skill was low and success poor. When a general policy, presented as a philosophy, would be dismissed as hogwash, inducing me to resort to directing detailed particulars, this course would be resented and resisted as usurping prerogatives. I never got it right.

Some people fail at this from romantic illusions. Others fail by reason of excessive cynicism, although where combined with insight into personality and the willingness to be flexible in personal dealings, cynicism seems to work well much of the time for some people, as it did for Napoleon and Lyndon Johnson. They were smart and favored rational methods of government but dealt with people – especially in the latter part of their careers – on the mistaken assumption that all springs of conduct are narrowly selfish, that people are motivated, and therefore can be influenced, only by fears and appetites so that nothing should be used but the carrot and the stick. And they assumed that when another person takes a position that he ascribes to principle he is cunningly raising his price, and if a high price is then offered and refused, he is simply a stupid merchant who has priced himself out of the market.

I am fairly realistic about these matters and owe my failure to neither romanticism nor excessive cynicism but to emotional limitations in dealing with others. Like Louis IX, from those responsible to me I earned respect, sometimes admiration, as a person yet could not obtain through them my sought results. I had more success in persuading judges, over whom I had no authority, than I did in inducing subordinate executives to follow my policy decisions. Most of the latter group regarded the company as their farm and me as a stump that they could not burn or blast but around which they must plow.

For almost half a century I devoted time and effort to family business enterprises. Compared to most of my other work, this task I did not do as well or enjoy as much. I sympathized with the Roman official whose bent was to be a philosopher but whose duties kept him directing military operations against alien enemies, in Michael Grant's words, "among the misty, melancholy swamps and reedy islands of the Danube." Family responsibility turned me to this and kept me from quitting. But what sent me in to work at business each day was no more duty than habit and the sense of a job: You have a job, you do it.

Although in the world of affairs my conduct has not been inflexible, my effectiveness in personal matters has been impaired by an unwillingness to yield where practical self-interest suggested compromise and no moral duty called for a refusal to budge. For example, once when I was eight or nine, my grandmother took me to a department store and told me she would buy me whatever I chose. The offer got me nothing because my first choice, a gun, having been denied, I refused any substitute.

My reactions to being denied resemble those of many people, more often wanting—and continuing to seek—what I cannot have than telling myself it was not really desirable. The former causes frustration and misses the emotionally practical consolation of the latter. It sometimes leads to renewed efforts that may succeed, but those efforts may be wasted, either in continued failure—throwing good money after bad—or in disappointing success. Thomas More's remark that the world's greatest punishment was to have our wishes probably makes a better aphorism than a maxim because to treat it as a rule of conduct would forbid much useful effort, and because fulfillment of wishes does not invariably disappoint.

In law, business and politics, the quality of my judgment has been average. I have some elements of good judgment: willingness to face those facts that one wishes were not facts, the capacity to see the central issue, the discernment of others whose judgment is good and sometimes the sense to rely on this judgment. But an important element I lack: accurate measurement of practical probabilities; that is, what will happen, or what would happen if.

Regretted mistakes are divided between those made in disregard of others' correct advice and those that followed wrong advice when I lacked confidence in my own judgment, found later to have been correct.

If vision can be regarded as a combination of capacity to discern future possibilities (imagination) and to measure future probabilities far enough ahead to where they tend to overlap but not merge, then my vision rates higher. My imagination has been substantial when applied to the world of affairs but weak when applied to my own emotions. That is, my emotional reactions to anticipated events tend to surprise me.

As to wisdom, regarded as a combination of judgment and vision, to estimate my own would be unwise.

Its element of discrimination makes loyalty inconsistent with uniform benevolence and therefore may put it on a lower moral plane, but the former quality more closely fits my taste, and my practice has followed the taste.

I have inflicted cruelty and received it. Have been played for a sucker, and without help from others have made a fool of myself. Have been both a somebody and a nobody. Have had some kinds of success, along with failures and defeats that encompassed more than political, marital, business, professional, scholastic and athletic.

In this age that rends the psyche, inner harmony has value, and I have wished to be less torn within. But to come to terms with the world in all respects, rather than reducing the discord between one's own selves, is a poor way to live. Hindsight suggests that my errors have tilted on the side of excessive nonconformity, even though one should kick against the pricks.

Some of my learning has come from reading, listening and observation. Much has come from doing stupid things.

Looking back on many of my undertakings, I have felt, if not regret, at least a wish for another chance to improve the performance. But *To Be A Politician*, in its 4th edition, was about as good as this writer could make it. (In certain passages clarity should not have been sacrificed in the interest of compression. As Horace put it, *Brevis esse laboro, obscurus fio*.) The best writing that has been published about the nature of the politician's profession, this book's deficiencies reflect the limits of my ability, not a failure to use all I had.

Nothing written or spoken by me since my mid thirties and addressed to the public has given me regret.

Not having sought to make my life a work of art

gives me no regret, although to have lived more gracefully, with clothes, decor, entertainment and food, would have been a better course. It would be satisfying to become half as civilized as Anatole France.

By the standards of the time and place, I became a good lawyer and as such contributed to my community and profession.

I helped to build and rebuild parts of downtown Seattle, leaving socially desirable structures.

I gave land for parks, gave money for education and culture and helped build the Bullitt Foundation into a constructive philanthropy. Over the years, most of my worldly goods have been given away. That part given to worthy causes is about equal to what I have left. The bulk of charitable giving has gone to the Foundation, to which I have given so far between a fifth and a sixth of what it has been given. Many of the choices made have been perplexing, but giving never has taken moral effort.

In athletics, when young I won some fights, when middle-aged placed in ski races and in my seventh and eighth decades did mountain climbs of a kind that challenges young mountaineers.

As a husband, I failed. Pleasure was neither given nor received. With women, there were plenty of good times, a few friendships, no deep attachment or contentment.

Some of my practices have been moderate, but except for a precarious equilibrium between self-acceptance and self-mastery, about the only balance in my life has been that of alternating excesses.

I learned to cease to bear a grudge.

I sought to fill the roles in which I had been cast: Perform duties, adhere to principles, use skills, do some things well and have some fun. At heart, however, I have longed not for virtue, power, wisdom, wealth or a smile from God, but for glory. If offered one of what is God's I would forego the kingdom and the power and take the glory. I would rather have been a hero than a saint, a sage or a success.

Like Halifax, wishing at the same time to attain the glory of high rank and the glory of despising it, I found the latter not as hard. My devotion to work does not contradict or deny my wish to be a hero. You may fill your days with work, seeking to achieve, even to achieve the glory of high rank, but you cannot pursue the glory of heroism through methodical routine and daily effort.

Some people's conduct inspires others to improve their own. If my example has had constructive effect on others it is unknown to me. Despite having put much into my work and taken much out, whatever significance my life might have to others will be less what the work was worth than the total mix of my life itself (e.g., Carl Sandburg, William O. Douglas and Malraux).

Although we all must balance efforts among duties, ambition, survival and pleasure, many of us concentrate on a single aspiration, often a career vocation. My diverse interests and goals, not choosing between "perfection of life" and "of the work" or a formal career, have helped me avoid the narrow development that my friend Bill Sumner called becoming a "delta function," but at the price of excellence in a single field.

As for many, my experience has oscillated between loneliness in solitude and impatience in company, but not as extreme as Rousseau, of whom it was said that he was equally intolerant of attention and indignant at neglect. Much of my life, whether or not in sight and sound of others, has been spent alone, often by choice. Most of this time has been more satisfying than it would have been if engaged in intercourse with others that might make me impatient for something else. Yet although I have made successful efforts to make and keep friends, I have not done enough to arrange my practices to spend more time among those whom I enjoy. Often I turn to conversation with friends to keep myself from losing touch with reality, as well as for the common rewards of friendship.

Someone said we should beware of longing for something because we might get it. We all resemble the Three Princes of Serendip. I sought fulfillment in politics and failed but was granted it in writing on an aspect of that life. I hoped for sons who would express my values and instead got daughters who did. Likewise in mountain climbing, results often differ from expectations and hopes. On two McKinley climbs, I looked for a triumphant score, got defeat, exhaustion and friendship, then on the third try success as well, again surprise.

As one might expect from a man who had designed his home, and helped as well to design his country, Jefferson designed his gravestone. It gives his name, the dates of birth and death, and then only this: "Author of the Declaration of Independence and the Virginia Statute for Religious Freedom and Father of the University of Virginia." I would prefer to be remembered as an honest and competent lawyer, author of some works worth reading, a constructive citizen, a loving father, a loyal brother, an amusing companion and a staunch friend.

As an alternative, my gravestone could bear my good fortune from some felicitous personal relations.

My parents set good examples and treated me pretty well. My sisters love me. My children have provided me joy and satisfaction. Adherence to a few friends has gratified me. Like children, they are less an achievement than a blessing. Over many years, their loyalty has sustained me, their congenial company has warmed me, and their examples have elevated my life.

4/1/93

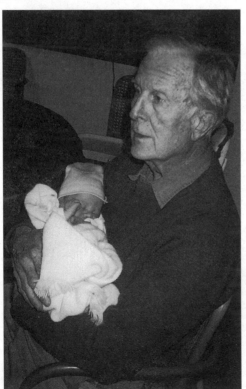

INDEX

MORE TITLES
FROM WILLOWS PRESS

By Stimson Bullitt

To Be A Politician	Hard Cover	$22.95
	Soft Bound	$15.95
River Dark and Bright	Hard Cover	$22.95
	Soft Bound	$15.95
Ancestral Histories of Scott Bullitt and Dorothy Stimson	Hard Cover	$29.95

By Lawrence Kreisman

The Stimson Legacy: Architecture in the Urban West	Hard Cover	$55.00
	Soft Bound	$35.00

You may order these books directly from the publisher. Please include $3.00 for postage and handling (and 8.2% state sales tax if you are a Washington State resident). Allow two weeks for delivery.

Willows Press
1204 Minor Avenue
Seattle, Washington 98101

Please send me _____ copies of _____

@ $ _____ per copy, for a total price of _____ , including tax.

Name: _____

Address: _____

City/State/Zip: _____